GEORGE CONDO
HUMANOIDS

GEORGE CONDO

HUMANOIDS

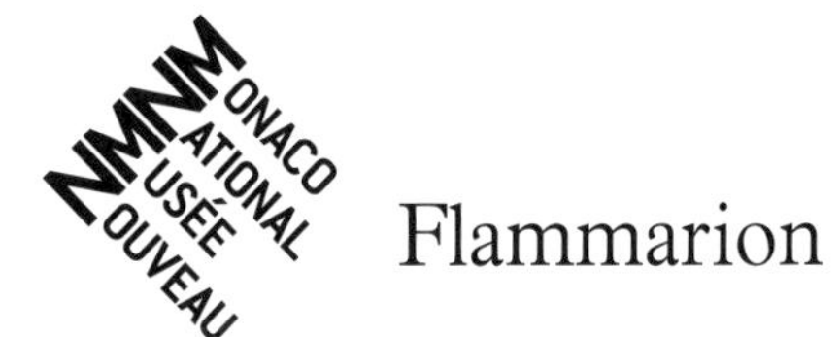

Flammarion

This book is published on the occasion
of the exhibition

"Humanoids" by George Condo
NMNM, Villa Paloma, March 31, 2023–
October 1, 2023

Editorial Directors
Julie Rouart, Kate Mascaro (Éditions
Flammarion), Guillaume de Sardes (NMNM)

Text Contributors
George Condo, Didier Ottinger, Jean-
Christophe Maillot, Guillaume de Sardes

Editorial Coordination
Yaël Rusé, Helen Adedotun (Éditions
Flammarion), Floriane Spinetta, Stéphane
Vacquier (NMNM)

Administration Manager
Delphine Montagne (Éditions Flammarion)

Translation
From French to English: Peter Behrman
de Sinéty

Copyediting and Proofreading
Kate van den Boogert
Floriane Spinetta, Stéphane
Vacquier (NMNM)

Graphic Design
Amélie Boutry

Picture Research
Lucía Pasalodos (Éditions Flammarion)

Production
Élodie Conjat (Éditions Flammarion)

Color Separation
Les Caméléons, Paris

Printed in Italy by
Musumeci SpA

Published by
Nouveau Musée National de Monaco
Éditions Flammarion

Published with the support of

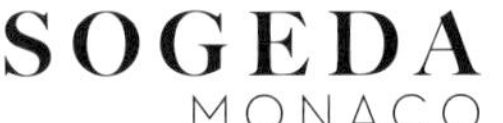

Simultaneously published in French as
George Condo: Humanoïdes
© Éditions Flammarion, Paris, 2023
© Nouveau Musée National de Monaco, 2023

English-language edition
© Éditions Flammarion, Paris, 2023
© Nouveau Musée National de Monaco, 2023

All rights reserved.
No part of this publication may be
reproduced in any form or by any means,
electronic, photocopy, information retrieval
system, or otherwise, without written
permission from Éditions Flammarion.
82 Rue Saint-Lazare
CS 10124
75009 Paris

editions.flammarion.com

23 24 25   3 2 1

ISBN (NMNM): 978-2-492121-12-8
ISBN (Flammarion): 978-2-08-041968-2

Legal Deposit: 03/2023

"Humanoids" by George Condo

Director of the NMNM
Björn Dahlström

Guest Curator
Didier Ottinger

Scenographer
Christophe Martin,
assisted by Alisson Mimil Baysset

General Coordination
Emmanuelle Capra, Clémentine Sassi,
and the entire NMNM team

Lighting Concept
Ugo Cerina (Reliefs)

This exhibition would not have been possible without the friendly support of George Condo, his team, and Princess Alexandra of Hanover.

Special thanks to private lenders, museums, cultural institutions, and all those who wish to remain anonymous:
George Condo; Collection Frac Île-de-France; David J. Fiszel; Andrea Caratsch Collection, St. Moritz; Bernard and Joann Kruger; Les Ballets de Monte-Carlo; Anton Massini; Moeremans d'Emaus Collection; Ringier Collection, Switzerland; H.R.H. The Princess of Hanover; H.R.H. The Princess Alexandra of Hanover

And all those who contributed to this project:
Condo Studio: Michelle Janevicius, Garrett Swanson, Elizabeth Warfel;

Les Ballets de Monte-Carlo: Jean-Christophe Maillot, Directeur; Francesca Dolci, Jean-Marc Genestie, Annabelle Salomon Favier, Peggy Semeria, Patrick Wante;

Hauser & Wirth: Cristopher Canizares, Senior Director; Caitlin Foreht, Associate Director; Sophie Nurse, Senior Artist Liaison;

Carol Asscher, Jean-Luc Biamonti, Rahel Blättler, Jean-Philippe Calestrini, Andrea Caratsch, Steve Cohen, Safia El-Malqui, David Fiszel, Xavier Franceschi, François Fernandez, Chloe Geary, Martin Guesnet, Marine Guerbois, Sandy Heller, James Lavender, Béatrice Lecouturier, Bernard Massini, Carine Menache, Tara Nikolla, Simon de Pury, Ellen & Michael Ringier, Anna et Misha Moeremans d'Emaus, Christian Roti, Véronique Simian, Emmanuel Van Peteghem, Vincent Vatrican, Véronique Verhaaren

Partners:
Direction des Affaires Culturelles
Direction de la Communication
Direction de l'Éducation Nationale, de la Jeunesse et des Sports
Direction du Tourisme et des Congrès
Le Méridien Beach Plaza

Nouveau Musée National de Monaco

Board of Directors

President
H.R.H. The Princess of Hanover

Vice-Chairman
Patrice Cellario

Board Secretary
Françoise Gamerdinger

Board Members
Jean-Luc Biamonti, Daniel Boeri, Céline Caron-Dagioni, Jean Castellini, Olivier Gabet, Pierre Nouvion
Honorary Member
Valerio Adami

The Nouveau Musée National de Monaco is a public institution headed by the Prince's Government.

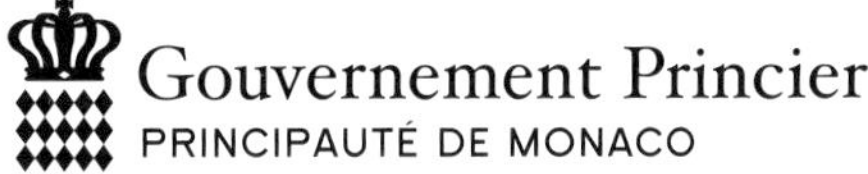

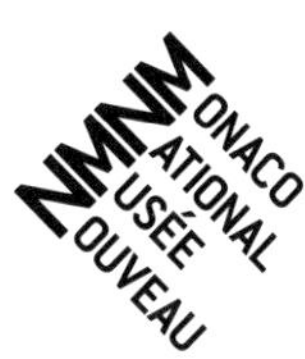

Direction

Director
Björn Dahlström

Administrative and Financial Department

Administrative and Financial Manager
Angélique Reyné

Administrative and Financial Assistant
Danièle Batti

Secretary
Emily Battaglia

Production Manager
Emmanuelle Capra

Assistant to the Exhibition Production Manager
Clémentine Sassi

Technical Registrars
Florent Duchesne, Benjamin Goinard

Ticketing Officers
Florentin Certaldi, Christine Mikalef, Robert Pelazza

Chief Supervisor
Richard Fonteix

Security Officers
Federico Castellon, Henri Cavandoli

Collections Department

Chief Curator
Célia Bernasconi

Curatorial Assistant
Romy Tirel-Marill

Collection Registrars
Damien L'Herbon de Lussats, Marie Zdyb

Preventive Conservator
Annaé Annenkoff

Development Department

Development Department Manager
Guillaume de Sardes

Development Assistant
Ksenia Redkova

Communications and PR Manager
Élodie Biancheri

Archives and Edition Manager
Stéphane Vacquier

Edition Assistant
Floriane Spinetta

Public Manager
Benjamin Laugier

Cultural Coordinators
Sharon Jones, Coline Matarazzo

George Condo is one of the major artists of recent decades. His paintings drive the art market into a frenzy and are collected by the world's most prestigious museums. This phenomenal success conceals a delightful, discreet, and cultivated man, remarkably gentle and generous, and fascinating in his conversations.

I cannot separate George Condo the artist from George Condo my friend: the more you have the chance to spend time with him, the more you realize how much of himself he puts into his paintings. Paradoxically, for a painter who became famous by appropriating the style of the Old Masters and championing "artificial realism," his work is a model of authenticity. A detail can tell you much about a man: his success has never in the least altered his openness to others.

The Nouveau Musée National de Monaco exhibition that inaugurates this book is an apt initiative because it finally honors Condo, the artist, in a country that George, the friend, knows well. For though he is a familiar presence in Monaco and on the Côte d'Azur, it marks the first time he has exhibited his work here. His delicate *View of Cap d'Antibes* (1989–1990), very Matisse-esque in method, testifies to his trips to the region when he lived in Paris. In years since, he has become an inconspicuous but regular visitor of the Principality.

In time, the idea of a collaboration with Les Ballets de Monte-Carlo was born. In 1998, George Condo conceived of the stage curtain presented in this book. He then accepted to create the sets and costumes for Jean-Christophe Maillot's ballet *Opus 40*, set to a score by Meredith Monk, which premiered at the Monte-Carlo Spring Arts Festival on April 22, 2000.

The exhibition *Humanoids* gives us the occasion to relive these wonderful memories.

The Princess of Hanover

The human figure is at the core of George Condo's work. His paintings show the human form as a sum of contradictions and conflicts between multiple aspects of his personality, distinct emotions, diverse cultural legacies…. Through the process of artmaking that he has explored for decades, Condo grapples with other painters and the history of art, but he also tackles his own emotions or, to use a well-worn phrase, his inner demons. He offers, in turn, similar schizophrenic journeys to his viewers.

This is a characteristic of his painting and one of the objectives he has set for it: the canvas must convey an energy. This cathartic dimension is essential—doubly so, since to share his emotions with the viewer, he must first transmute them into the painting.

There are so many things to see, examine, appreciate, discover, in George Condo's art that we often forget just how much his paintings, like his sculptures, are explosions of sounds and harmonics. It is important to emphasize that he does not simply project ideas and sensations into his paintings: he also fills them with all the sounds that surround and haunt him, composing the uproar of our time. George Condo is a musician.

That is why it seemed important to create a connection between his sculptures, his works for Les Ballets de Monte-Carlo, and his paintings at the Villa Paloma. My sincere thanks to George for his generosity and his enthusiasm at every stage of this project, even sharing his writings, collected here, in which he offers precious insight into his artistic practice.

Björn Dahlström
Director, Nouveau Musée National de Monaco

George Condo

HU MAN OIDS

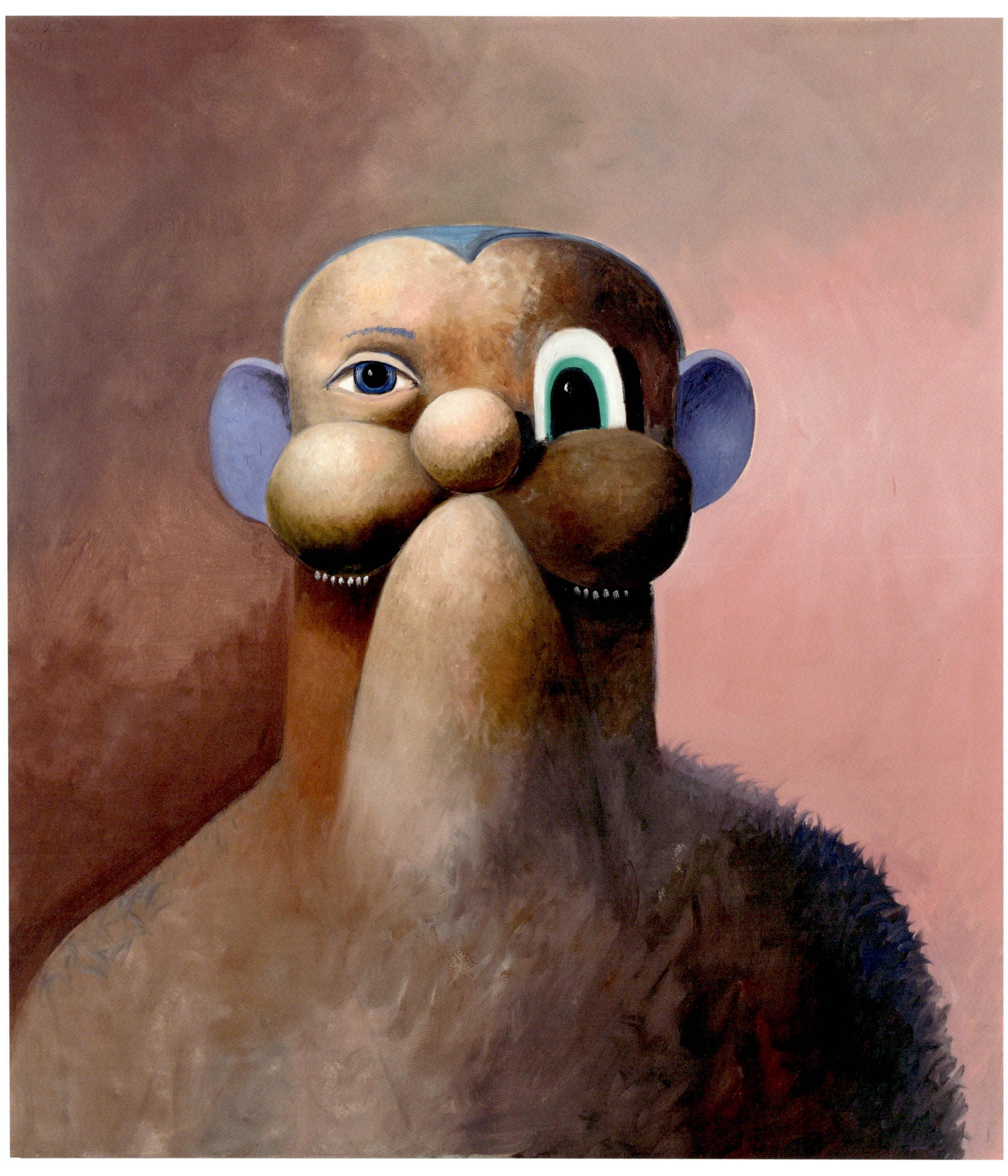

Modern Caveman, 2017
Oil on canvas, 5 ft. 4 in. × 4 ft. 10 in. (162.6 × 147.3 cm)

WHEN AND WHY I BEGAN TO PAINT HUMANOIDS

Humans weren't interesting anymore … they had been painted time and time again over thousands of years in every way known to man.

The human revolt had begun to transpose various earthly cultures into a synthetic representation of humanity … at which point abstract artists such as Kazimir Malevich sought to eradicate it, leading into pure abstraction, which Wassily Kandinsky followed, and Mark Rothko and Barnett Newman completed. At this point, what was left of the human in painting? What was there in the minimalist movement of Donald Judd and Robert Ryman … all the way up until Mark Dagley?

Here is where the line was drawn between the concrete reality of the known and the interpretation of the unknown….

Pop culture was the "next" answer after abstract expressionism and action painting. Consumerism was the economic driving force, hence mankind and the machine were the dominating hierarchy of the industrial world…. This world transformed itself at that time to space exploration, leading to the first man on the moon. Einstein's theories had already gone from relativity to the atom bomb, the world became nuclear and from its existential ashes the Humanoid was born … no stranger to the traditional means of painting but composed of the atomic man. The new human is one of technological advances and interplanetary resolve. A resolute being within its own right, the Humanoid came to me as a representation of the world. A world of artificial realism … the one we live in today, the world of disinformation, the world of similarities … the simulacrum … the realistic representation of that which is artificial or in essence manmade. That is the how and why I came to create the Humanoid.

What is a Humanoid?

An inverted form of abstract art in the form of an emerging being … a figure trapped in its own imagination of itself and therefore resembling on the surface that which he imagines in his mind.

It is a way of taking nature or industrial space and transforming it into a human-like being. I could be on an ontological journey into the psyche seen from the perspective of a cartologist who is mapping out the voyage of the "human" to the "other" … the fact that as humans we perceive that which is external to ourselves as real, does not mean that we consider our own self to be the way we perceive our own self. We may be inhabiting a self that is entirely our own to ourselves but not to those around us, who see it differently. Therefore, to arrive at the essence of oneself, could be perhaps irrelevant…. "I am" could mean "I am not."

It's a psychological composition based on experiences that to one's own mind is exactly what we think it is but not the way others see it. To capture this phenomena in a portrait is to be able to work from the "inside out" … to think for your subject in an entirely different way than the subject thinks for itself…. A Humanoid is then the closest thing to one's own perception in counterbalance to the perception of others … but also a composite of the meaning of persona or outward appearance…. The appearance in Hegelian terms of the self as opposed to the "being-for-self" which is an Aristotelian concept…. That which appears to be oneself then is itself, as opposed to that which is the being of oneself and perhaps only in the being but not appearance of the self. So the being becomes the question…. Is it a human being? Devoid of any perceptive rationale yet still in essence a self, or is it a self which has no resemblance to its perception of the being?

A conundrum of existence perhaps … that we as humans are of no particular identity other than the one imposed upon us by the rationale of others bereft of what is in our minds as ourselves. A Humanoid is born of this conundrum, it resembles to a certain extent a being … that resembles a human … yet it cannot think as an inanimate object, as a painting or a rock…. What is in the mind of a rock? Or anything devoid of a human mind…? What is in the mind of a painting—which is essentially a canvas with paint on it?

What has a mind and what does not within the realm of a Humanoid?

Does a human-like being possess reason? Reason that pertains to its own species, or could there be a language? Most people from one part of the world are unable to speak the language of a distant region of the planet….

So what then is the language of a Humanoid? Is it one that resembles his appearance … a fractured vernacular understood by others of the fractured kind? Or a faceless figure? How does it communicate without a mouth? In the representation of these Humanoids one can somehow imagine a spoken means of communication loosely based on one's own … regardless of the fact that a painting in and of itself cannot speak.

The return of an uncivilized civilization … vacated buildings in anonymous lots once home to the wealthy and prosperous, all of whom carried within them Humanoid hosts…. Living beings somewhat transparent whose reflections could not be seen in a mirror … but could and did appear on canvas. They inhabited those who they could emerge within, taking on the form of peripheral beings while simultaneously central to the direct source of the existence of the carrier…. In other words, they were the person in paint more than the person itself.

ANTIPODAL BEINGS

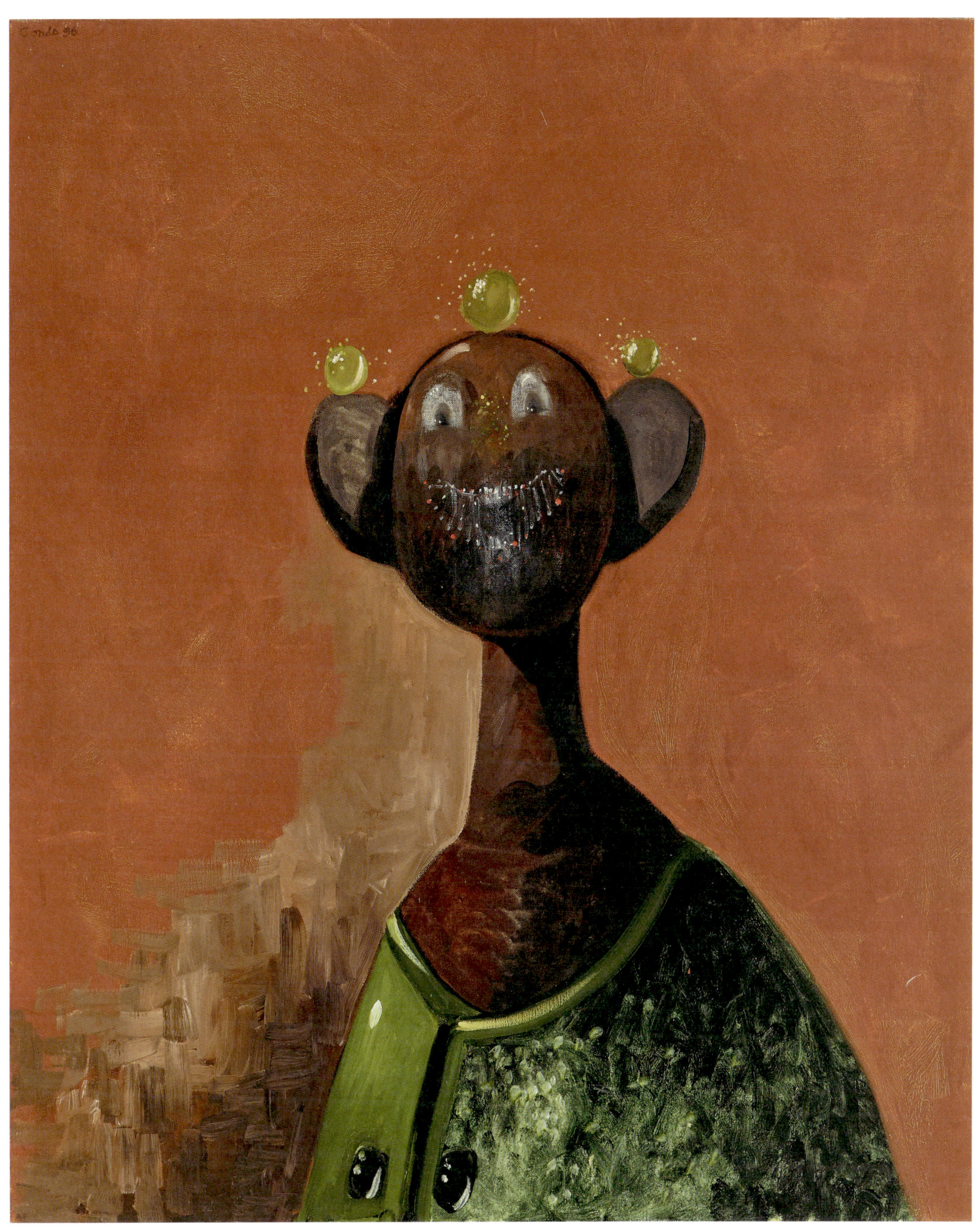

Smiling Pod Portrait, 1996
Oil on canvas, 4 ft. × 3 ft. 4 in. (121.9 × 101.6 cm)

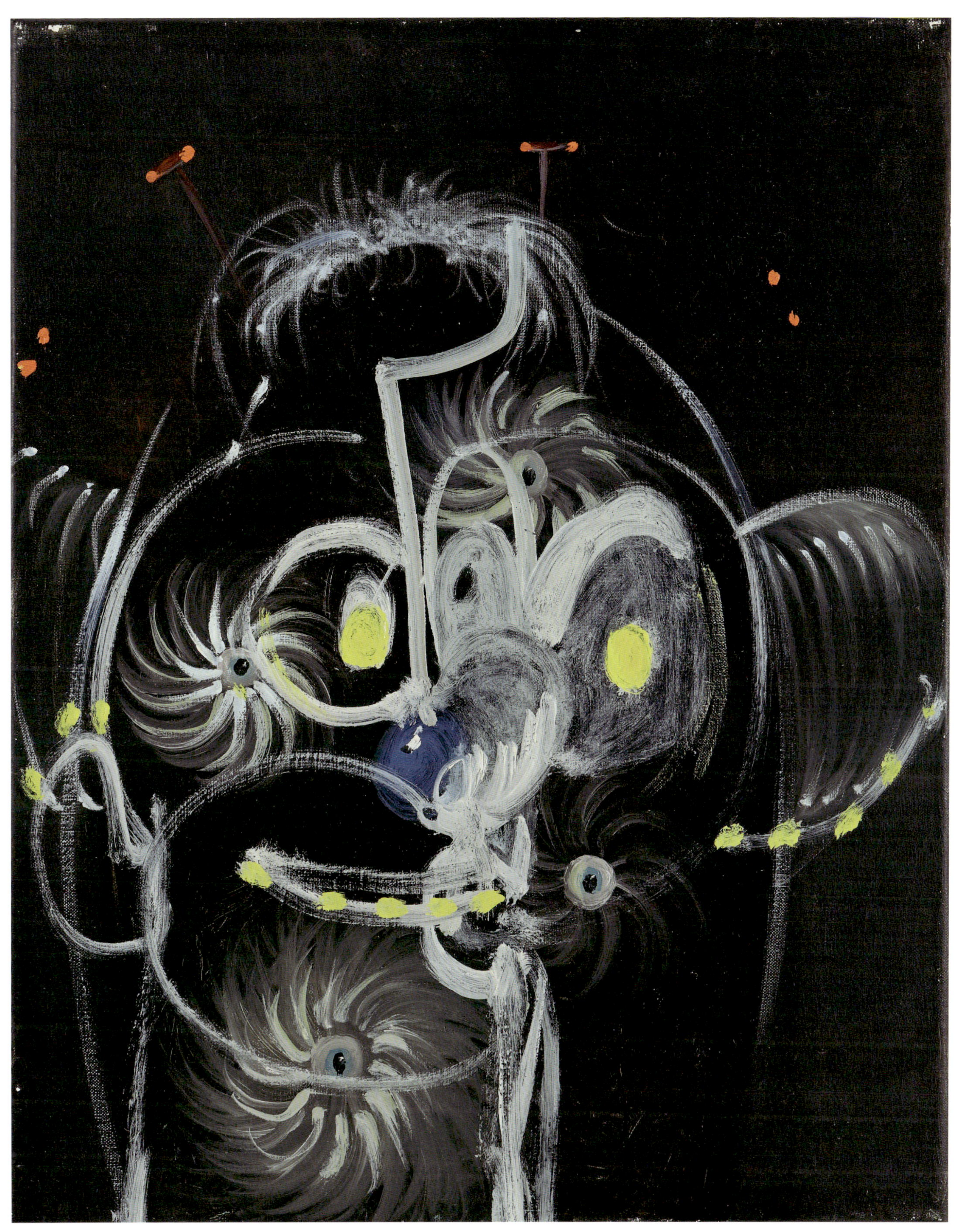

Space Being, 1988
Oil on canvas, 20 × 16 in. (50.8 × 40.6 cm)

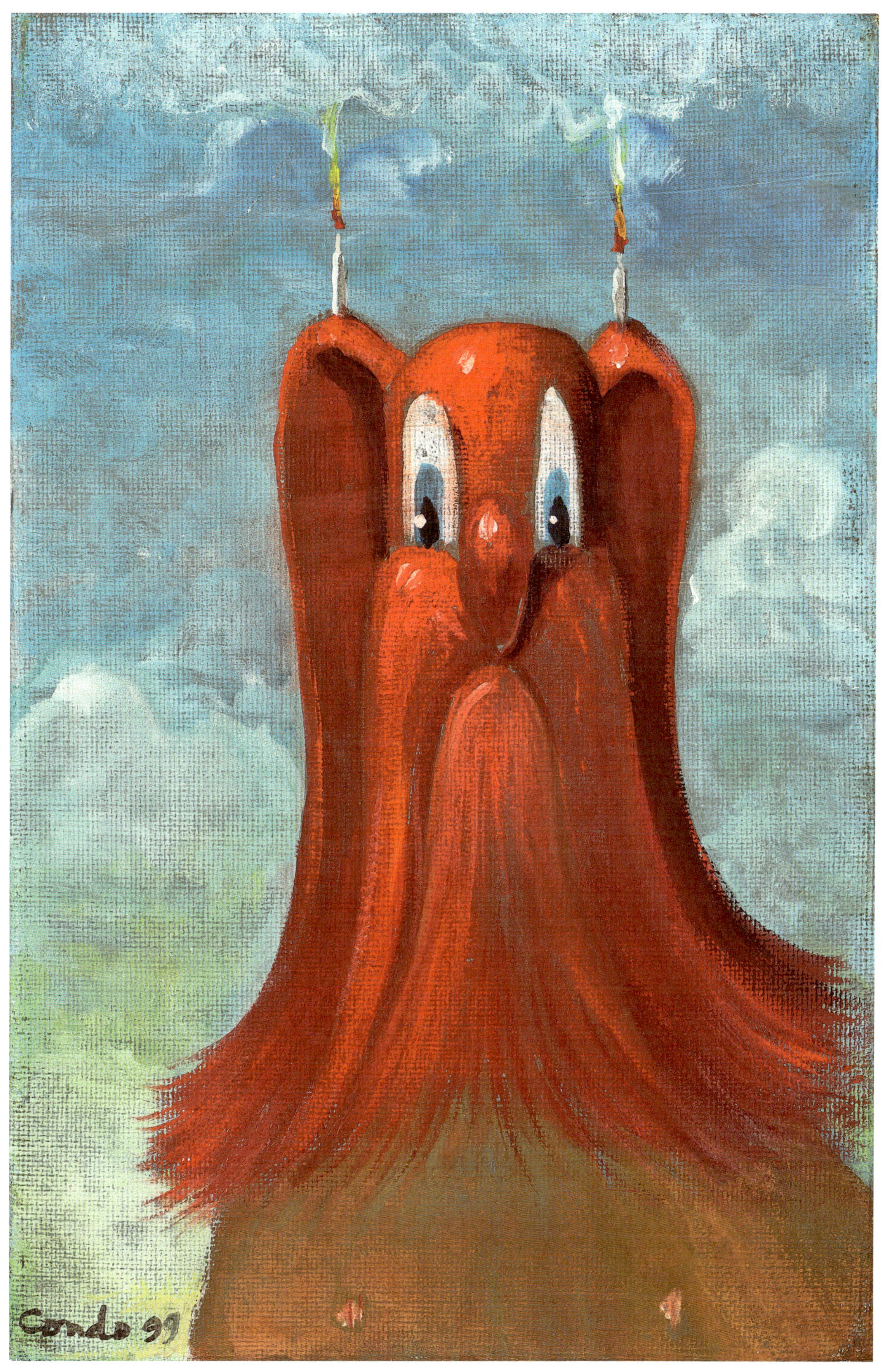

Grand Rouge, 1999
Oil on canvas, 9½ × 6⅓ in. (24.2 × 16.1 cm)

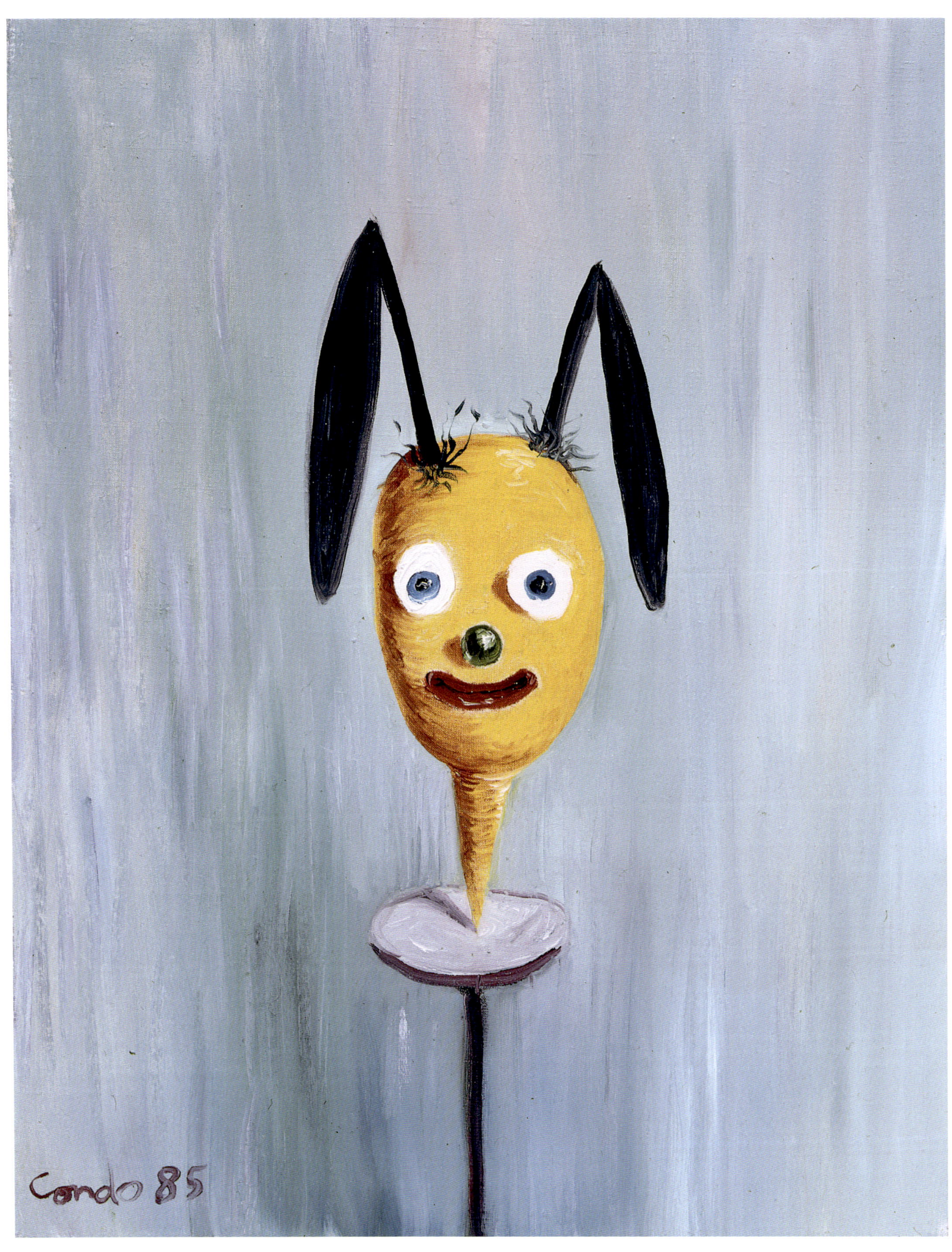

The Barber Shop Painting, 1985
Oil on canvas, 16¼ × 13 in. (41.3 × 33 cm)

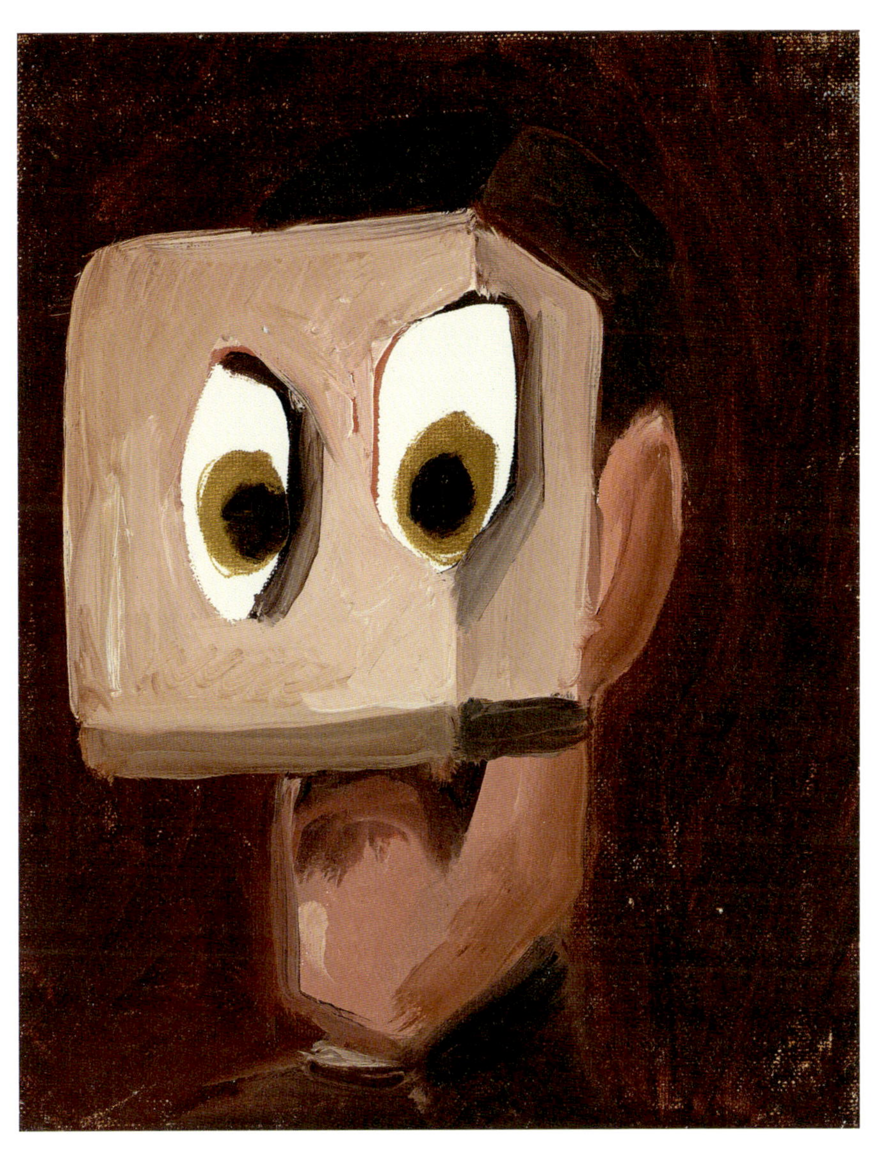

Masked Man, 1998
Oil on canvas board, 10 × 8 in. (25.4 × 20.3 cm)

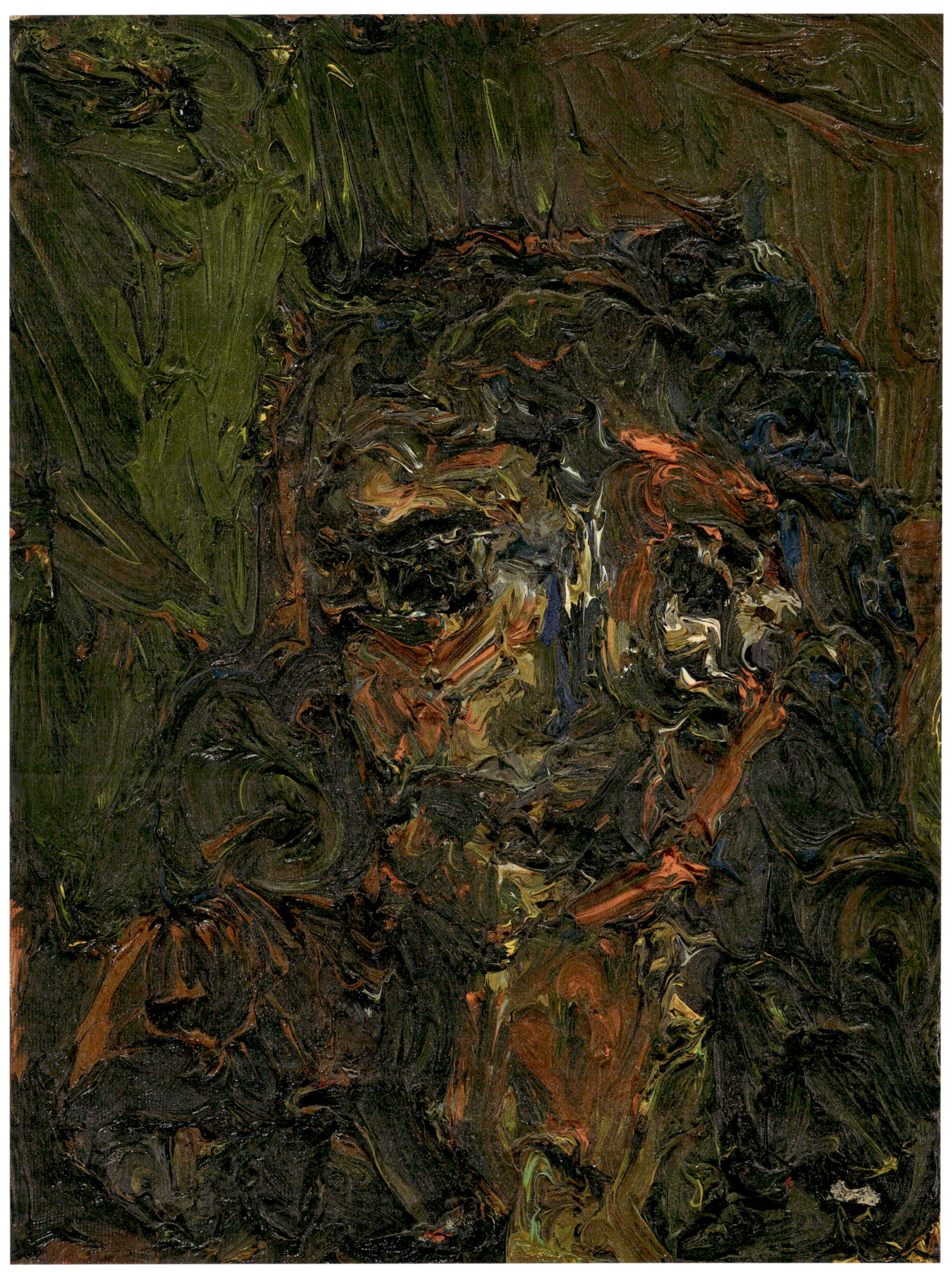

Female Portrait, 1987
Oil on linen, 14 × 10¾ in. (35.5 × 27.3 cm)

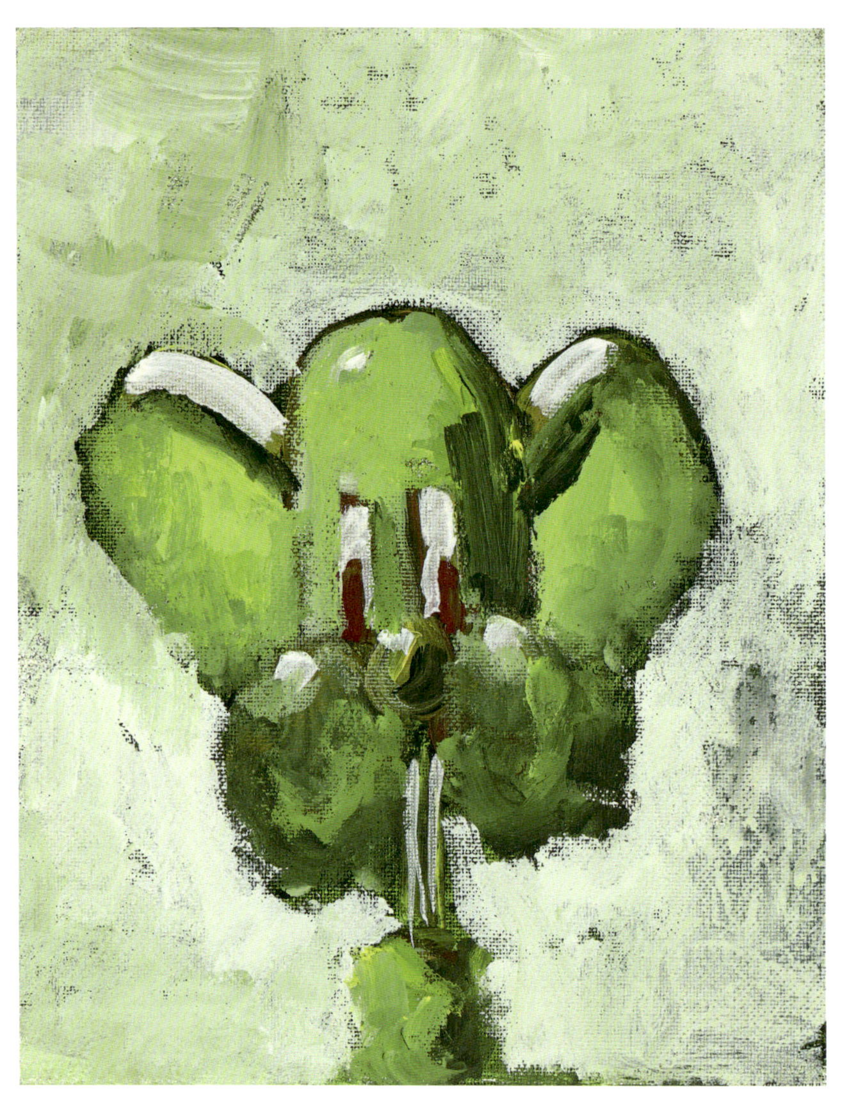

Green Pod, 1998
Oil on canvas board, 10 × 8 in. (25.4 × 20.3 cm)

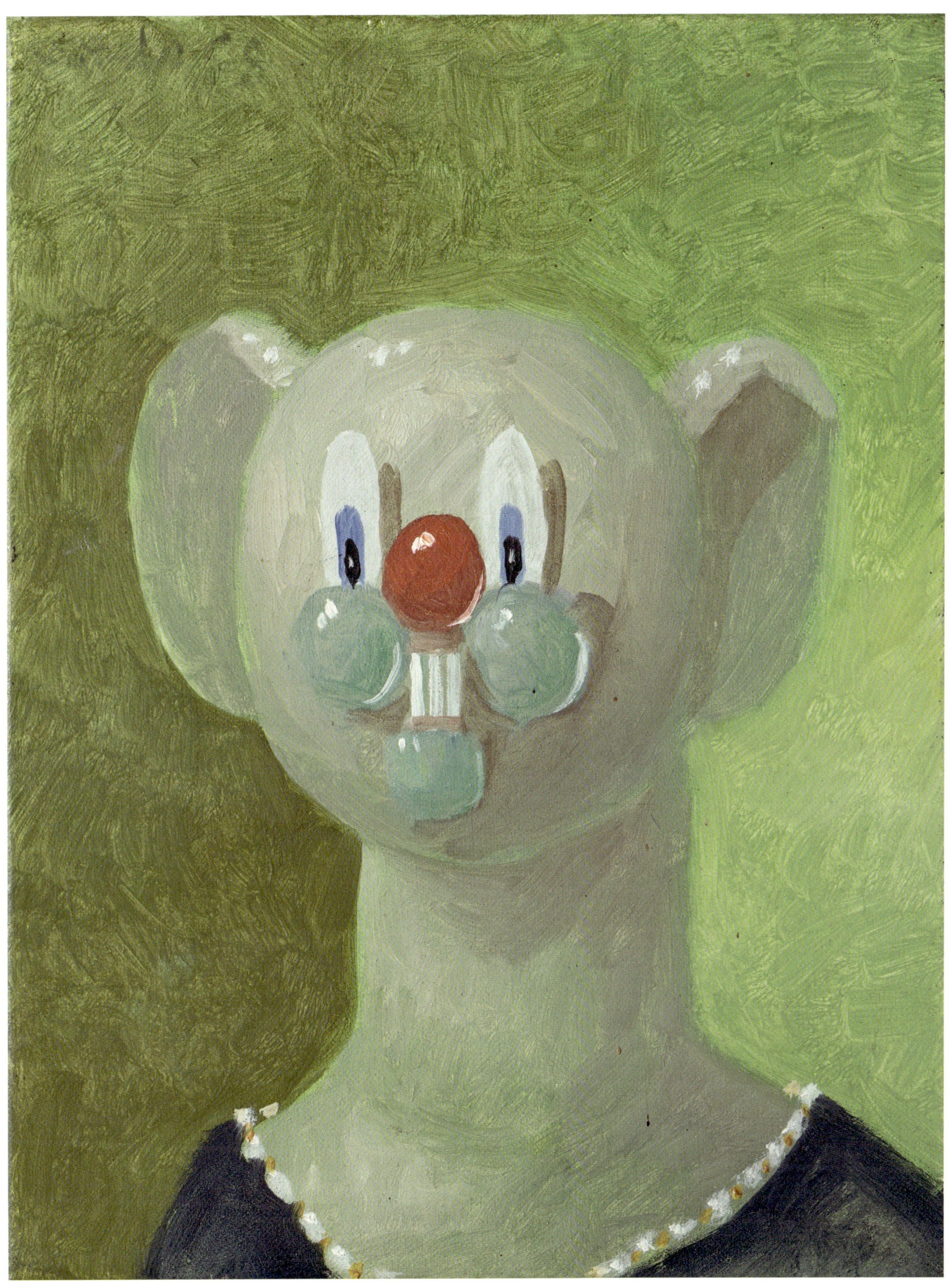

The Unnamed Antipodal Chipmunk, 1998
Oil on canvas, 7¼ × 5⅔ in. (18.2 × 14.2 cm)

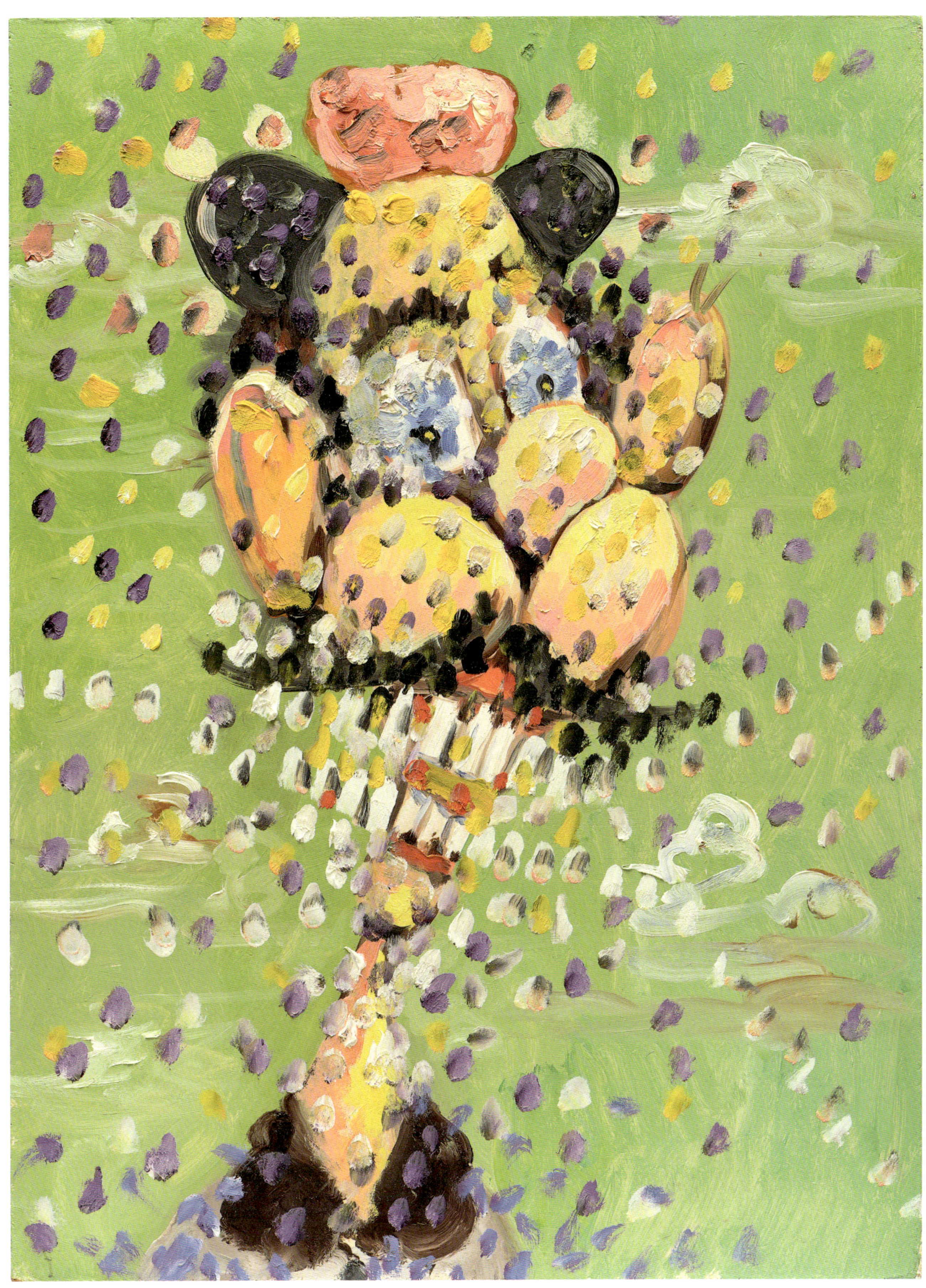

The Pointillist Pod, 1996
Oil on board, 24 × 18 in. (61 × 45.7 cm)

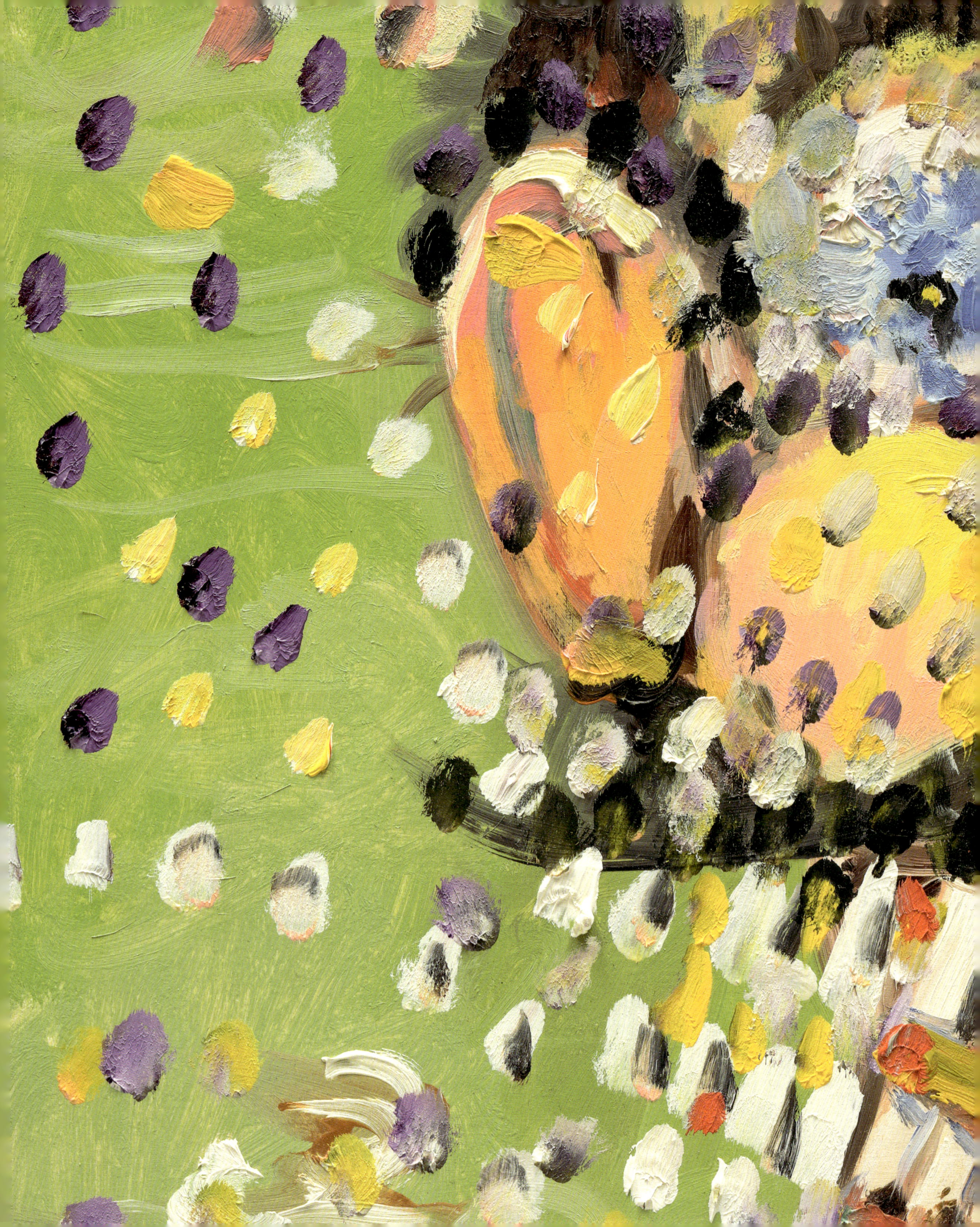

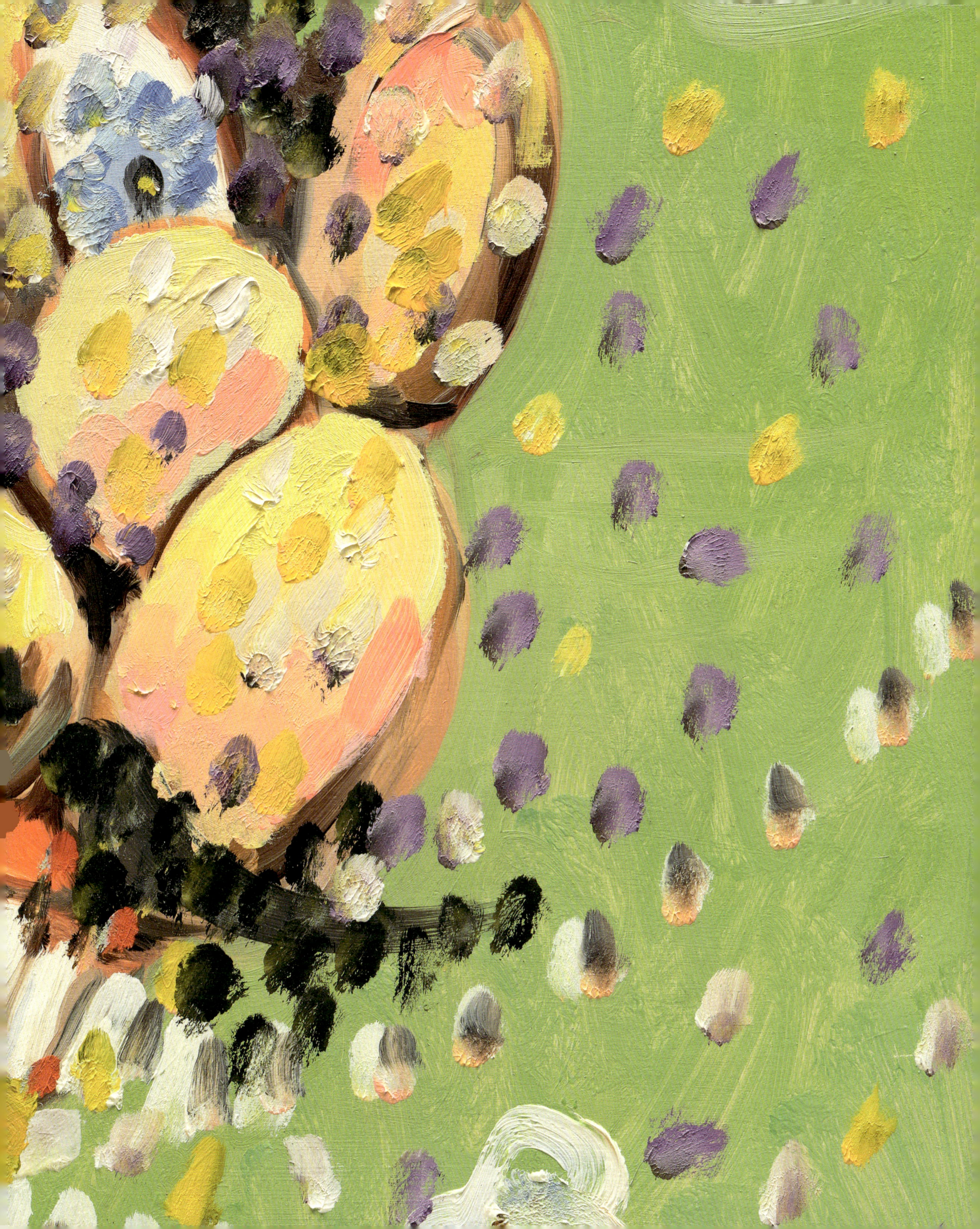

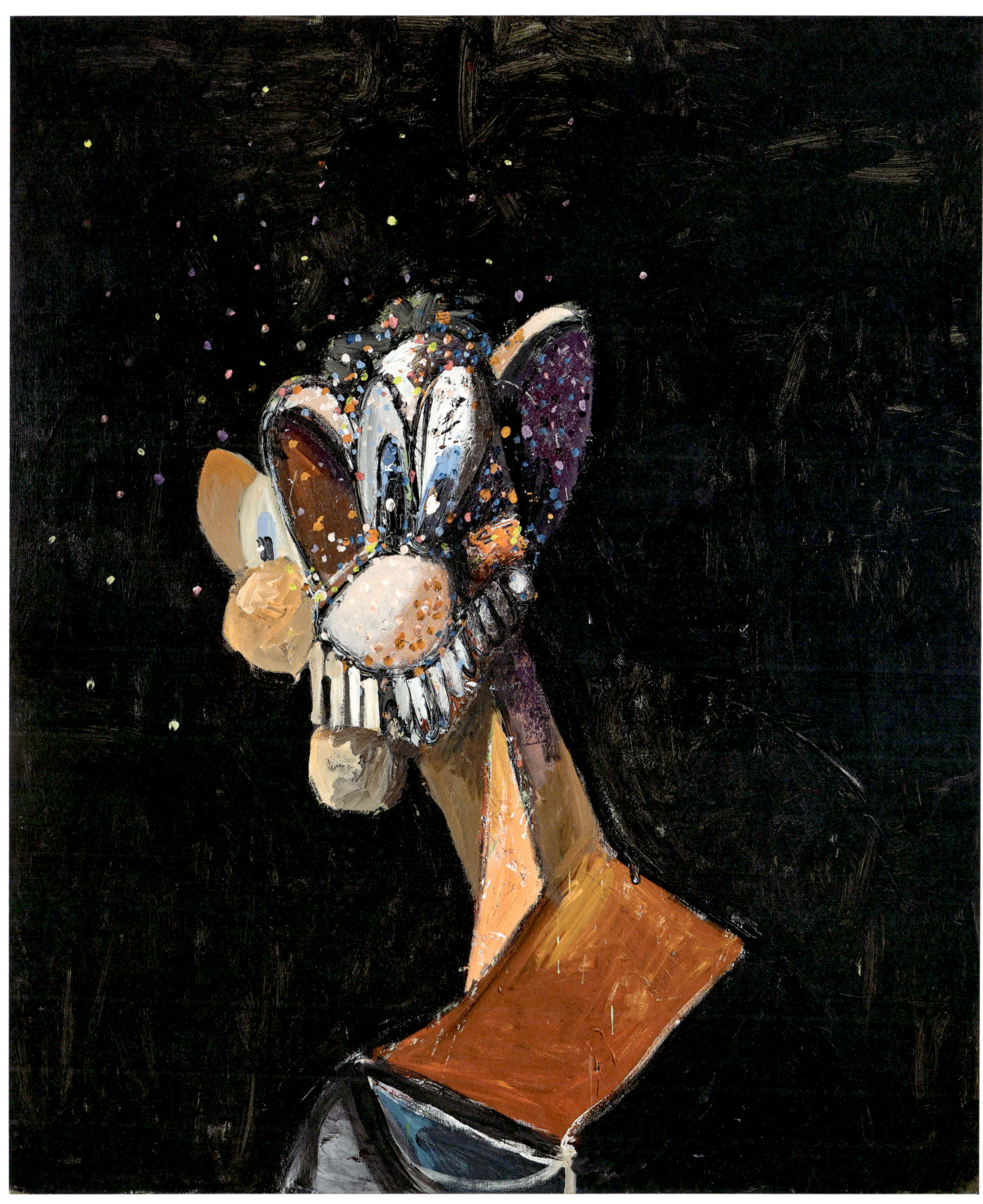

Antipodal Being, 1996
Oil on linen, 5 ft. 10⅛ in. × 5 ft. ¼ in. (178.1 × 153 cm)

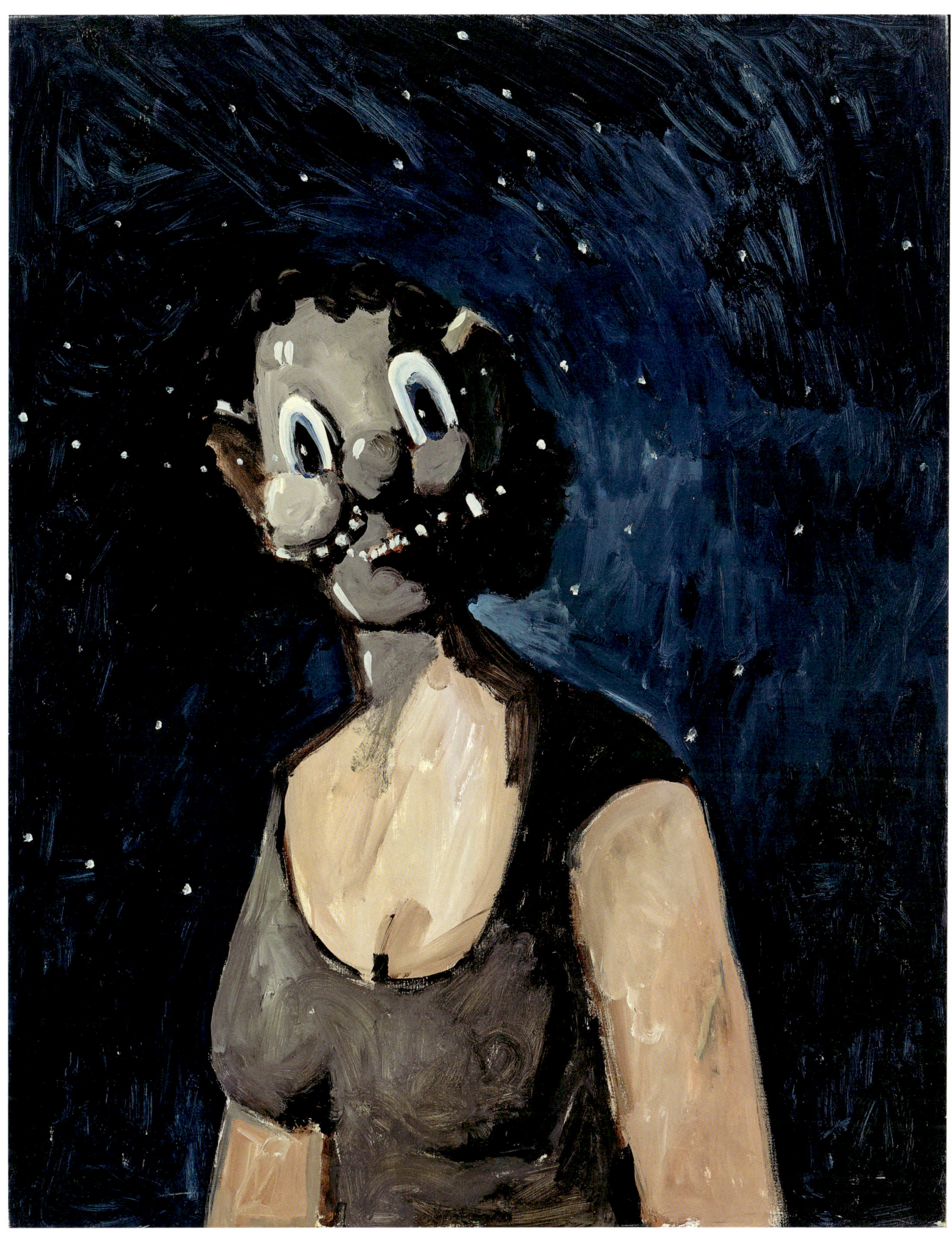

The Secretary, 1998
Oil on canvas, 4 ft. 2 in. × 3 ft. 4 in. (127 × 101.6 cm)

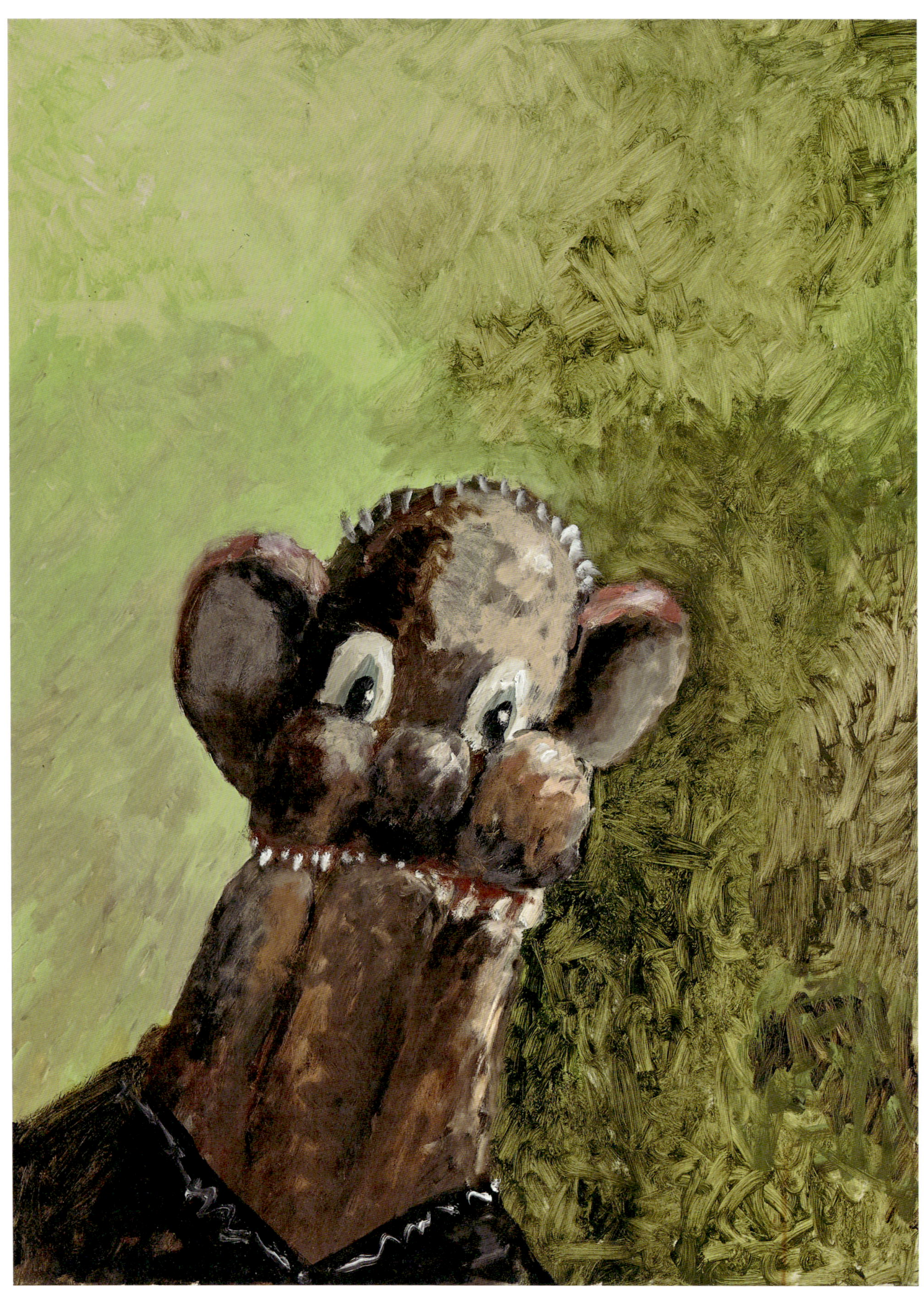

The Grave Digger, 1999
Oil on canvas, 3 ft. 4 in. × 2 ft. 6 in. (101.6 × 76.2 cm)

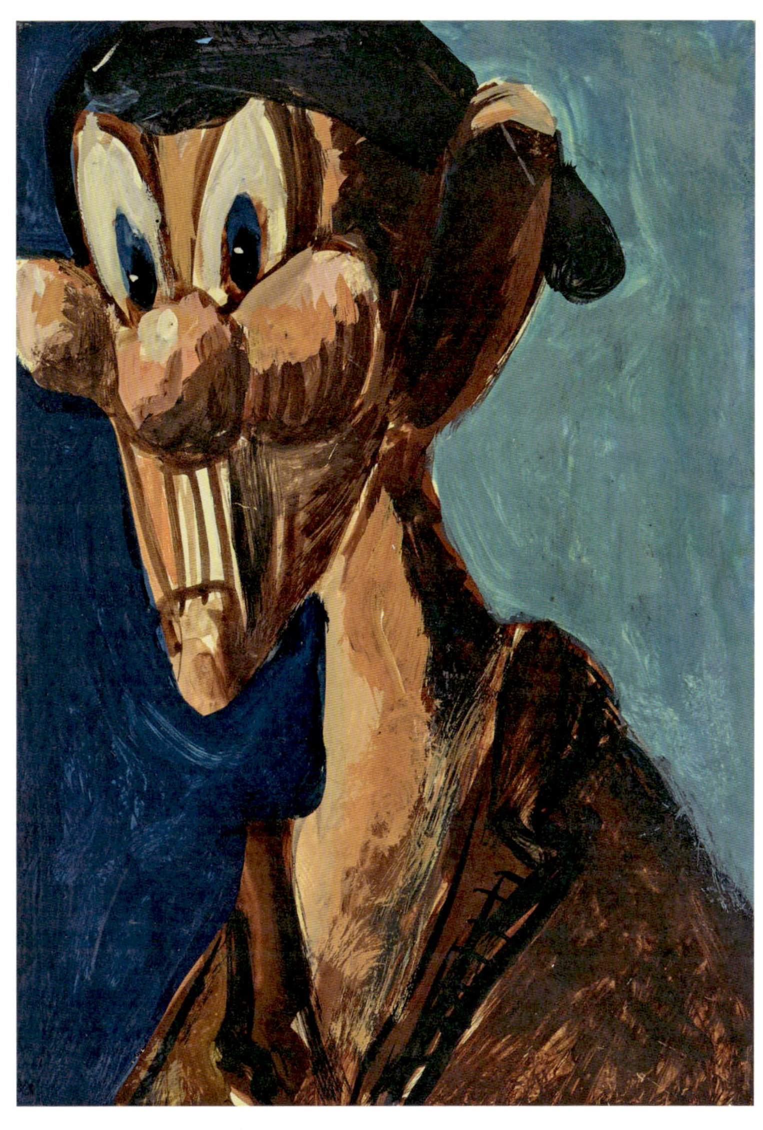

Jack the Ripper, 1996
Oil on masonite, 7 × 5 in. (17.8 × 12.7 cm)

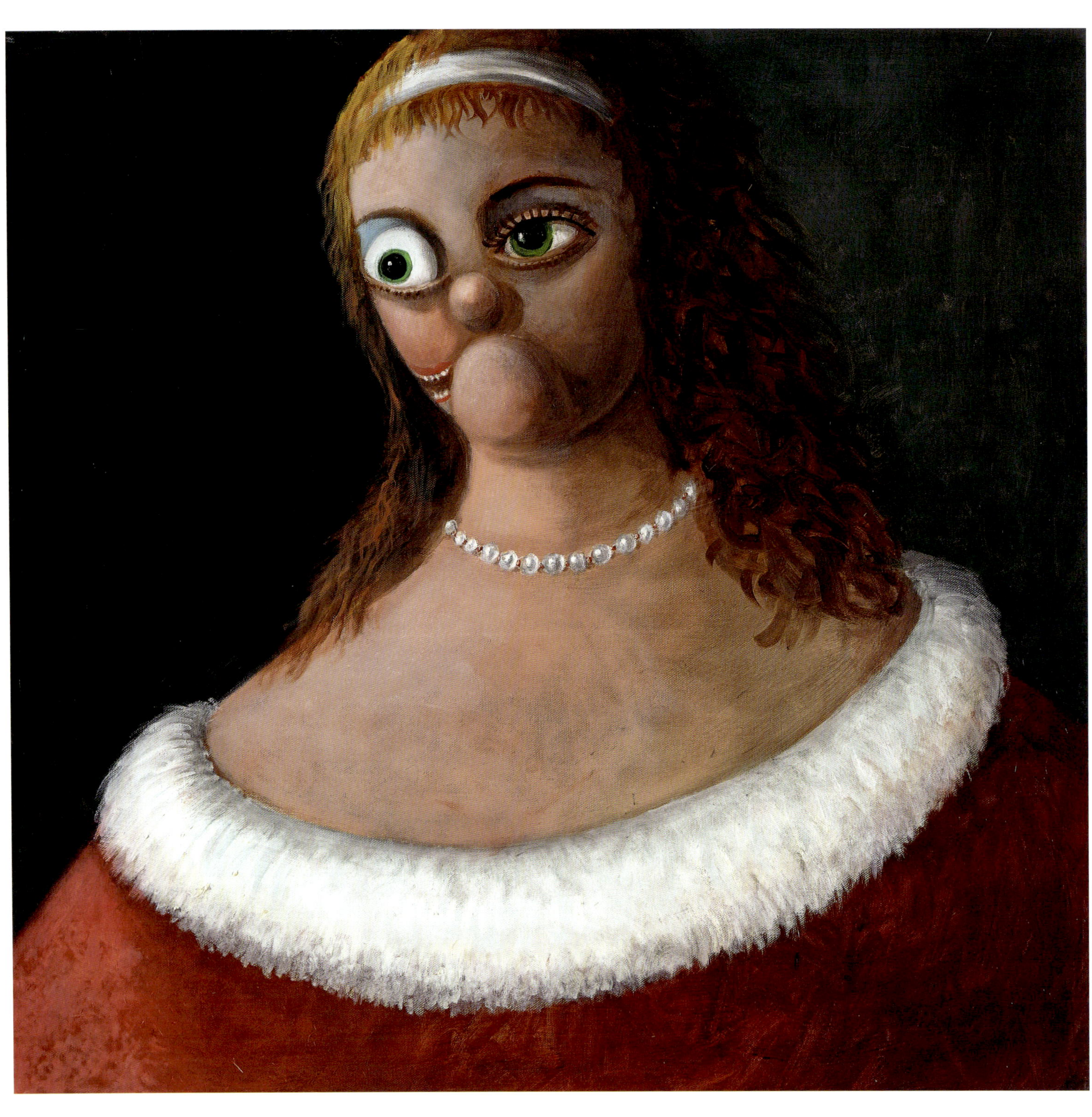

Girl with Pearl Necklace, 2019
Oil on canvas, 3 ft. 2 in. × 3 ft. 4 in. (96.5 × 101.6 cm)

COMPARATIVE ANALYSIS

So back to misconceptions about my work and the comparisons starting with Pablo Picasso, an artist I greatly admire and would certainly rate as a giant in the history of art.… But what is it that is different between the two of us? Picasso's first works were studies of pigeons. I always liked blue jays and cardinals. Perhaps the reason I painted so many cardinals in the religious format is a case of misplaced identity, that of bird to human, yet still a different bird and a different approach to art.

In the case of the nineteenth century, artists began from a complete understanding and education in the French school of neoclassicism and the studies found in the teachings of Charles Bargue. His book is clearly referenced in the early drawings of Roman plaster cast studies that Picasso copied in astonishing detail. From here the artist continued to paint in the realistic but still stylistic manner of these studies as can be seen in his beautiful ink studies of his father and eventually a copy of Philip IV *by Velázquez. He was clearly inspired by these masters and yet as he developed as an artist his eyes were opened to the new school of painters in Paris, namely Toulouse-Lautrec and Cézanne.*

From here he began to really take off disassembling the concept of space in an artwork, giving as much importance to negative space as was normally given to positive space. The seminal Demoiselles *was clearly a version of Cézanne's bathers with the audacious incorporation of African masks.… He then broke to a monochromatic transition to cubism and went through this cycle until he returned in 1918 to neoclassism once again, namely the classical Greek and Roman influence. In contrast to this I came into art from the year 1957 (the year I was born), a time when* Jackson Pollock and Franz Kline, Willem de Kooning and Barnett Newman *ruled the art world.… There was no parallel to them other than the extensive influence they had all over the world, that even threatened the French, the masters, and Picasso directly confronted this development, obliterating its importance. Now America had its own heroes.…*

So I came into a world where the rebellion was already in full swing and it was my mission by the time I reached my early twenties to now obliterate them.… To enter through the lens of abstraction and turn it back into realism … yet without the nineteenth-century representational manner, but with a new language composed of multiple presences simultaneous to those movements, and to use the styles applied to the standard format of the portrait.

These were not the portraits of lovers as in Picasso's work but the portraits of imaginary beings.… Humanoids that allowed me the freedom to interchange any period in art into a single iconic form. I could be thinking of Frans Hals and Franz Kline in the same painting.… I had no reason to impose an identity as an artist rather more of mistaken identities … to the extent that the critics were confused. Holding on desperately to old norms of analysis, trying to make sense of these defiant beings that assumed either the majestic presence of royalty or of dehumanized and rejected clowns, beggars and garbage collectors. No man or woman was greater than the other, no class or hierarchy existed, all were equals in my mind. Each character was like one you might find in a play or novel where the least expected one could pass on a message to radically change the story from a comedy to a tragedy.… This is the inherent difference in my work, never relying on anything but my mind, my memory and my reflections of the world as I saw it. The expression of grief, horror, joy, happiness, love and hate can all be seen at the same time in a single portrait because I gave myself the freedom to express my own emotions through the visage of the other.

FEMALE PORTRAITS

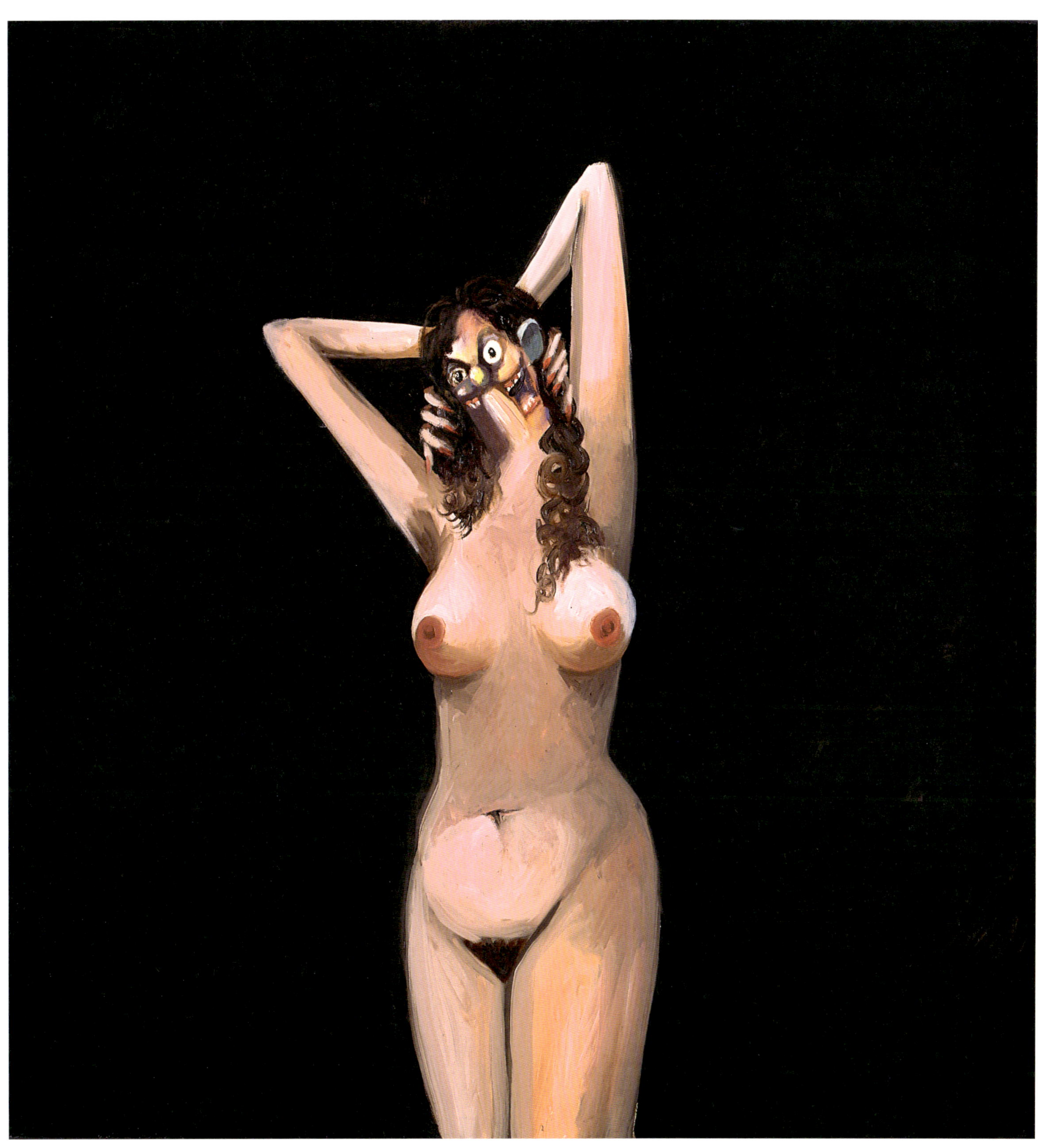

The Stranger, 2008
Oil on canvas, 4 ft. 2 in. × 4 ft. 2 in. (127 × 127 cm)

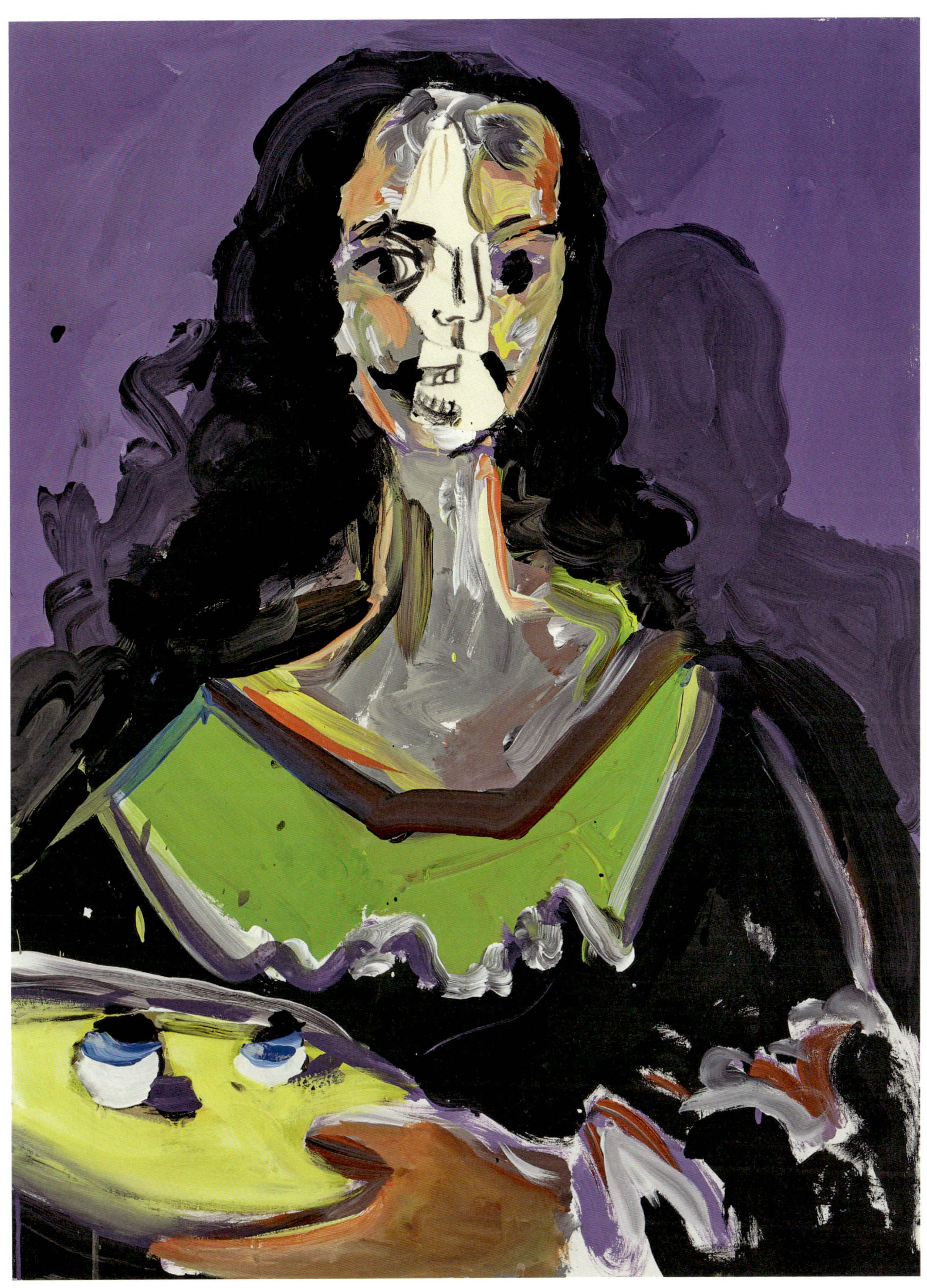

St. Lucy, 1992
Acrylic, charcoal, and collage on canvas, 3 ft. 4 in. × 2 ft. 6 in. (101.6 × 76.2 cm)

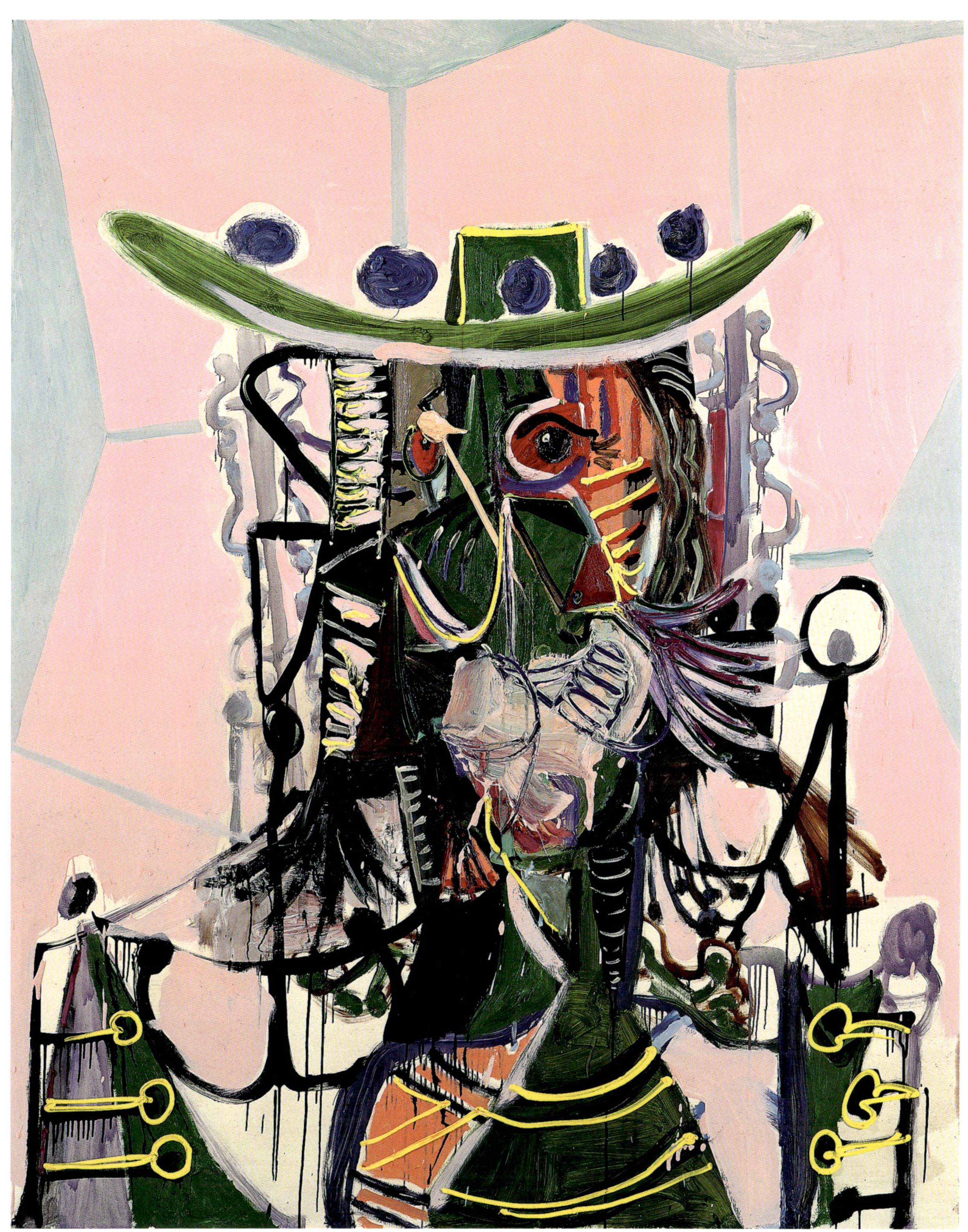

Memories of Picasso, 1989
Oil and acrylic on canvas, 6 ft. 4¾ in. × 5 ft. 3 in. (195 × 160 cm)
Frac Île-de-France, Paris

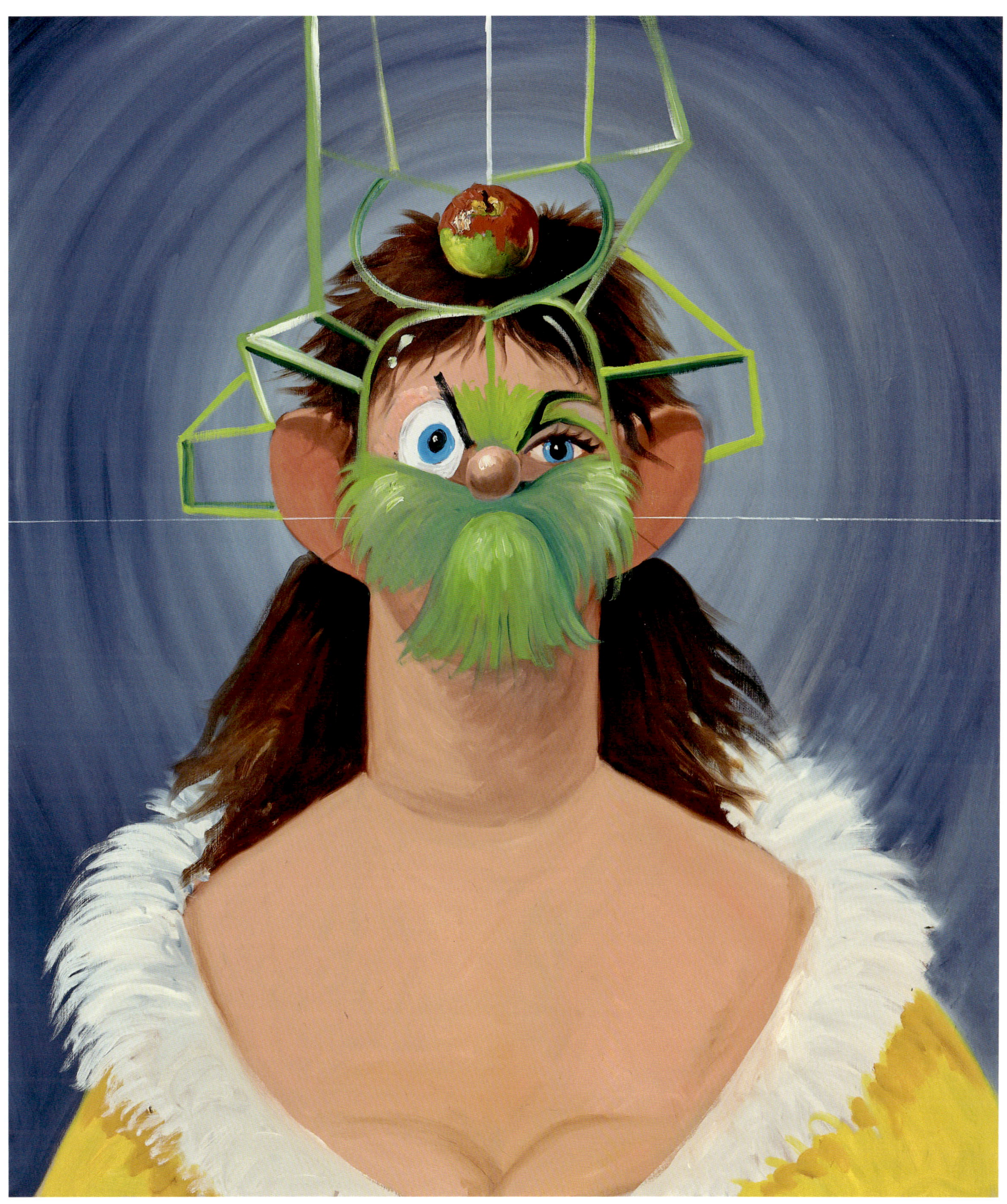

Snow White, 2009
Oil on linen, 4 ft. 5⅛ in. × 3 ft. 10¼ in. (134.9 × 117.5 cm)

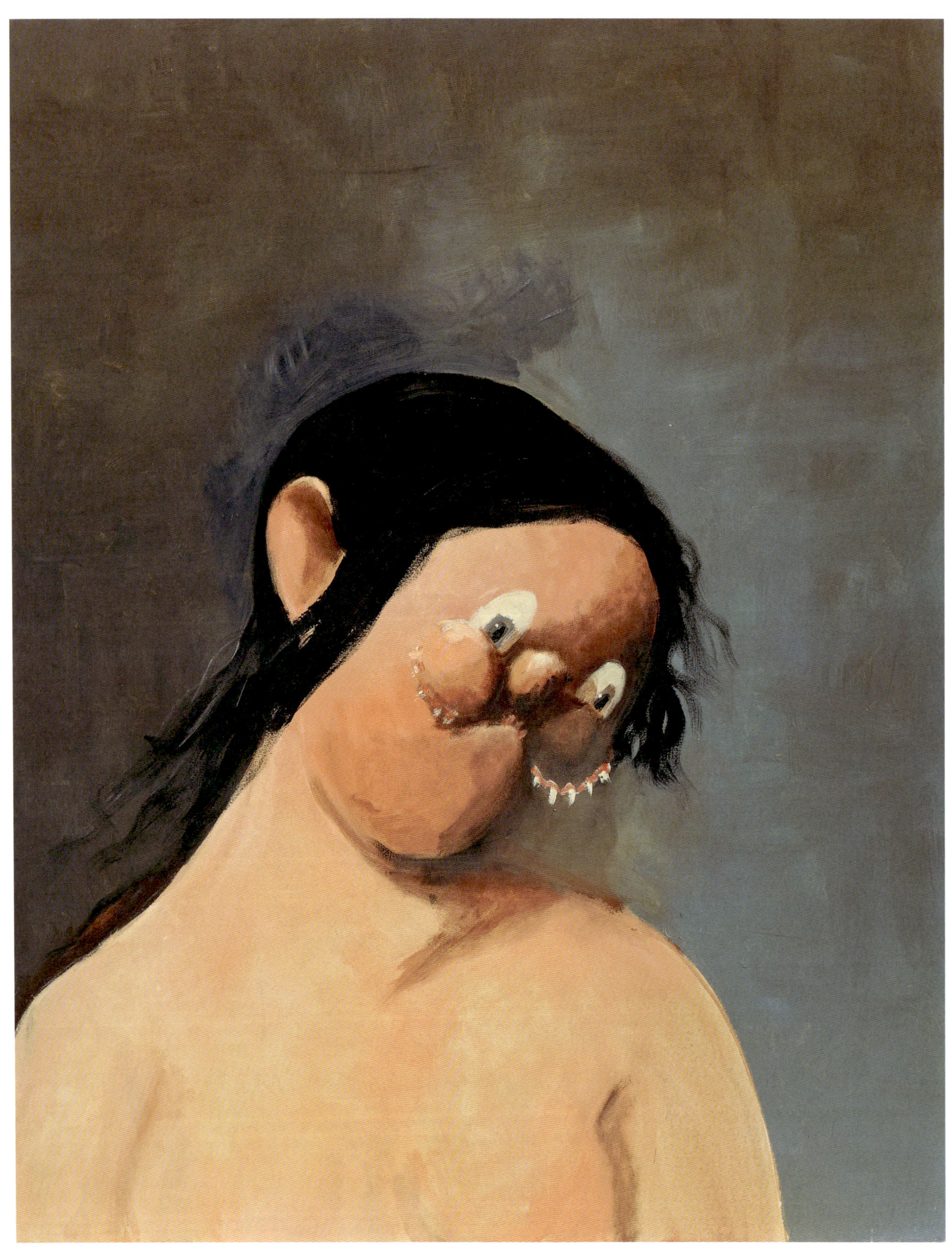

The Chinese Woman, 2001
Oil on canvas, 5 × 4 ft. (152.4 × 121.9 cm)

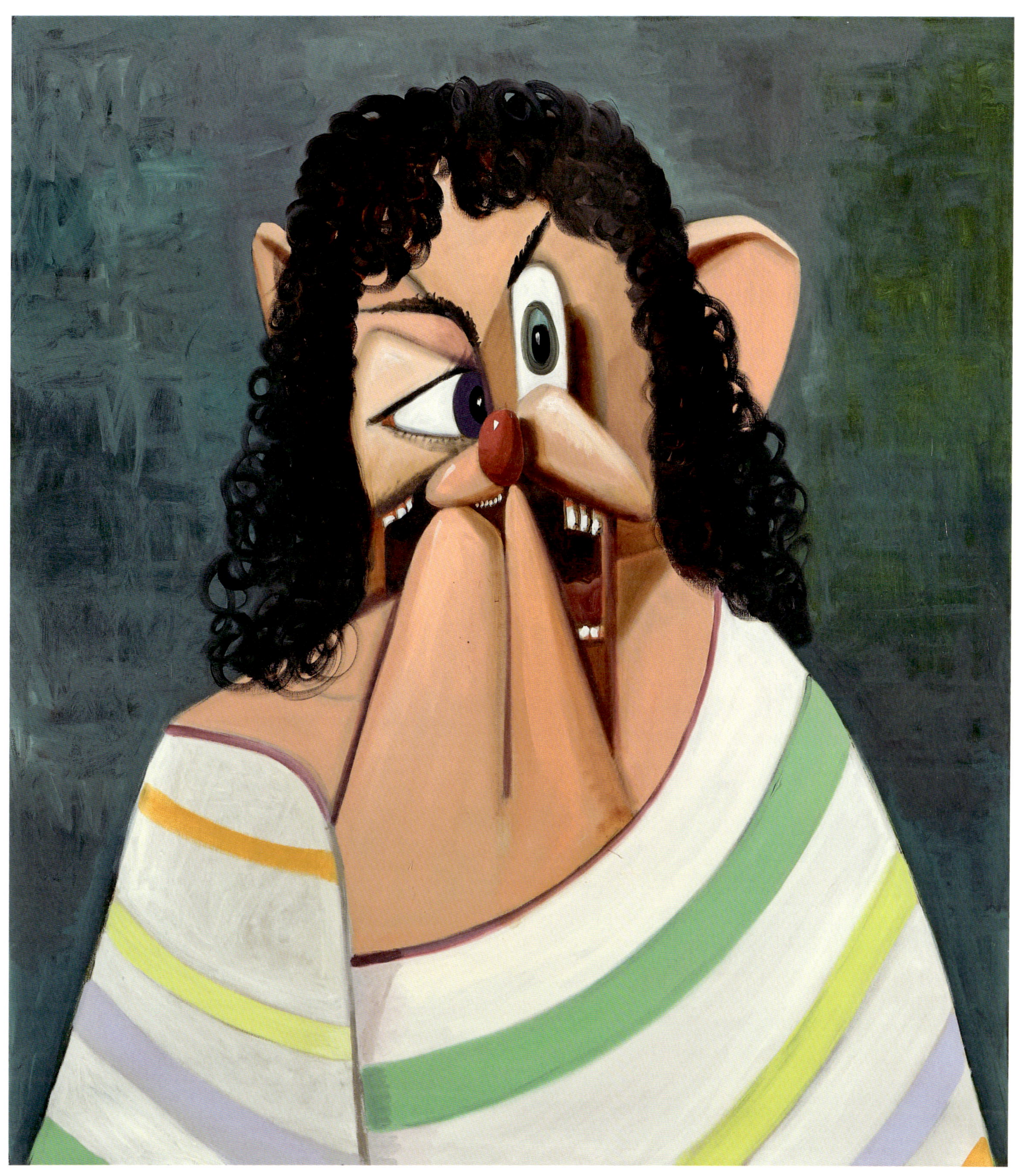

Rodrigo's Wife, 2011
Oil on linen, 4 ft. 6⅛ in. × 4 ft. ¼ in. (137.5 × 122.6 cm)

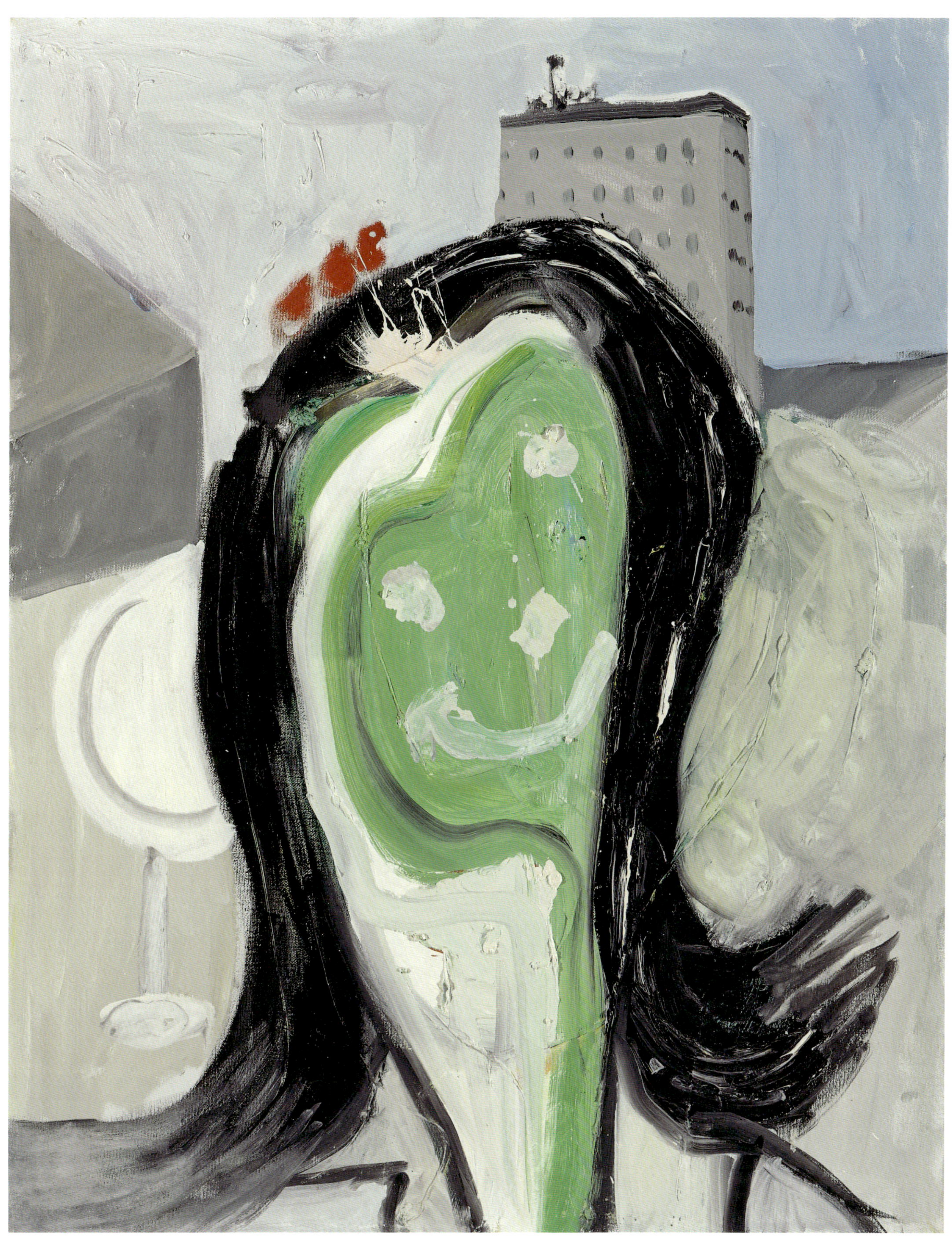

Girl with Red Bow, 1987
Oil on canvas, 30 × 24 in. (76.2 × 61 cm)

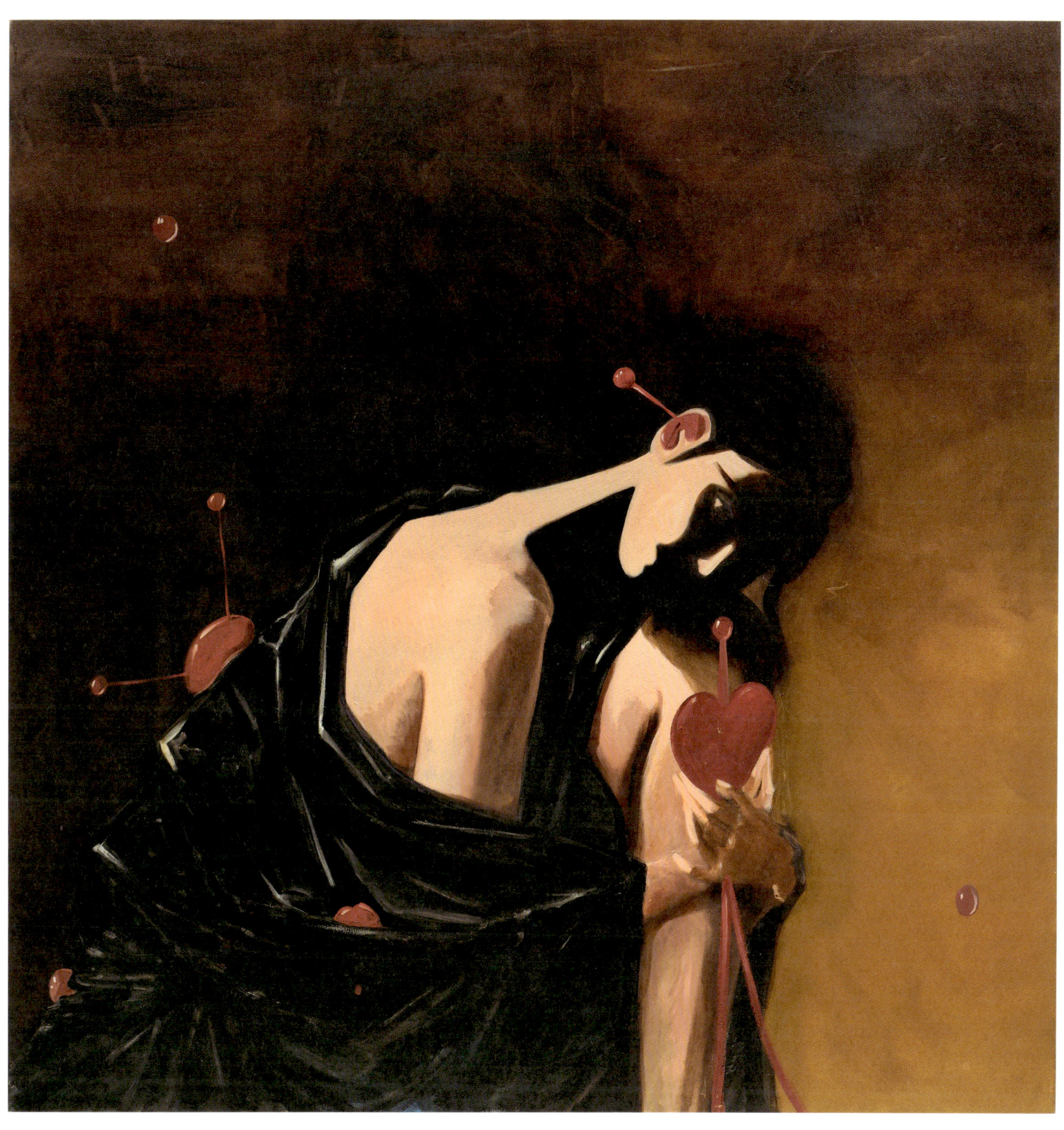

Lamentation, 2000
Oil on canvas, 6 ft. 6 in. × 6 ft. 6 in. (198.1 × 198.1 cm)

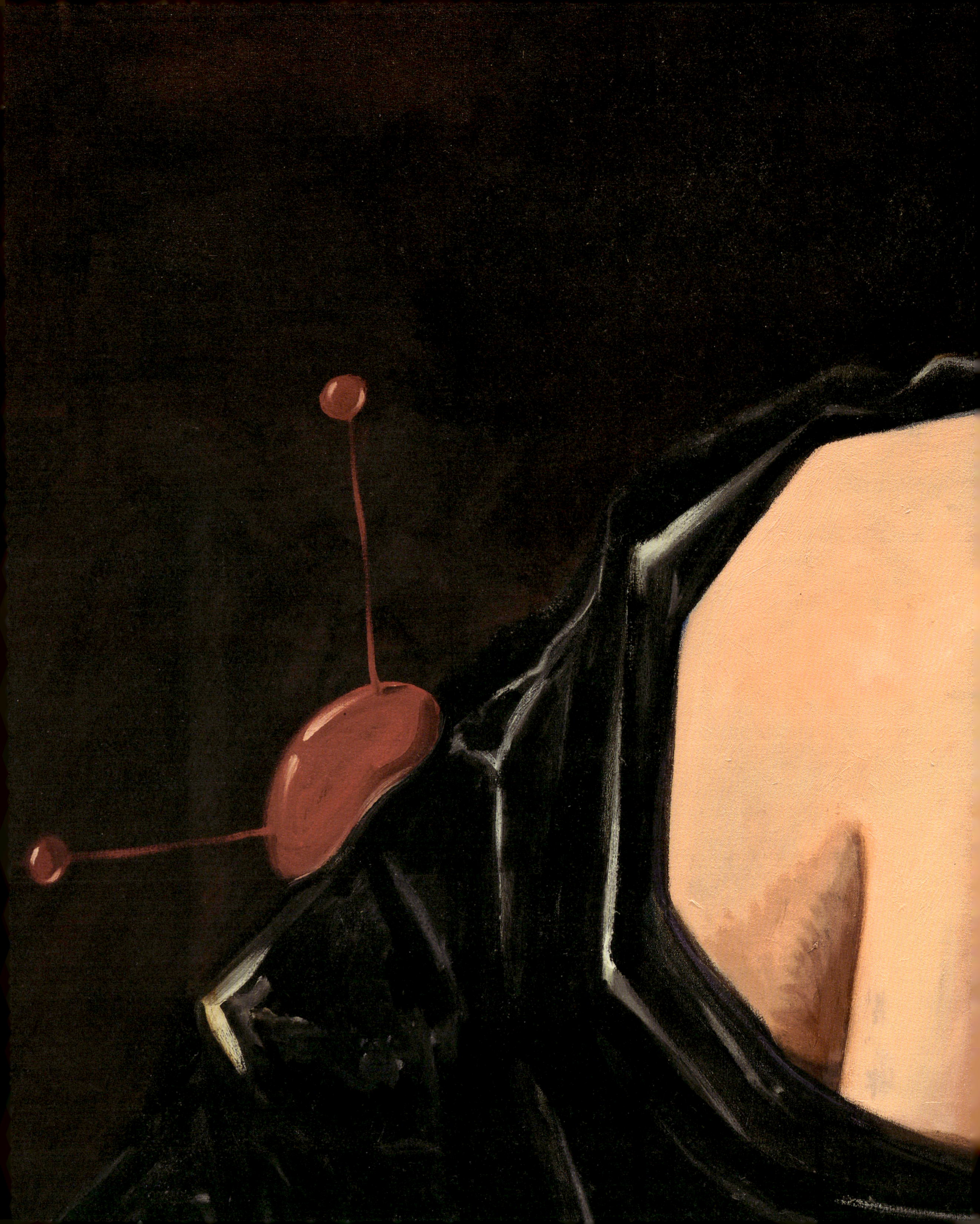

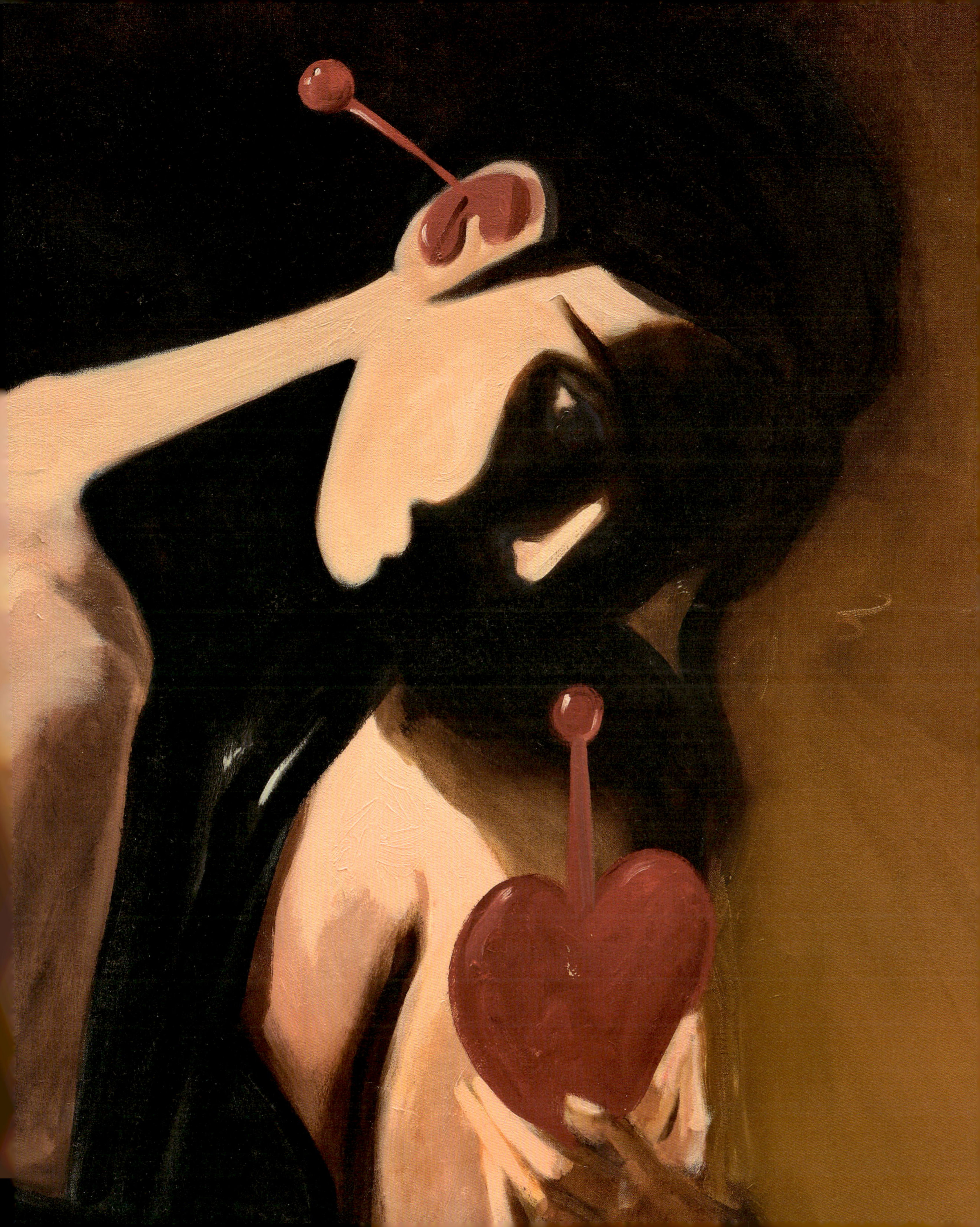

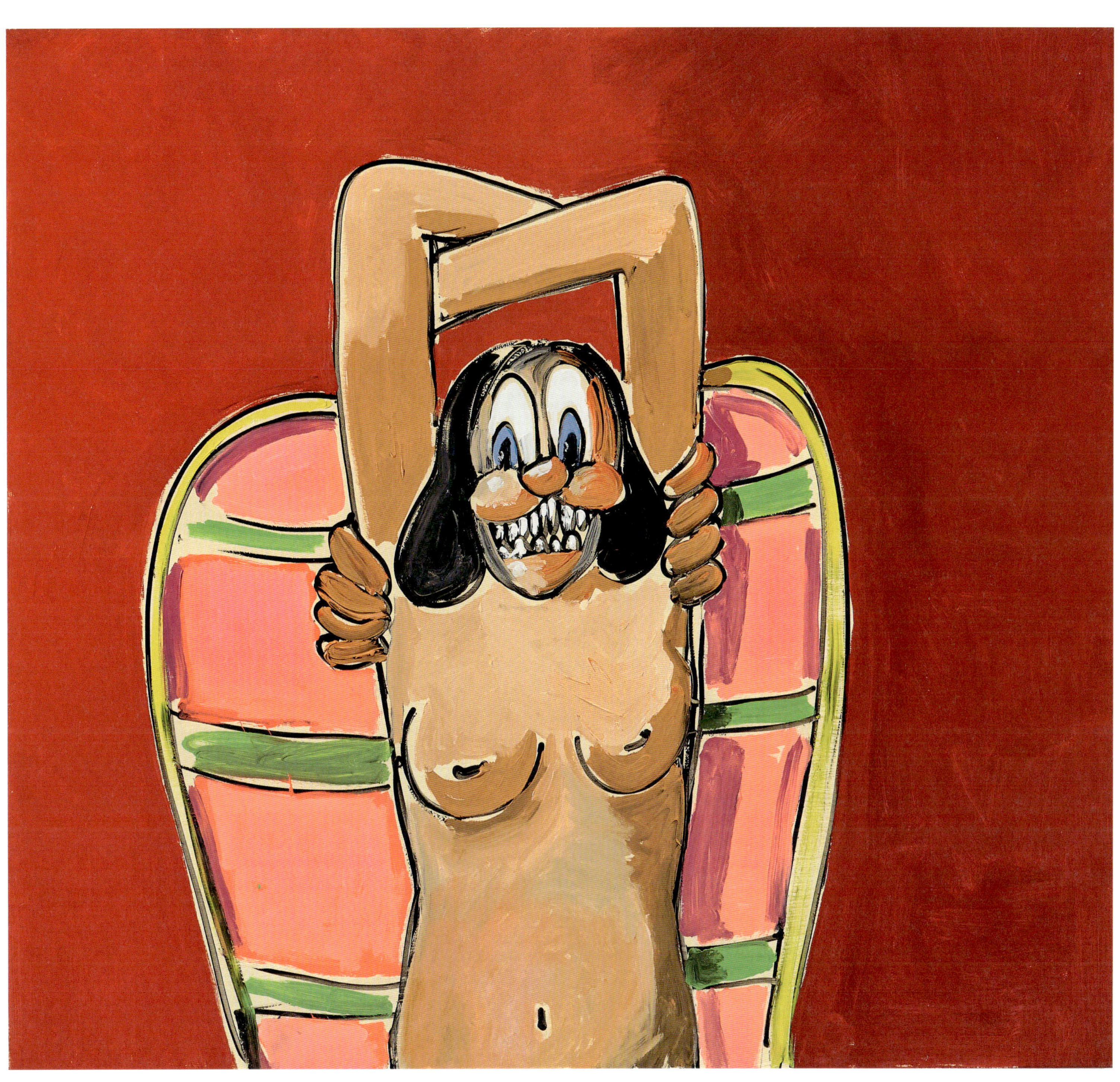

The Super Model, 1999
Acrylic on canvas, 5 ft. 5⅛ in. × 6 ft. (165.4 × 182.9 cm)

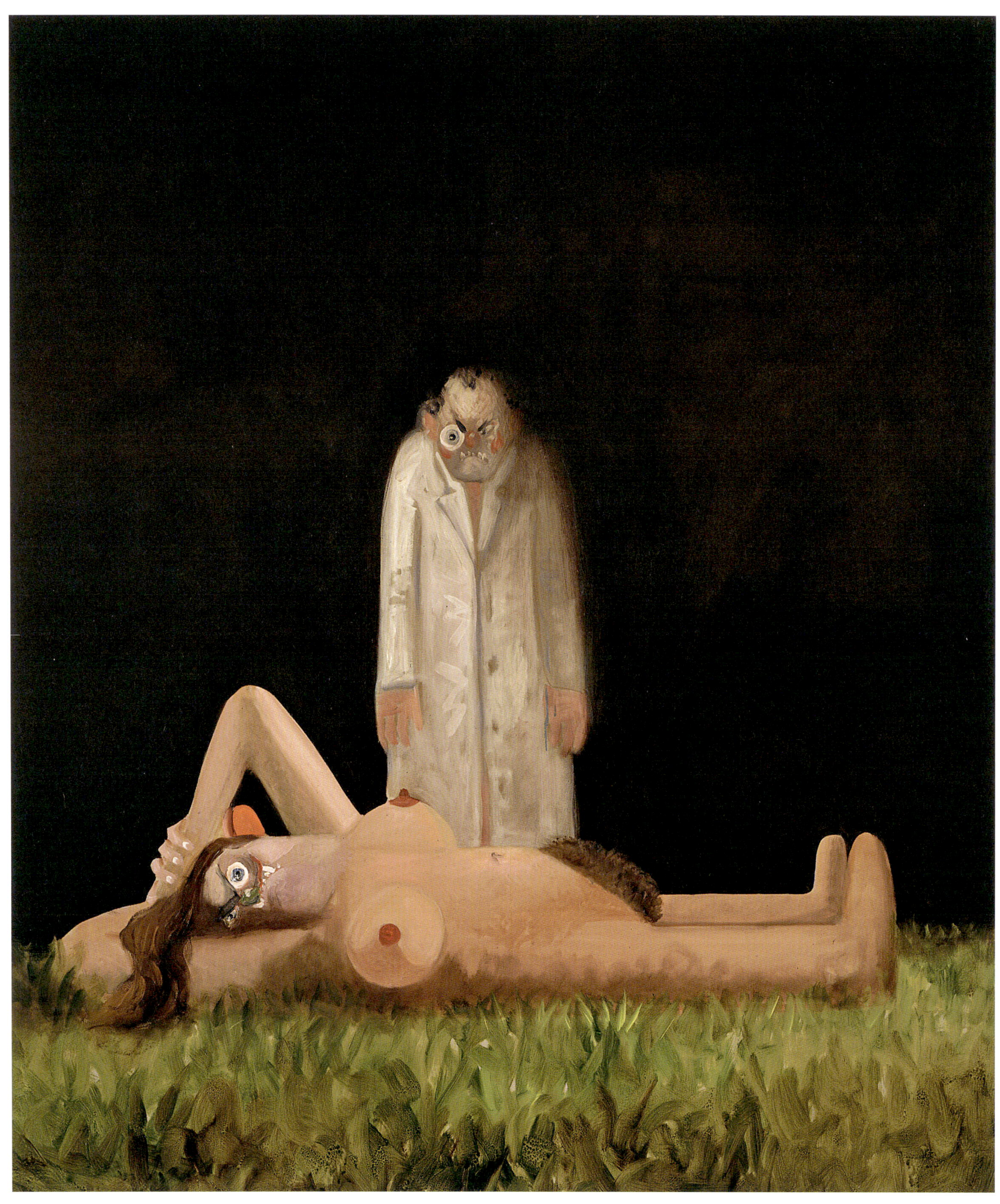

The Mad Scientist and His Wife, 2006
Oil on canvas, 5 ft. 2 in. × 4 ft. 6 in. (157.5 × 137.2 cm)

ART HISTORY

Like death, life lasts forever. From the ashes of thought a fire burns and the sun never dies … its heat brings life and destroys it. The artist is like the sun, his creations are life-long after his life has ended.… Only those whose works bring life to others will survive the rain coming from the minds of foolish thinkers … whose own thoughts are guided by fools who came before them. As a creator, art is the reflection of wisdom and the inner truth that knows itself to be in constant flux … never one but always at the same time the other … the other being that of the Humanoid, the ascending spirit of an untouchable dream … where the mind can live in another world within its own world. Creators live in this world within their world.

When will those who spent their days criticizing Claude Monet's paintings for being ugly go away? They did that to him back in the late nineteenth century, when most critics found his work insulting and blamed him for the death of art.… They couldn't see beyond the limits of what had preceded him.… Not understanding the difference between an artist whose life is devoted to evolution based on the principles of that which came before him, but with no certain ties to that which propelled those whom he admires into the context of art history.… One must do that to achieve greatness and secure a place amongst the gods … it would be foolish to ignore them and have no correlation, to exist in a vacuum and never be heard, seen or recognized. One must include all that he loves in art as did Picasso and Cézanne in order to become one of a family … they all do.… Let's face it, each great artist is marked by his predecessors and what he has done to add or subtract to create his own species of mankind.…

The Humanoids are my imaginary people, ones who can play the role of all the lovers and the mad and lonely, the hierarchy and the lowlife.… Like Bruegel's beggars, the homeless drinkers I painted in Double Elvis *at the Venice Biennale were there on display in majestic proportions dwarfing the rich and self-indulgent. Serving up a platter of homeless idiots in the midst of conversation, clinking bottles of cheap booze the way two fund managers may toast themselves with a glass of Château Margaux.… It was not that way for the great thinkers like Félix Guattari or William Burroughs who keenly detected my originality and set me apart from those who came before.… It was the way David Sylvester understood Francis Bacon, or Jean Genet Rembrandt, or Sigmund Freud Leonardo da Vinci.… It takes an original mind to see one.*

It's relative … I have destroyed the linear constructs of history by interchanging the languages from various centuries simultaneously and without sacrificing my own ideals and the portrayal of an iconic singular being. I found a way, like Amedeo Modigliani, to turn the real into a special species of my own type.… Who would ever want a painting by Vincent Van Gogh of simple academic representation rather than one that comes from his passionate vision of life? Who would want one by Modigliani? Who cares whether Rothko could draw? Nobody cares. What they want is the artist to be true to himself and be relentless in his path to individuality without the approval of anyone other than his own soul. Nobody would ever ask if Turner could turn the sunrise down a notch, or if Rembrandt wouldn't mind using colors other than brown as he reached the end of his life and limited his palette to the most rudimentary tonalities and hues of color.… But look at those Rembrandts photographed in black and white … you will see the master at work almost photographically capturing the most minute of physiological details in his self-portraits. Long after he abandoned so-called color … and was criticized for doing so … nobody can match the sheer perfection of these paintings. It is the honest truth that those which everyone seems to hate the most eventually become the most beloved.

FAKE
OLD
MASTERS

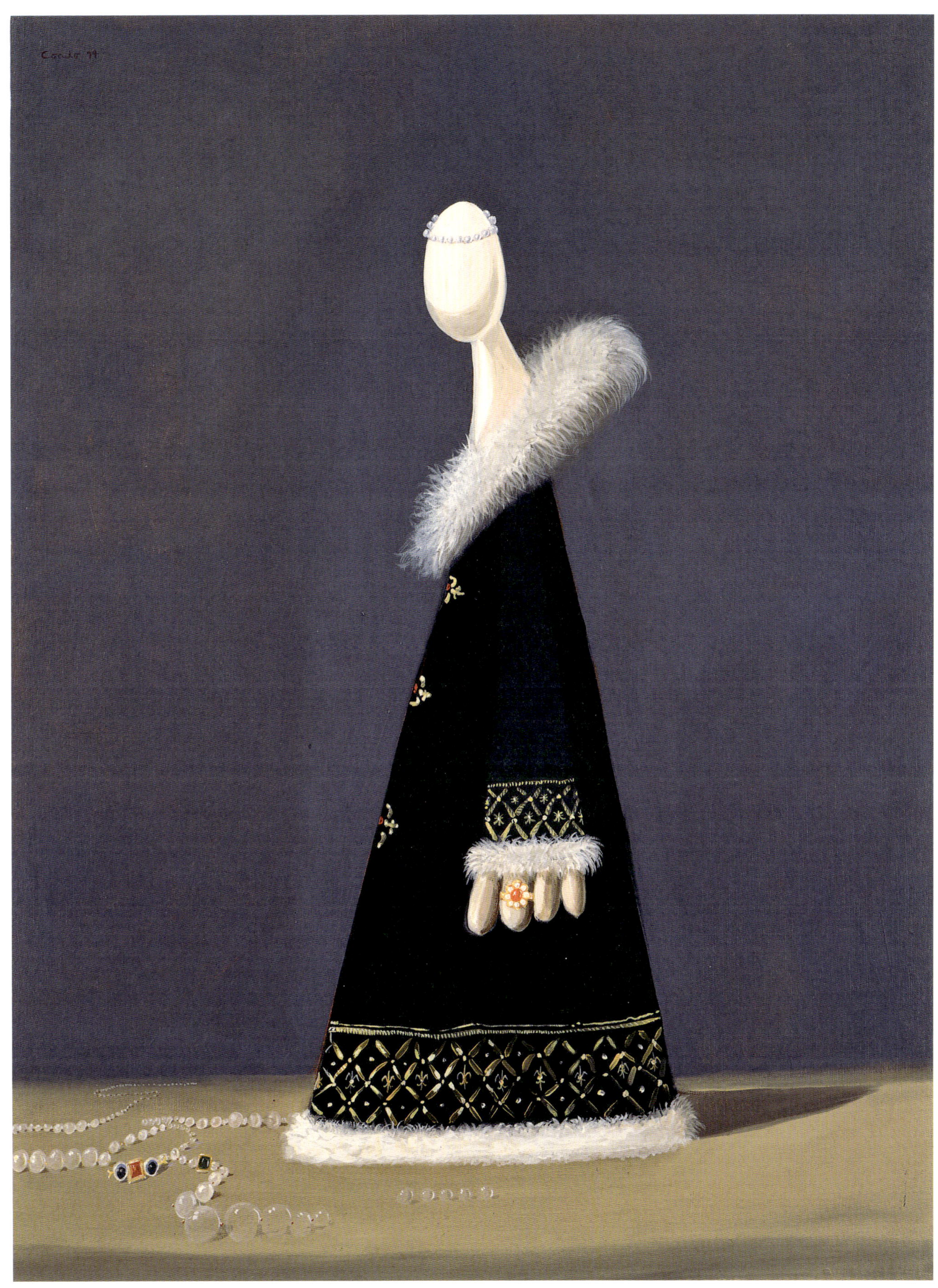

The Objective Idealist, 1994
Oil on canvas, 3 ft. 4 in. × 2 ft. 6 in. (101.6 × 76.2 cm)

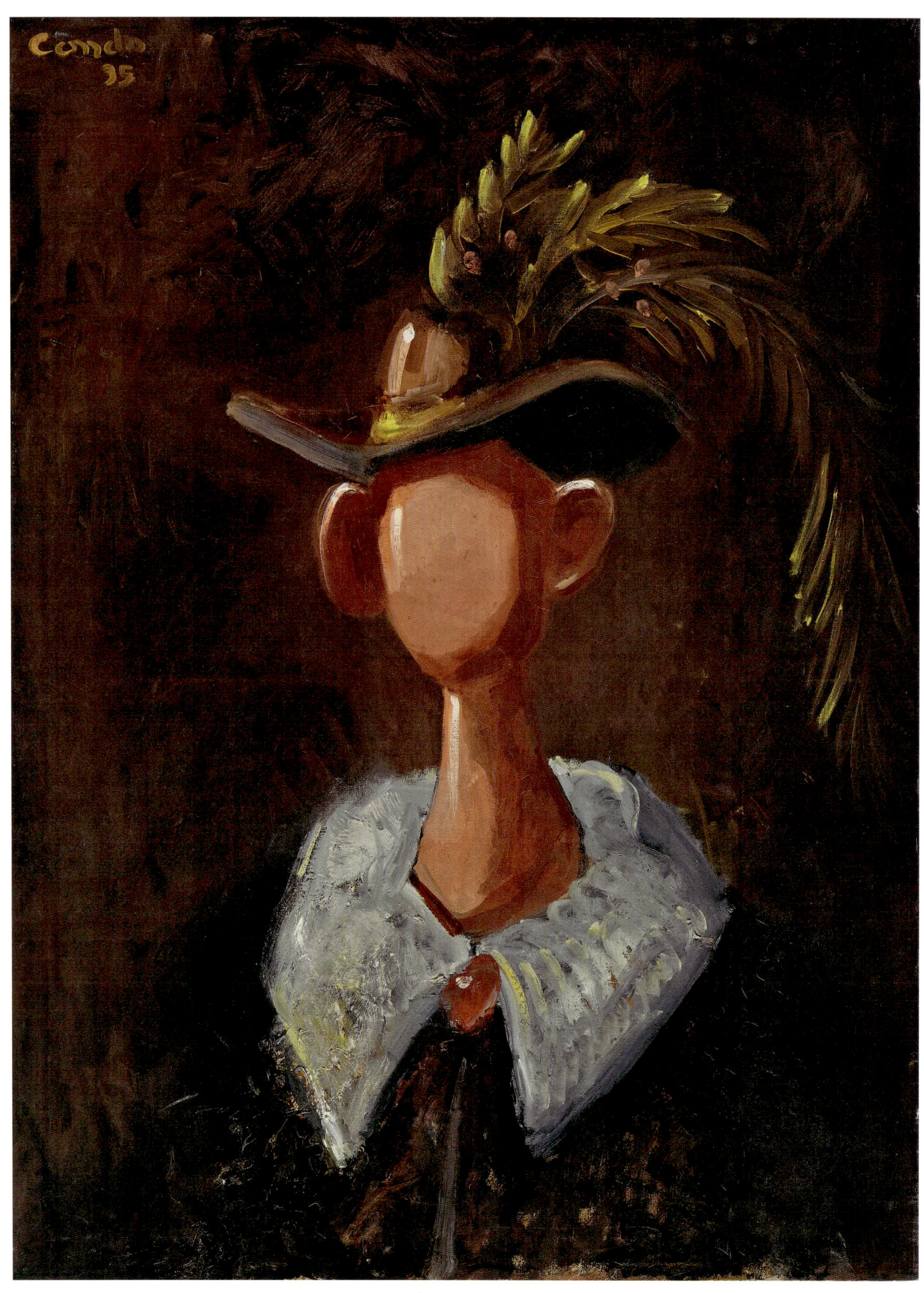

Memories of Frans Hals, 1995
Oil on linen, 3 ft. 4 in. × 2 ft. 6 in. (101.6 × 76.2 cm)

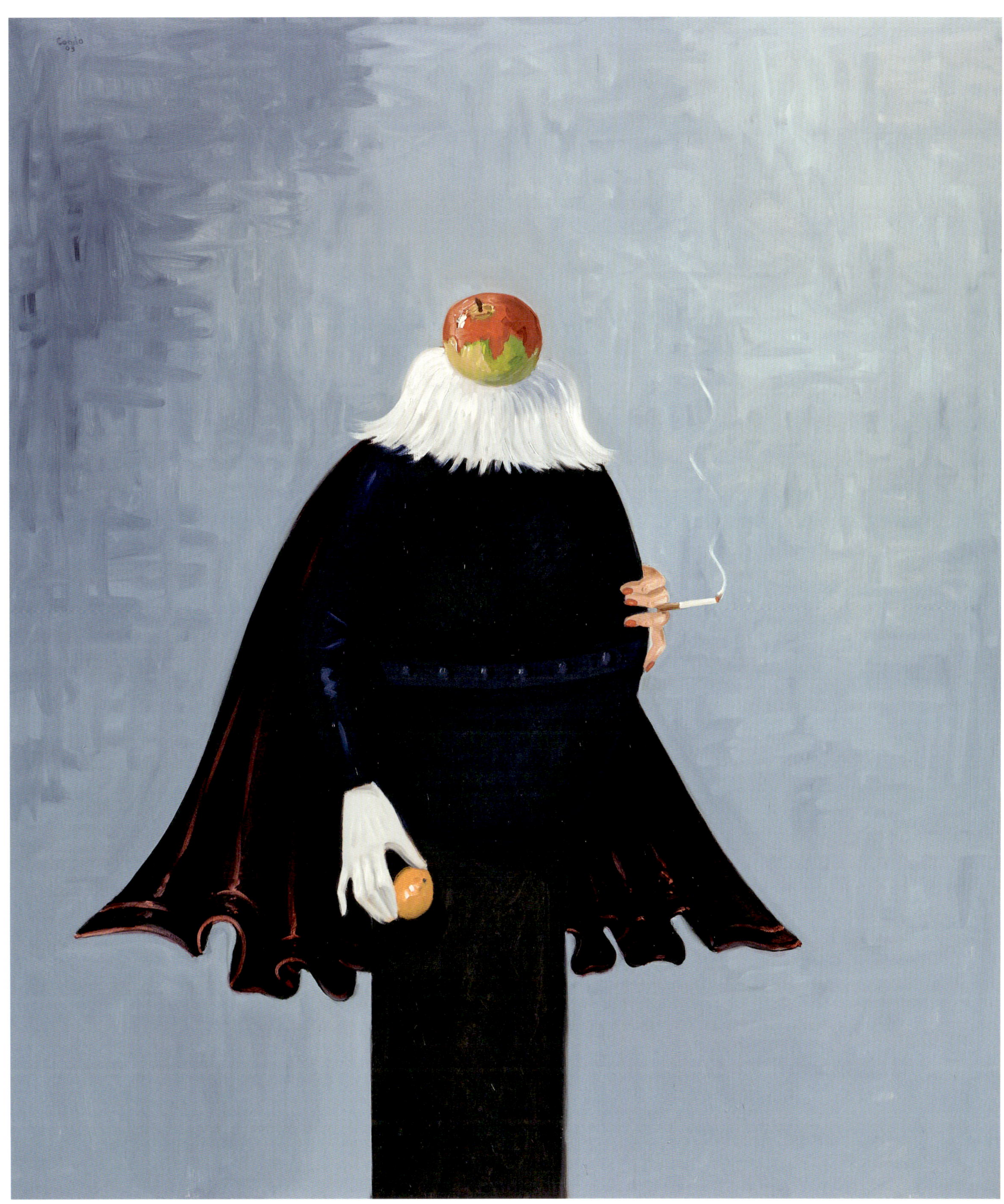

The Apple Picker, 2009
Oil on linen, 5 ft. 2 in. × 4 ft. 6 in. (157.5 × 137.2 cm)

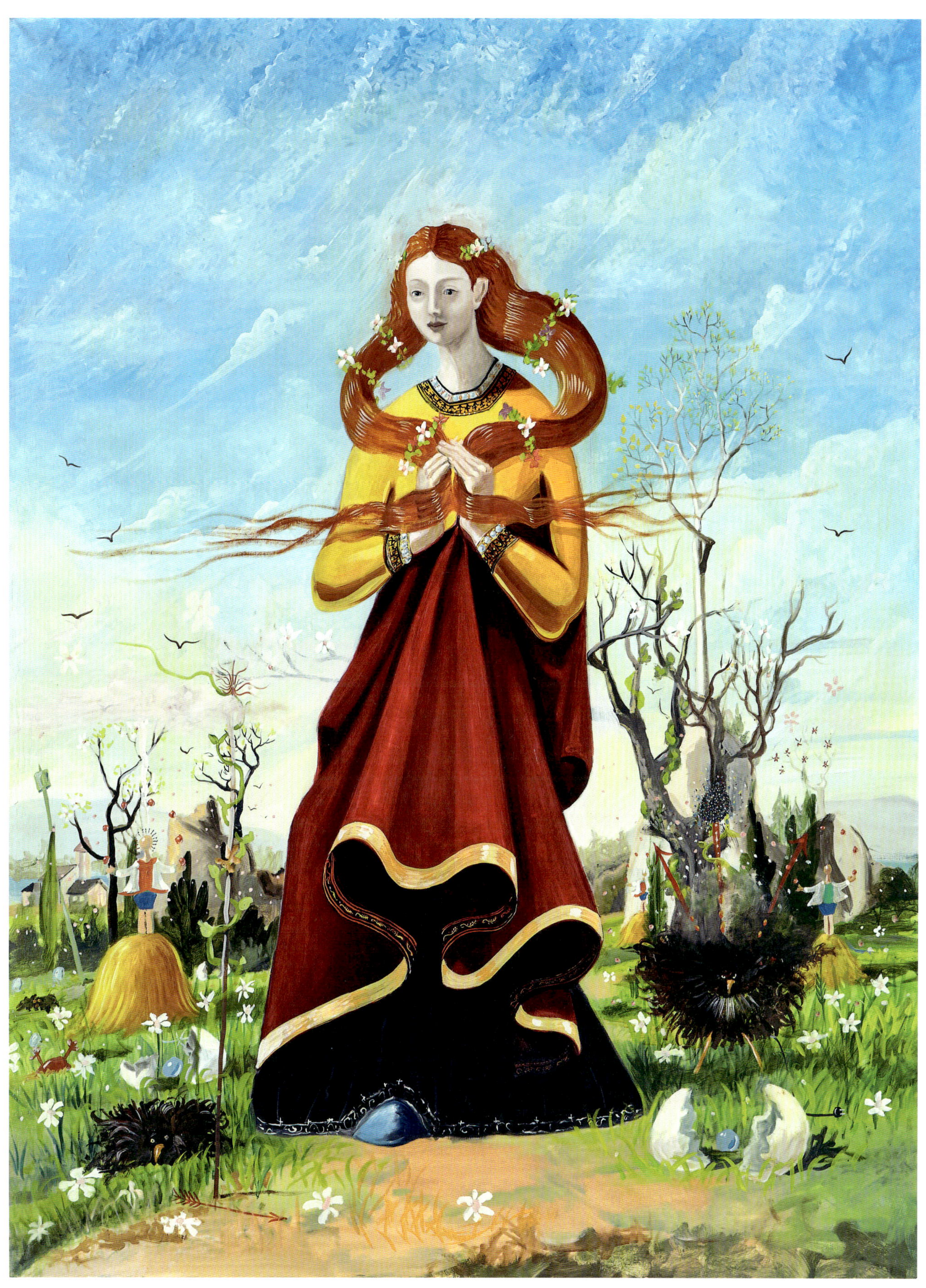

Interchangeable Reality, 1994
Oil on canvas, 6 ft. 6¾ in. × 4 ft. 11 in. (200 × 149.9 cm)

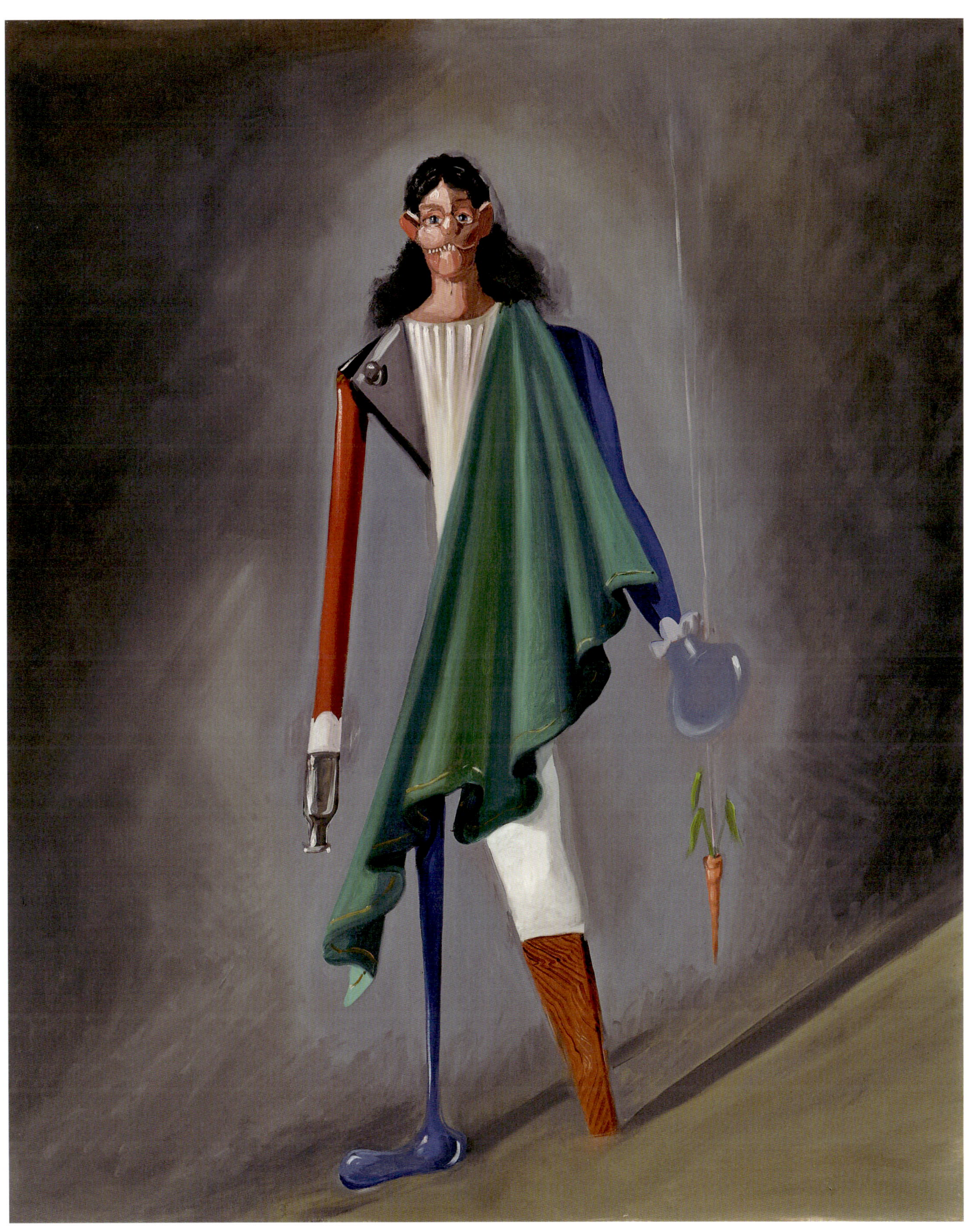

Yankee Doodle, 2003
Oil on canvas, 5 ft. × 4 ft. 2 in. (152.4 × 127 cm)

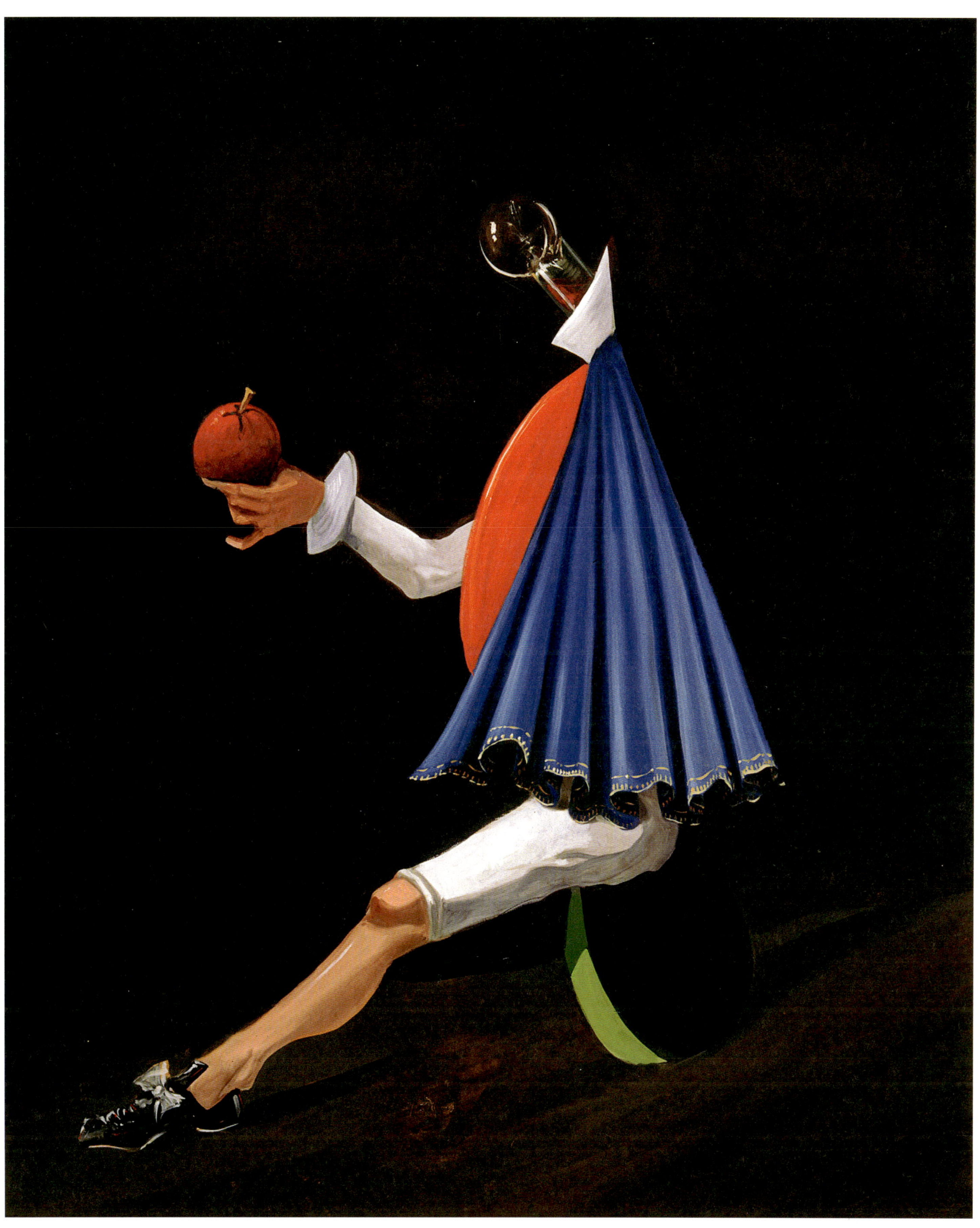

William Tell, 2003
Oil on canvas, 5 ft. × 4 ft. 2 in. (152.4 × 127 cm)

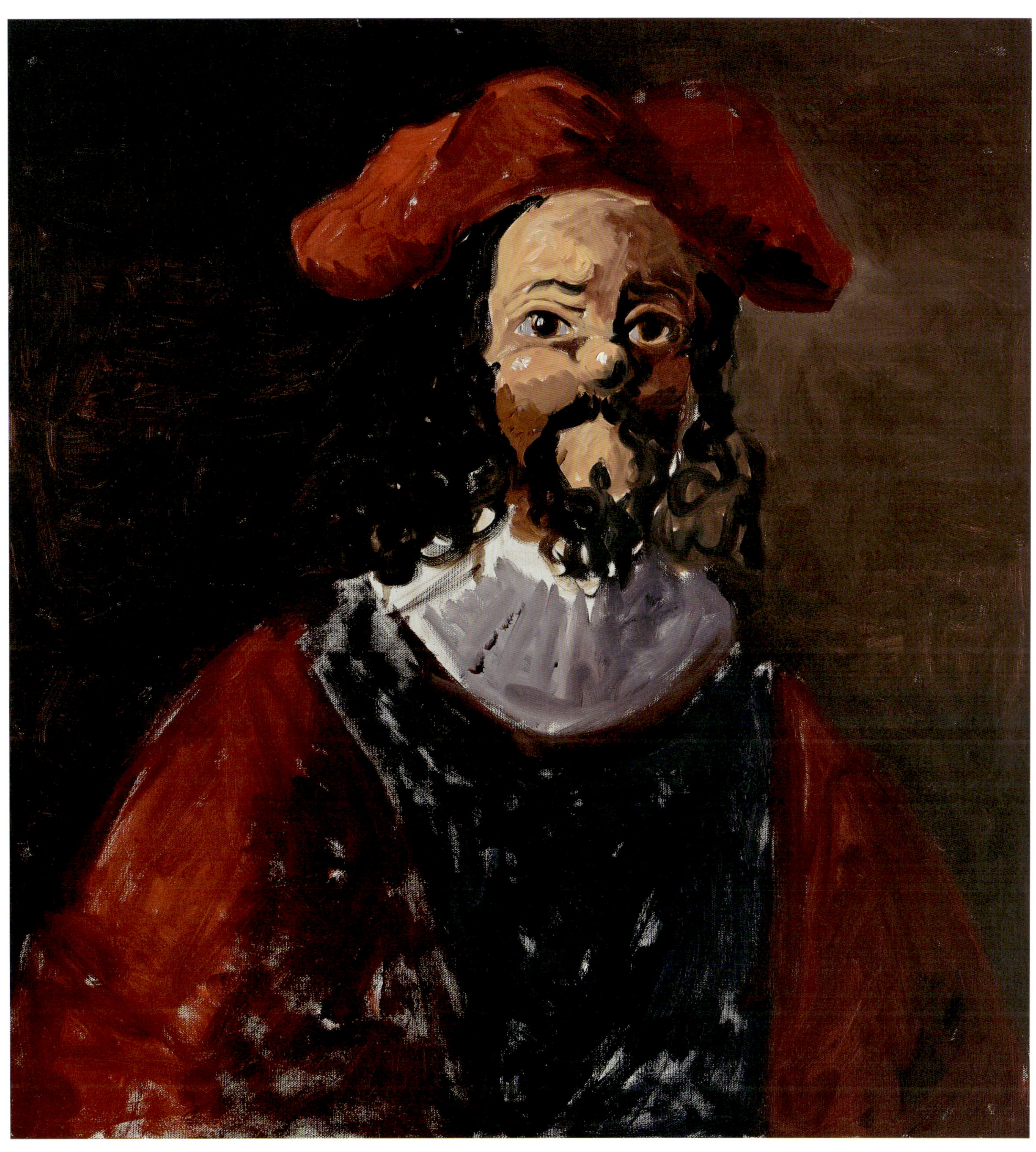

The Return of Polish Rider, 2010
Oil on canvas, 3 ft. 4 in. × 3 ft. 2 in. (101.6 × 96.5 cm)

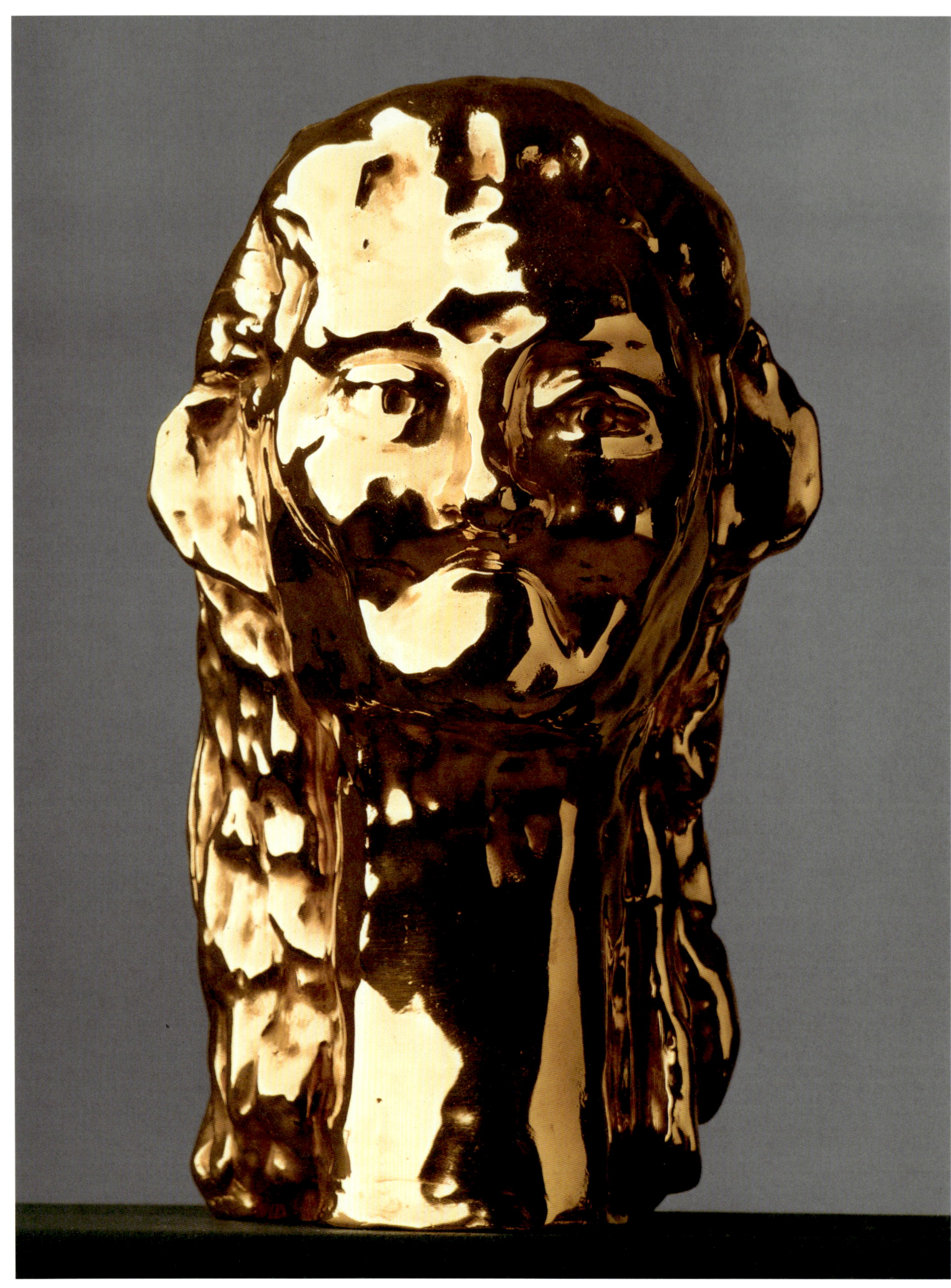

The Old Sea Hag, 2002
Gilded bronze, 10 × 6¾ × 8 in. (25.4 × 17.1 × 20.3 cm)
Artist's proof, edition of 3 and 1 artist's proof

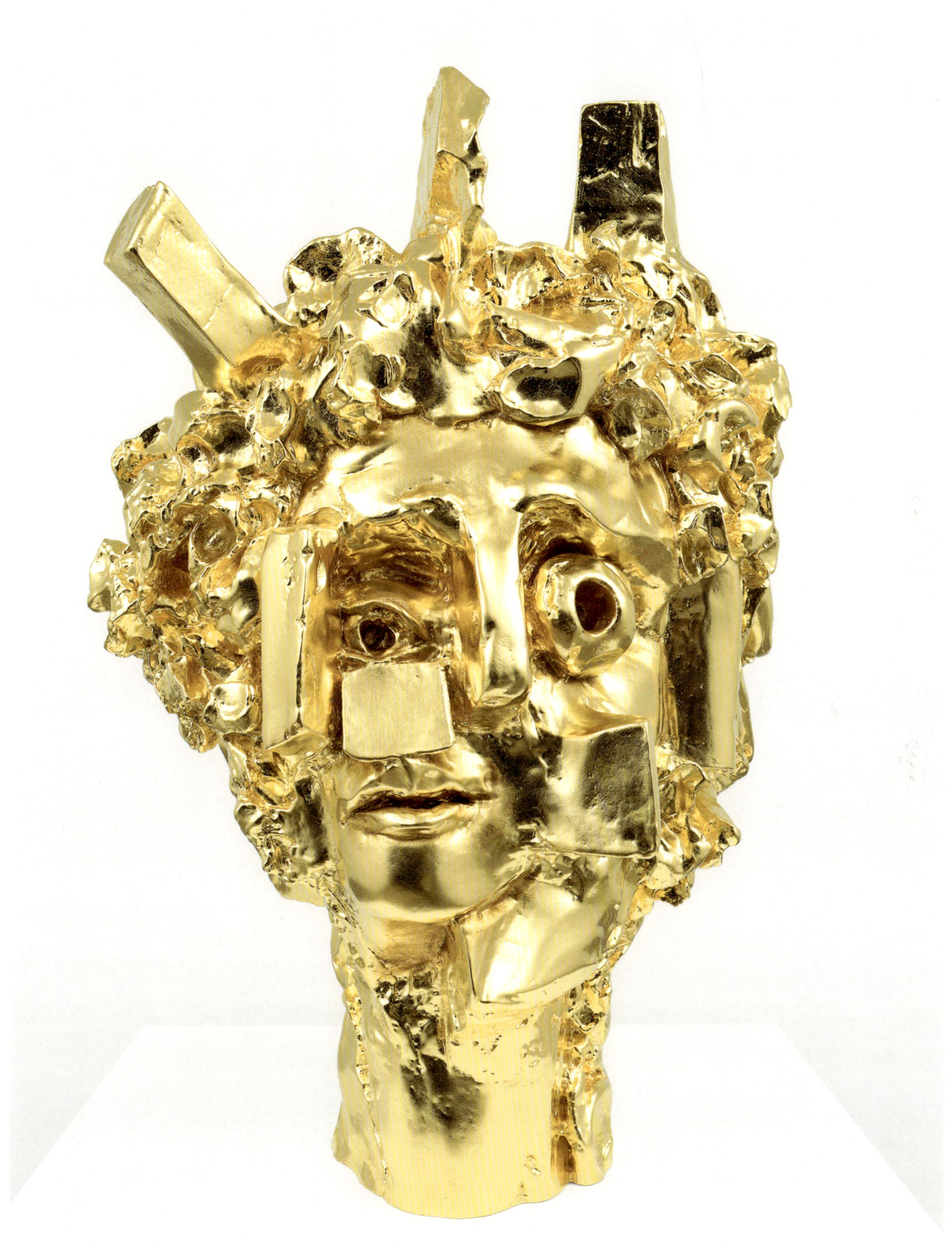

Constellations II, 2022
Cast aluminum with gold leaf, 31 × 21¾ × 20¾ in. (78.7 × 55.3 × 52.7 cm)
Edition No. 1 of 10 and 2 artist's proofs

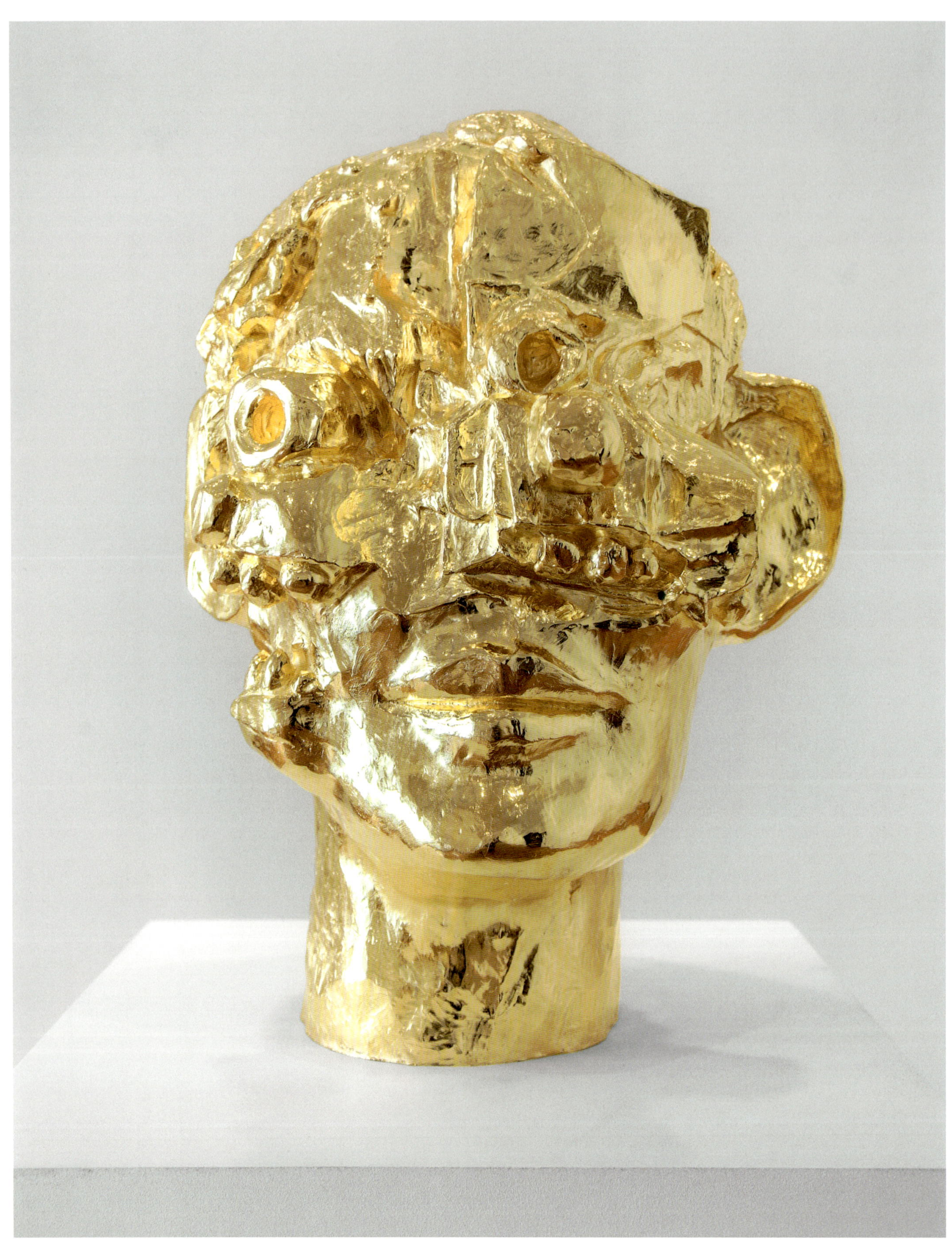

Robot Girl, 2012
Gilded bronze, 28½ × 20 × 24½ in. (72.4 × 50.8 × 62.2 cm)

ROBOT GIRL

Aside from any referential material … including citations or quotes from the great masters of philosophy, my aim is to be somewhat naive like the original thinkers before thought was analyzed into "thinking" and perhaps even ruined by interpretation … dissected like an animal only to find out later it was a human. Like drinking gasoline in the moment of great thirst in search of water. The elements as they first appeared, fire and water, were somewhat unexplainable and only left to the philosophers to bring light upon them. As was the kingdom of beasts upon the planet for the caveman to scrawl across the caves in the human endeavor to record his existence thus proving what he had encountered, that its natural beauty did exist … the beauty of the world in which he thrived, and that with being … life brought him life…. The robot has brought us life, today it has done man's job, it has created the medical facilities to cure that which doctors are unable to achieve … it has no mind, it has only function…. The Da Vinci of the fifteenth century has been replaced by the Da Vinci of the medical instrument world created by the Intuitive Surgical company; it has far more capacity to remain steady during surgery than the trembling hands of a drunken doctor called up in the middle of the night to replace a broken hip. It is far more reliable and its being has no soul. It is the thanks that we impose after successful surgery that brings this humanoid machine a heart and soul, for it is "us" that imbue upon the machine a human existence, it is us that give it thanks and praise for its miraculous healing powers…. Not a god, not a doctor, but a robot … an extension of the human being, in essence a Humanoid, a replicated hierarchy of our own selves to determine our wellbeing…. Its beauty perhaps in the days of Kant would have been shunned as form but in function praised…. There is no maiden or god to be worshipped here, only the glory of functionality…. Michelangelo, best known for the Sistine Chapel, is now a 3D airbrush used by contemporary artist Avery Singer to create her own mental metropolis of hybrid metahumans. One exceeds these outdated modes of distinction and brings us into today's world, not the one Rembrandt or Caravaggio sought out when questioning the spiritual religiosity of their times, but the one of today, where lives are saved not by prayers but by a robot.

Collective consciousness

If there is such a thing as collective consciousness, then what about collective imagery? Many minds meet as one … so therefore could never be represented as a single being rather a collective number of beings all in one visage … a symposium of minds in one head. It's the reason that a fractured face may not be of a single person but a divarication, a conflation of many faces ultimately adding up to the singular image in which many heads are seen at once … or many emotions or thoughts are seen all together at the same time…. Not a fracture in the sense of a bone but more of a brain … one that has been interrelated with many other brains all at once. Not clinically or medically but in the act of observance … at the moment when multiple viewpoints are being expressed and can only be seen in a glimmer of time at one moment.

What is defined as collective consciousness in the mind of a single being…? What robotic heaven- and hell-related antipodal being was informed to drive his microscopic forklift in my head and arrange my molecules? Who told god he was god? What are the bleachers in the auditorium of the subconscious and why were they put there … is it our hard drive? The one connected to an invisible cord that contains all that has been downloaded and dropboxed into our minds since birth, inaccessible without the painters' gift to replicate one that is not us but that potentially we see ourselves within…. The knowing, serious eyes of Van Gogh's subjects, the sinuous lines of Rubens' nudes, and the monstrosities of Goya's royal portraits all play a role in our creation of a self.*

* Reference to Aldous Huxley,
Heaven and Hell, 1956.

IMAGINARY PORTRAITS

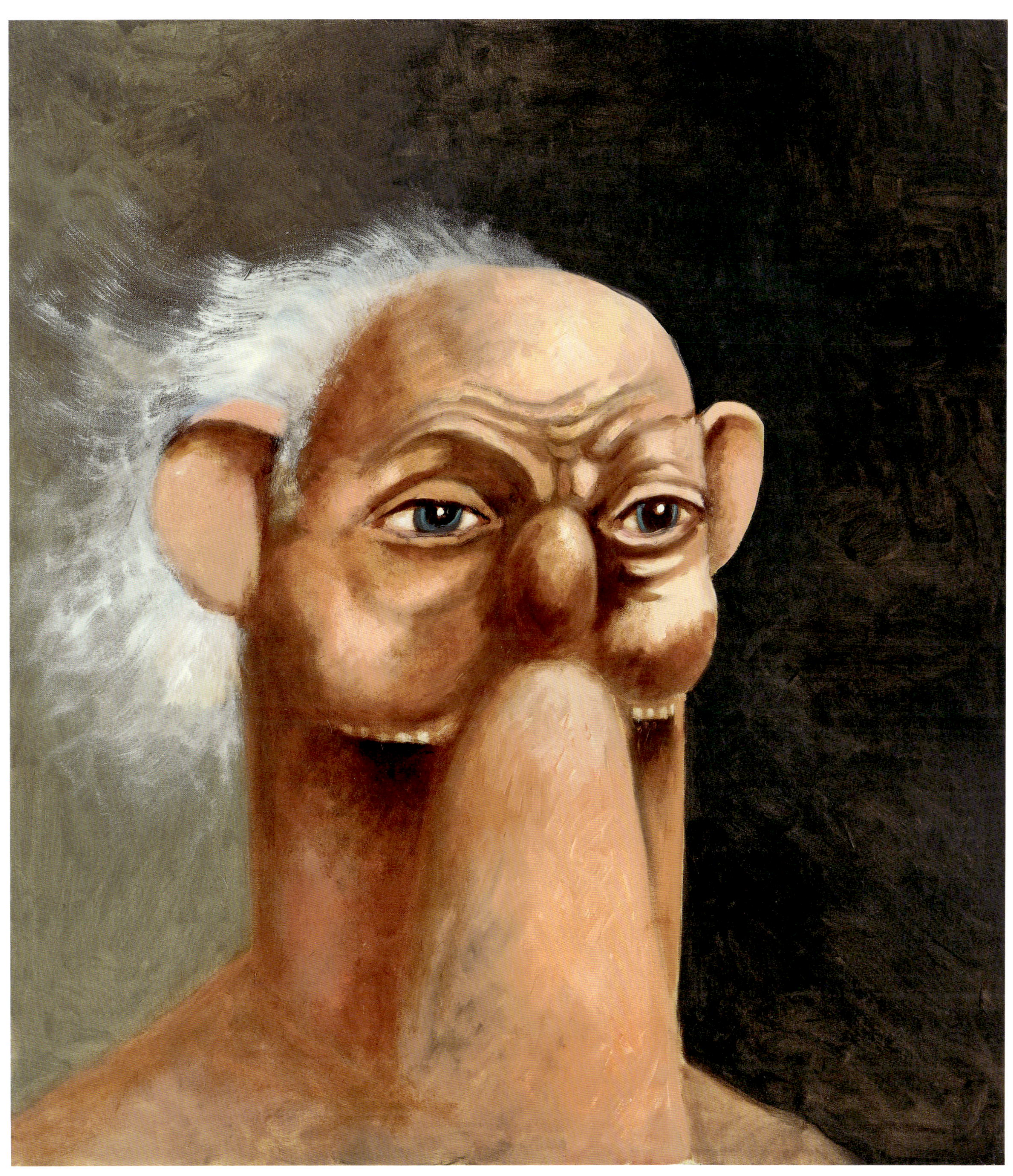

Old Man Portrait, 2011
Oil on linen, 3 ft. 6⅛ in. × 3 ft. 2⅛ in. (107 × 96.8 cm)

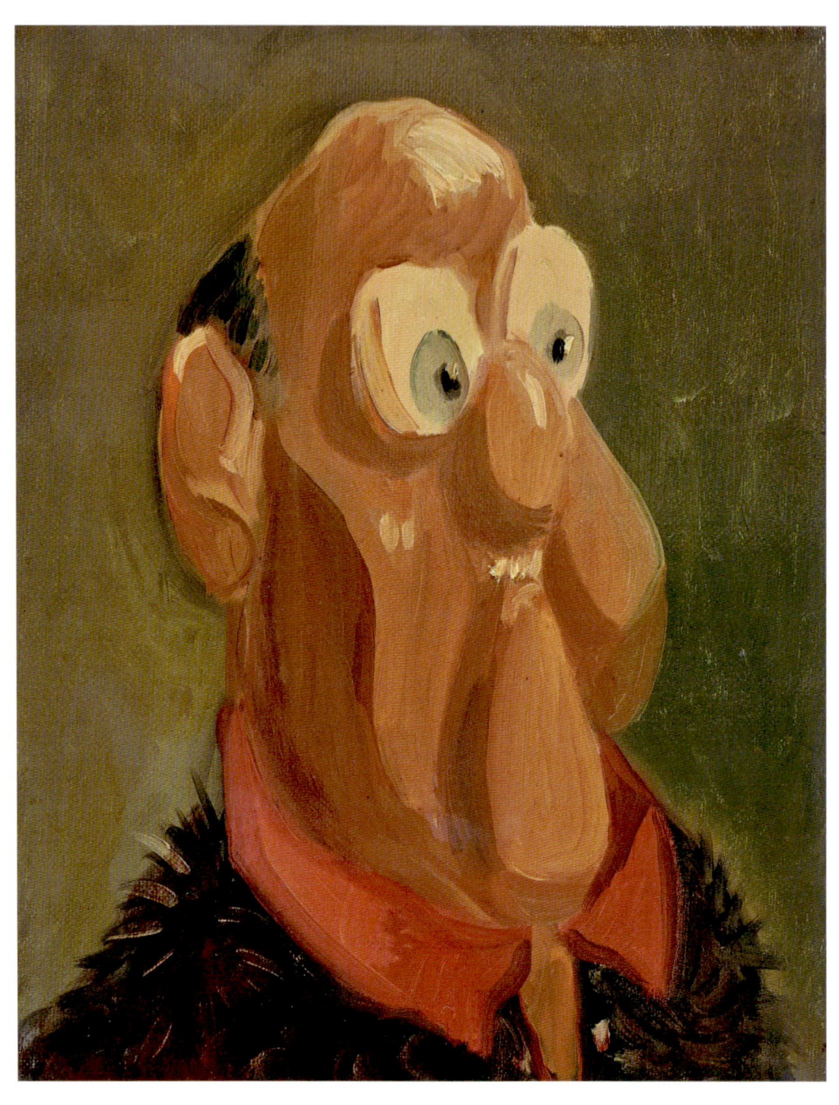

The Boss, 1995
Oil on linen, 10 × 8⅛ in. (25.4 × 20.6 cm)

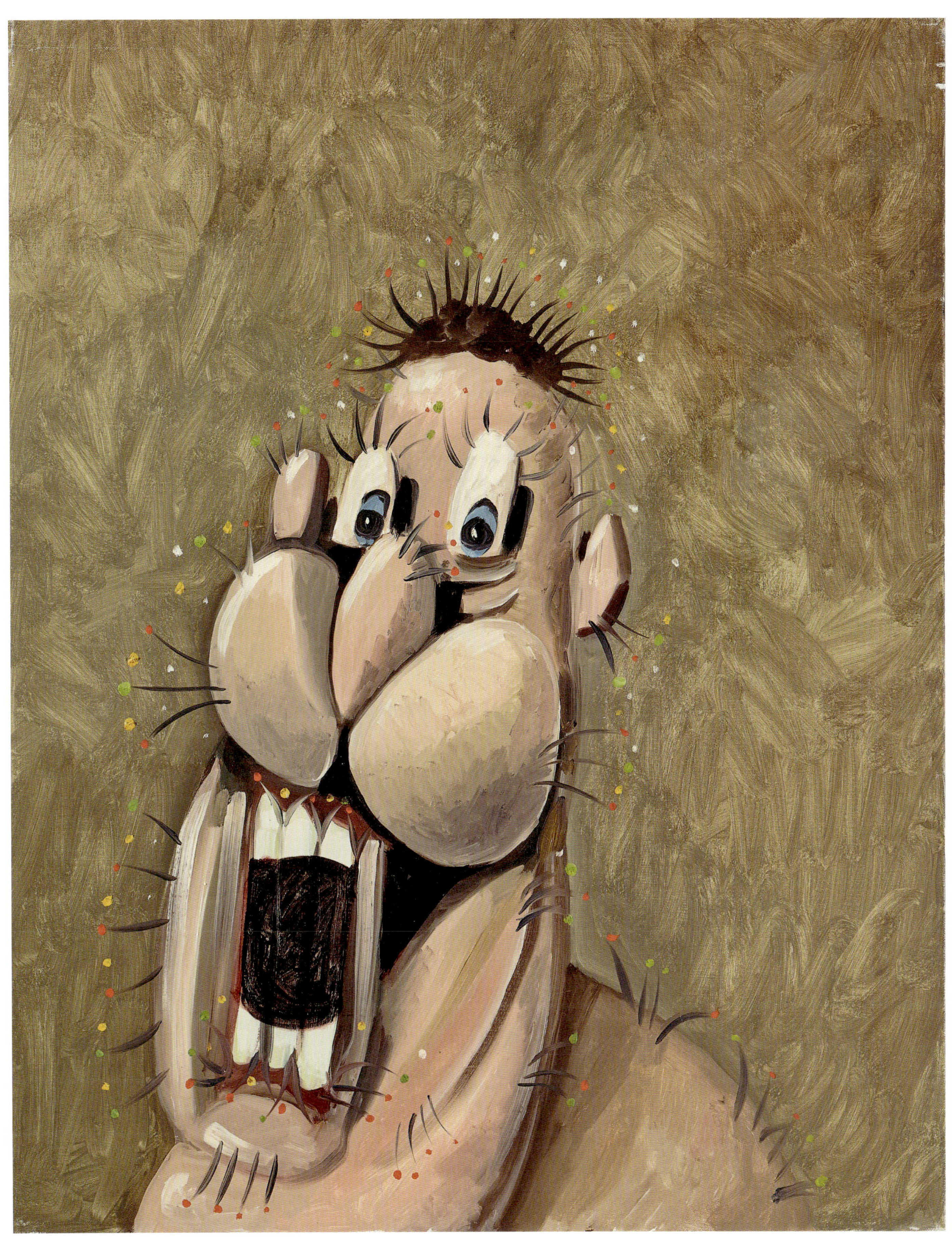

Portrait of Marc Glimcher, 1994
Oil on canvas, 30 × 24 in. (76.2 × 61 cm)

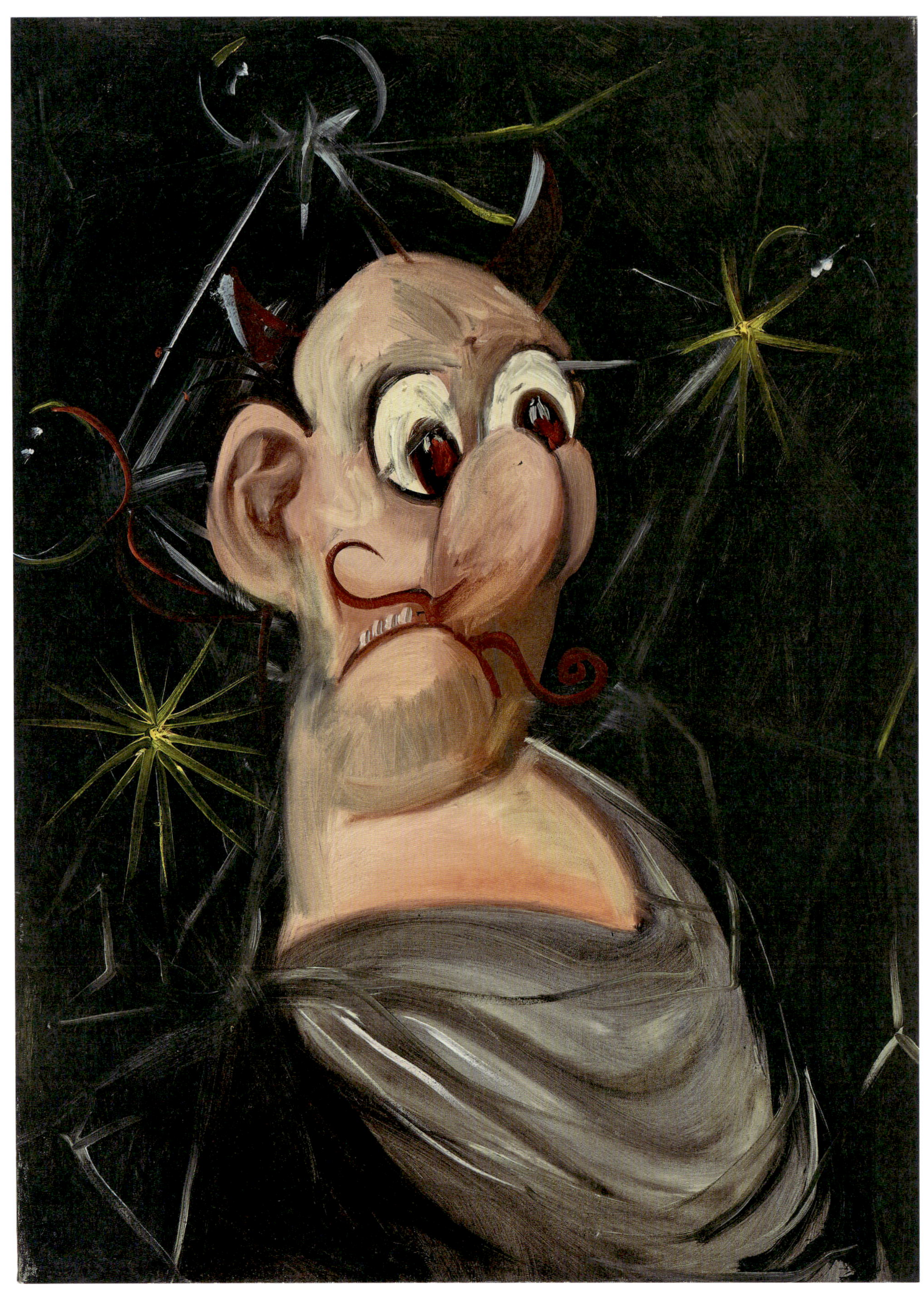

The Astrologer, 1993
Oil on linen, 3 ft. 4 in. × 2 ft. 6 in. (101.6 × 76.2 cm)

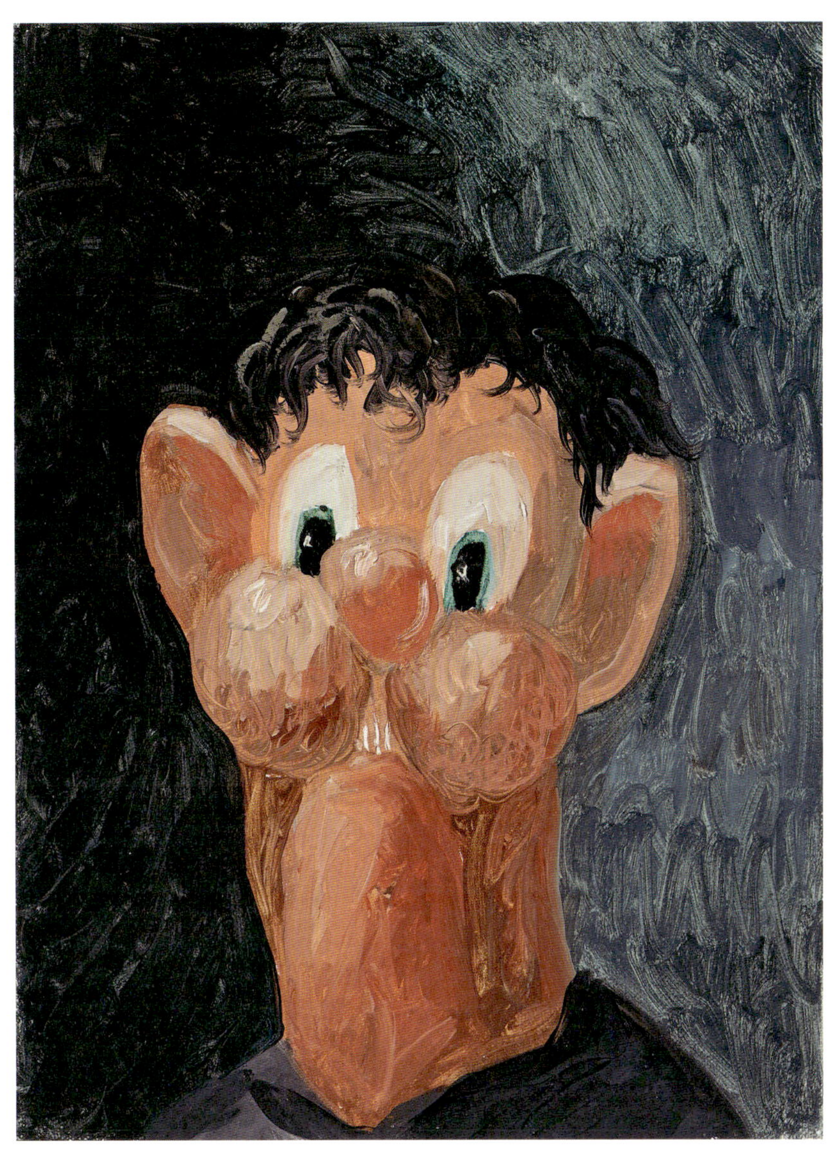

The Undertaker, 1997
Oil on linen, 12 × 9⅛ in. (30.5 × 23 cm)

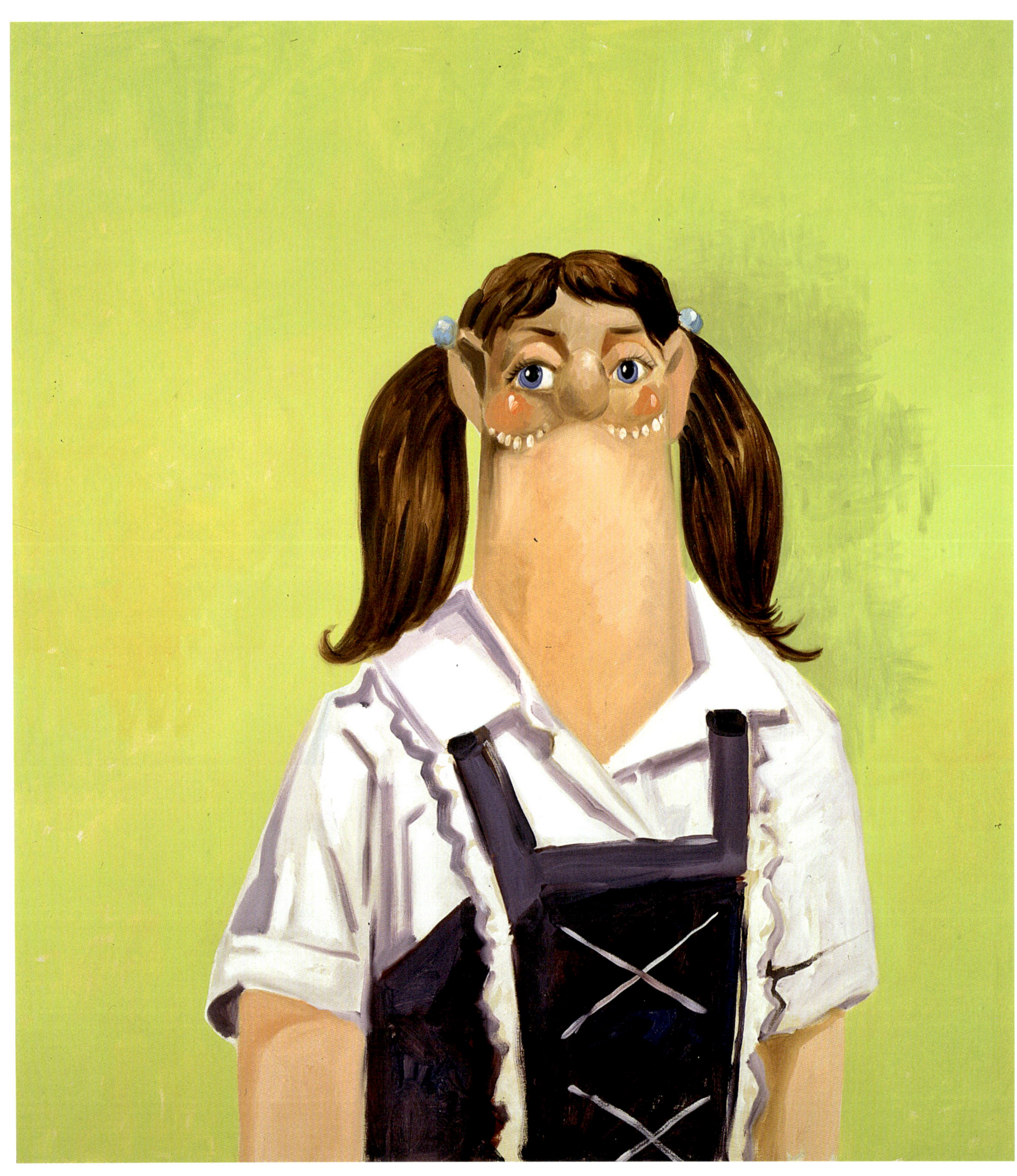

Farmer's Daughter, 2004
Oil on canvas, 5 ft. × 4 ft. 7 in. (152.4 × 139.7 cm)

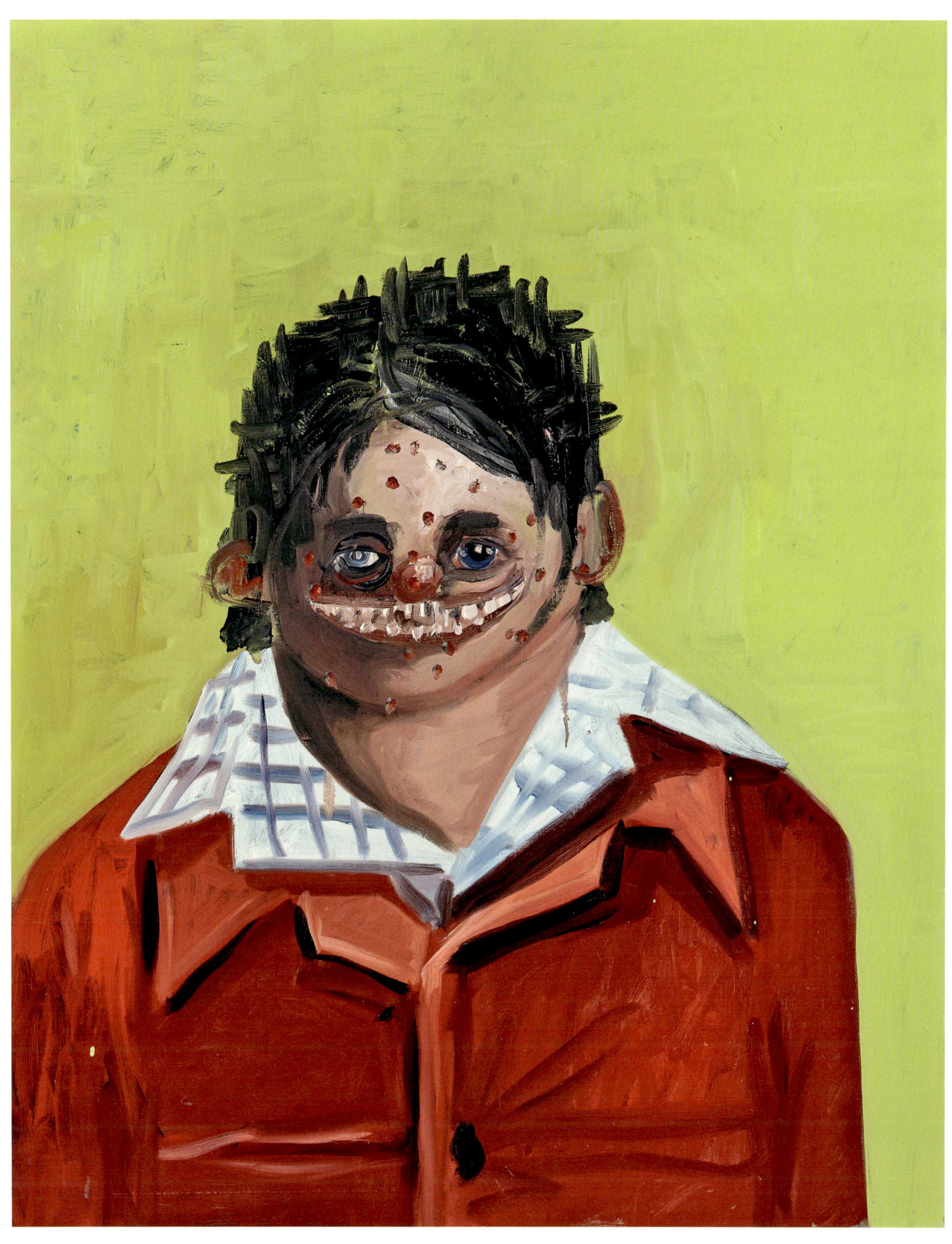

Little Billie, 2004
Oil on canvas, 4 ft. 2⅛ in. × 3 ft. 4¼ in. (127.3 × 102.2 cm)

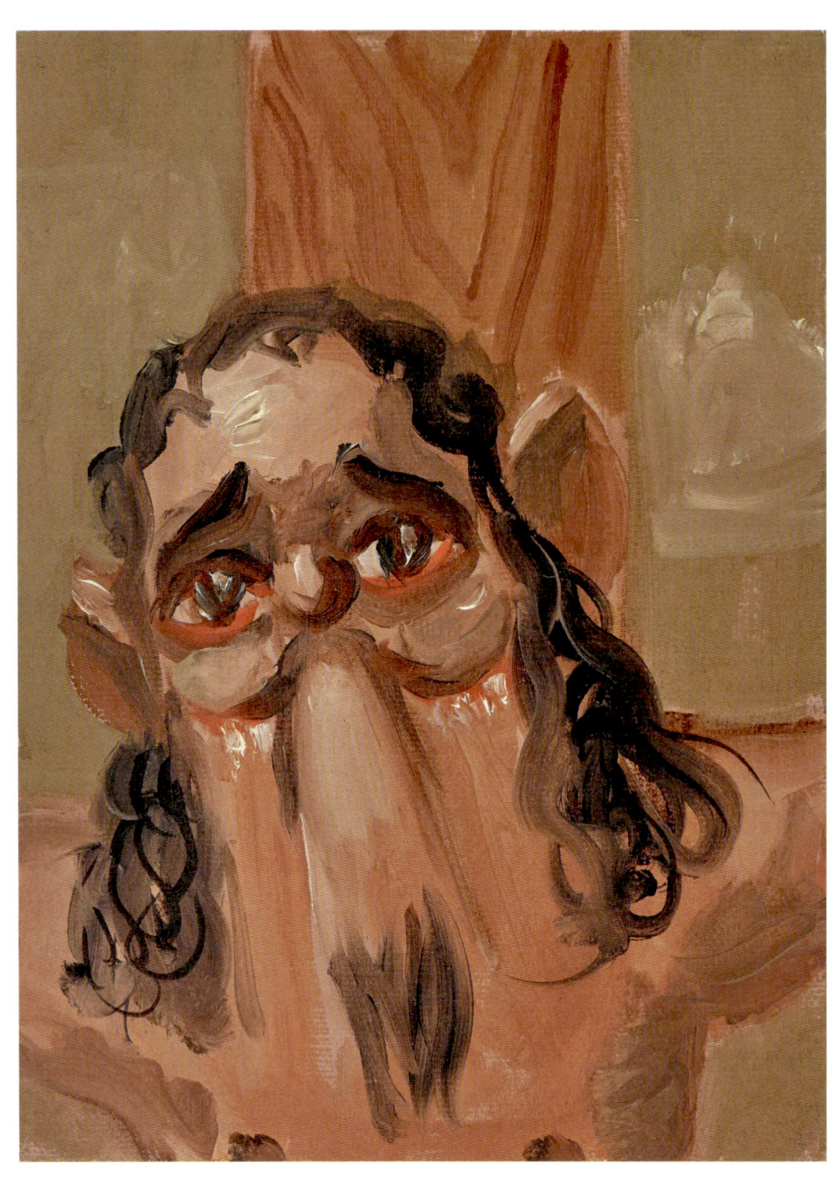

Small Crucifixion, 2007
Oil on canvas, 8 × 5⅞ in. (20.3 × 14.9 cm)

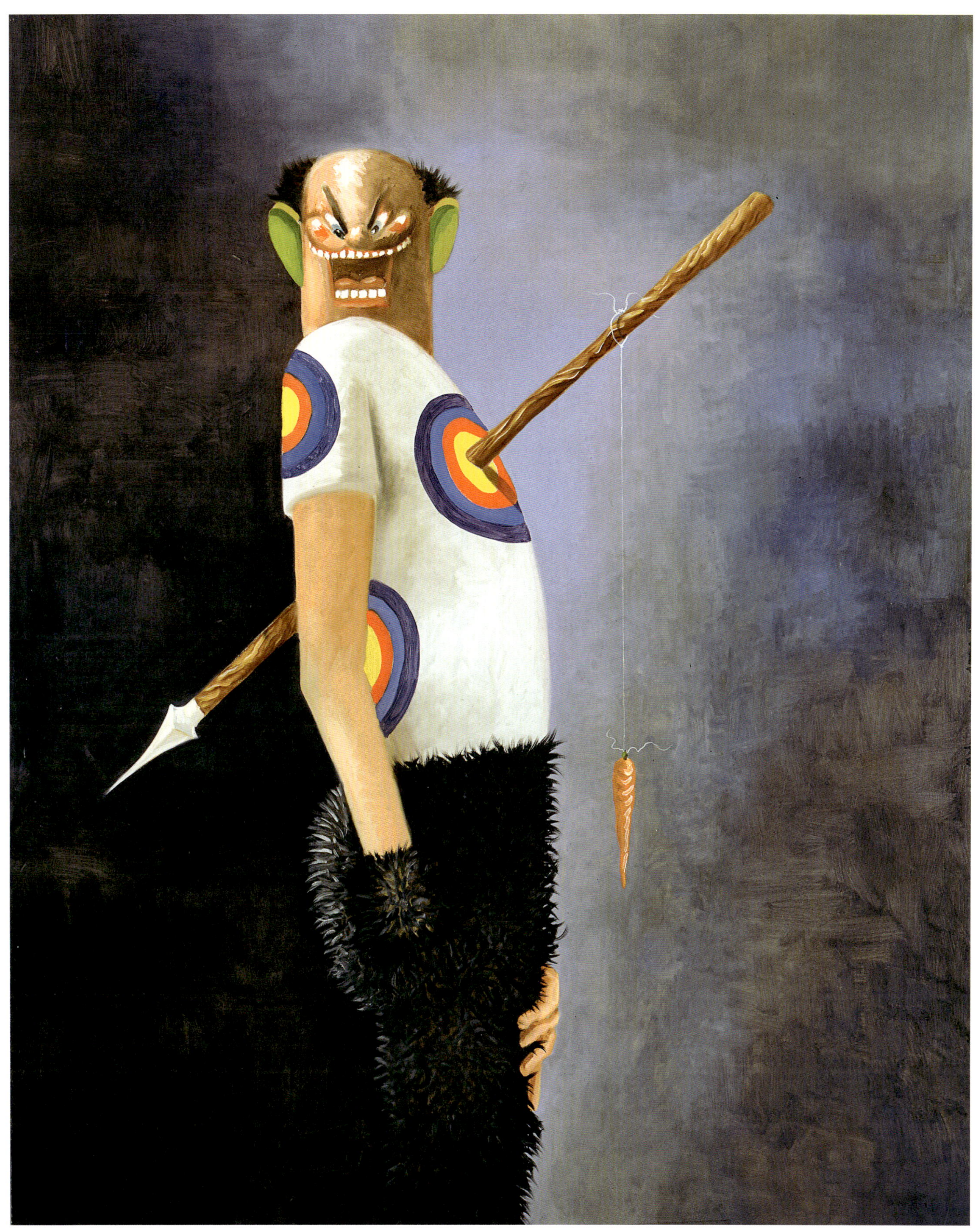

The Smiling Sea Captain, 2006
Oil on canvas, 6 ft. 8 in. × 5 ft. 5 in. (203.2 × 165.1 cm)

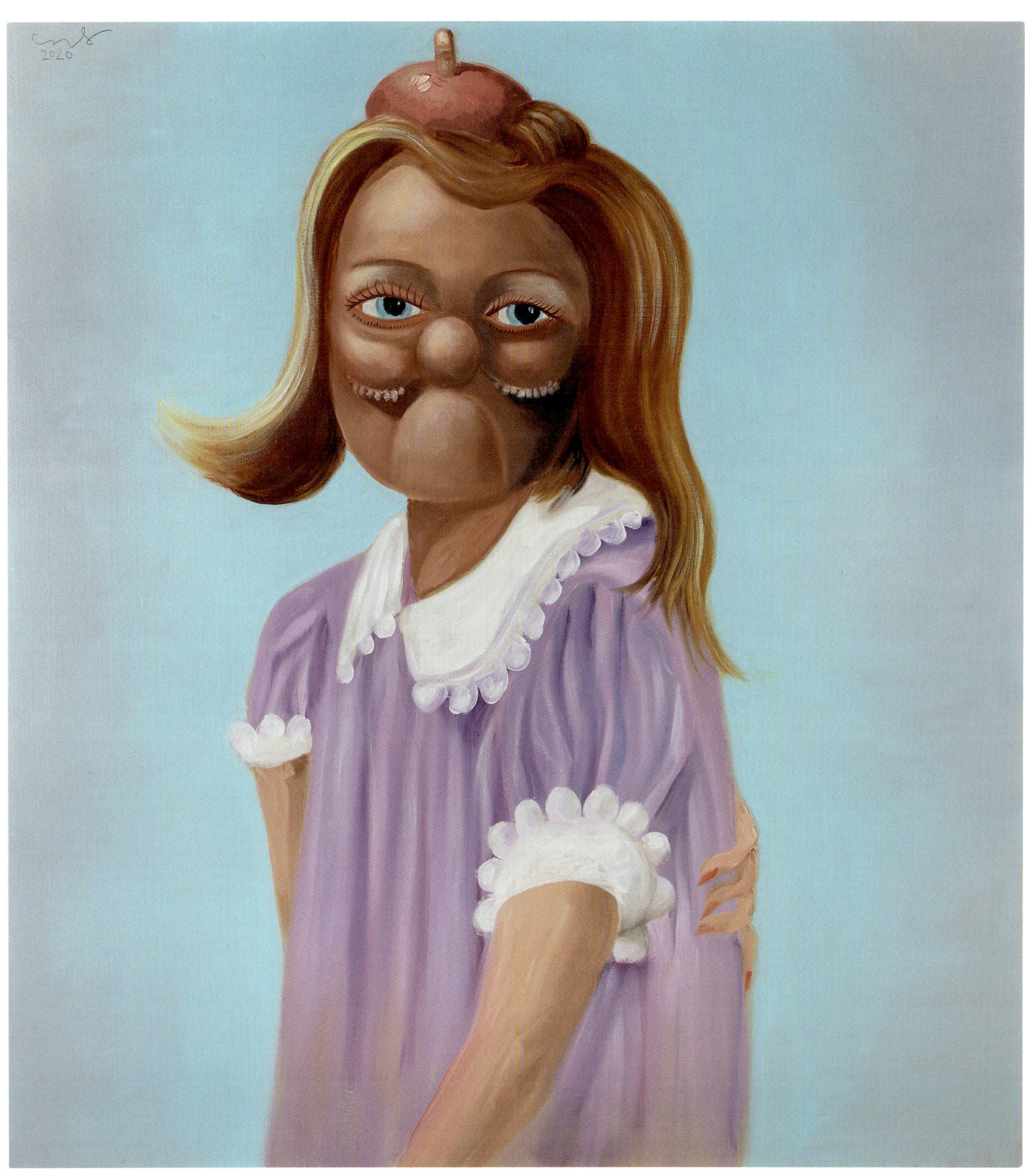

The Little Girl, 2020
Oil on linen, 4 ft. 4 in. × 3 ft. 11 in. (132.1 × 119.4 cm)

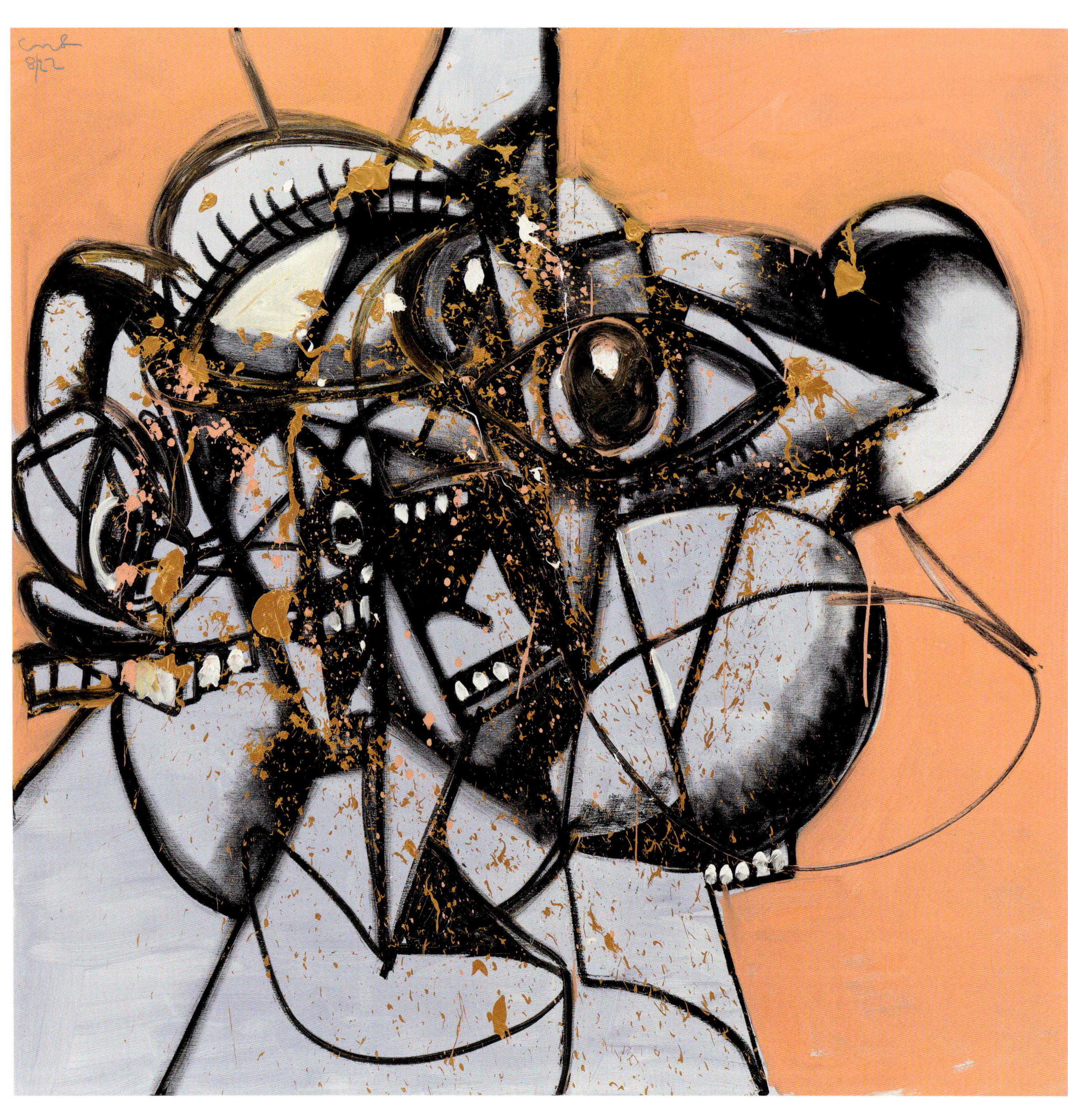

The Dream, 2022
Acrylic, pigment stick, and metallic paint on linen, 6 ft. 10⅛ in. × 7 ft. (208.6 × 213.4 cm)

THE WILL TO EXIST

March of the Humanoids and the will to exist…. In the rise of the Humanoids as real people came the transference of all familiar traits and juxtapositions. It was the inter-relationship between styles of painting that gave birth to them and eventually set them on the path to becoming more predominant than the representational. They are representational of many aspects of humanity and refer to the individual by being a construct of multiple beings simultaneously … they are one in many.

The Humanoid is not a science fiction monster, it is a form of representation that uses traditional means to bring out the inner emotions onto the surface of a person … one of whom could potentially be myself. Are all imaginary portraits self-portraits? Are all paintings that have been created to describe a being greater than oneself in fact a self-portrait as one greater than one's self? Could it be that the Humanoids are simply a series of introspective reflections upon my own inner emotions and they are disguised in order to hide from those inner feelings? That the screams and howls, the crack-toothed, broken-faced, fractured heads are all of myself?

The hysterical lines and applications of paint are all the makings of an infant in his high chair throwing baby food at the wall. Screaming and crying out for attention by doing "bad" things … only to be held and quieted by his mother and brought up to his crib to nap. (Who is the mother? Is the mother that an artist seeks out in this stage of life something symbolic?) These temper tantrums on canvas are the primordial expressions of growth … such as the pain that comes with teething…. And as the screams and relentless howls emerge from the canvases out come the teeth … the mouths wide open screaming in agony wishing it would all stop. The pain of emerging energy…. Yet there it remains alive and in paint for all to see and make their own associations and analysis. To create a narrative based on their own art historical references, many leaving out the fact that all the paintings will undoubtedly have an incestuous relationship with the history of art … but in a far more reckless way than has been previously noted … it is simply baby food to be splattered onto the walls of the kitchen where all the cooking is done and the floors are the easiest to clean up after. It's the "wreck" room later in life where the 8 year old hurls his skates through a window and shatters the glass. Leaving the fragments and pieces all over the floor and where things are mucked up and made dirty for someone else to clean. As one gets older the temper tantrums continue but become informed by intellect and less the result of raw emotion or simply accidental…. They have an intention, a force directed by the mind in all coherency to manifest itself in the form of some kind of artistic statement….

Having forgotten childhood and looking far forward into the adult world of acceptance and behavioral patterns that the older generation will comprehend as meaningful, added to a willingness to learn to control emotions, affect the results. The next phase is putting to use what has been learned through trial and error with technique and analysis … how things are made. To put it simply, it's for some to understand how bicycles are made piece by piece or a refrigerator, a doctor would want to know how humans are made in order to treat the conditions that come with being human … a painter will want to know how a painting is made. I wanted to understand how a painting was made…. What were the means to produce the illusions of a palpable reality higher perhaps in its essence than the one I seemingly resided in? The primitive instincts that began before one can remember your first birthday party when only one candle stood on the cake have become the same principles today when there are now sixty-four of them.

FRACTURED FIGURES

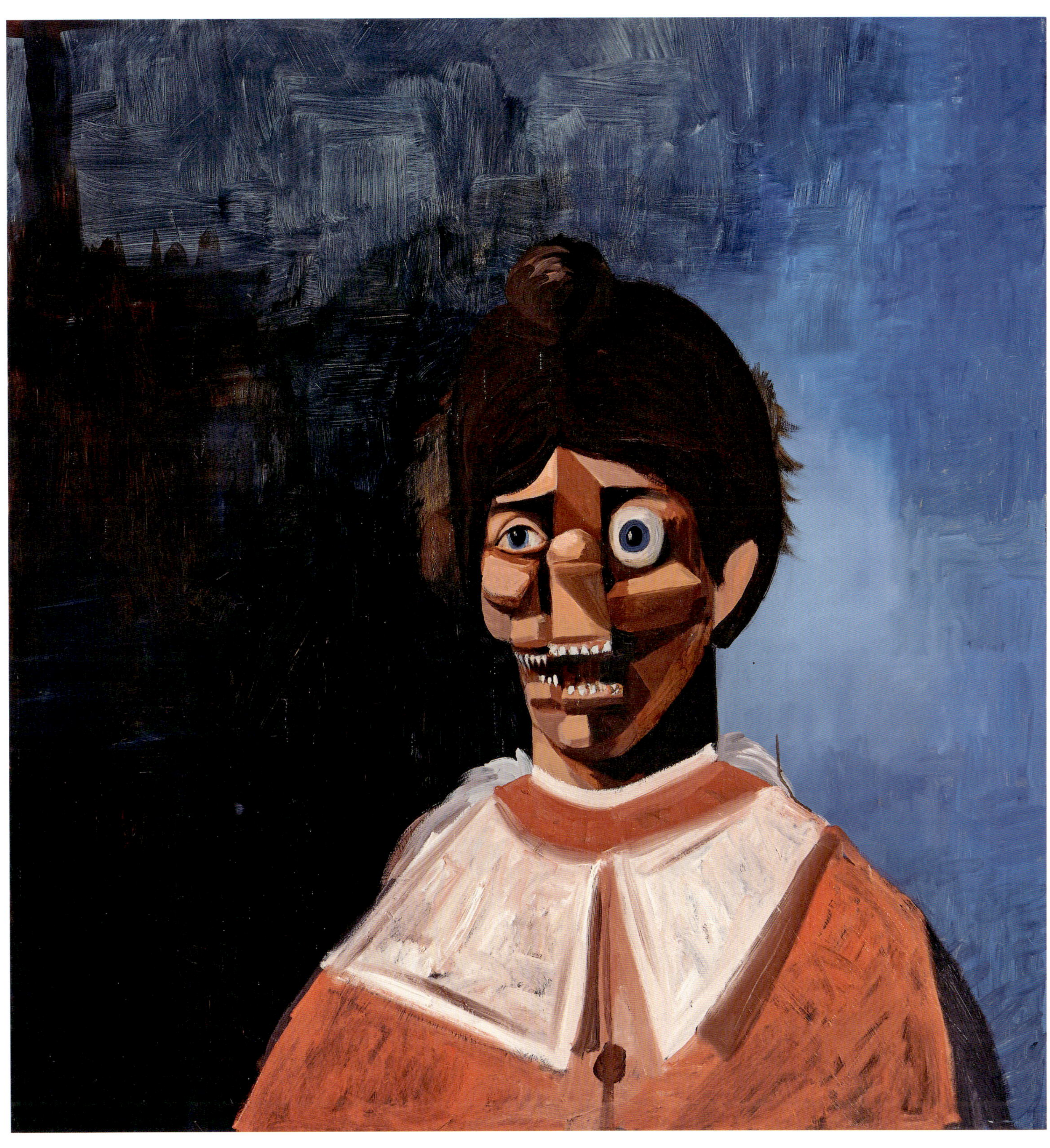

The Nervous Breakdown, 2004
Oil on linen, 4 ft. ⅛ in. × 3 ft. 10⅛ in. (122.2 × 117.2 cm)

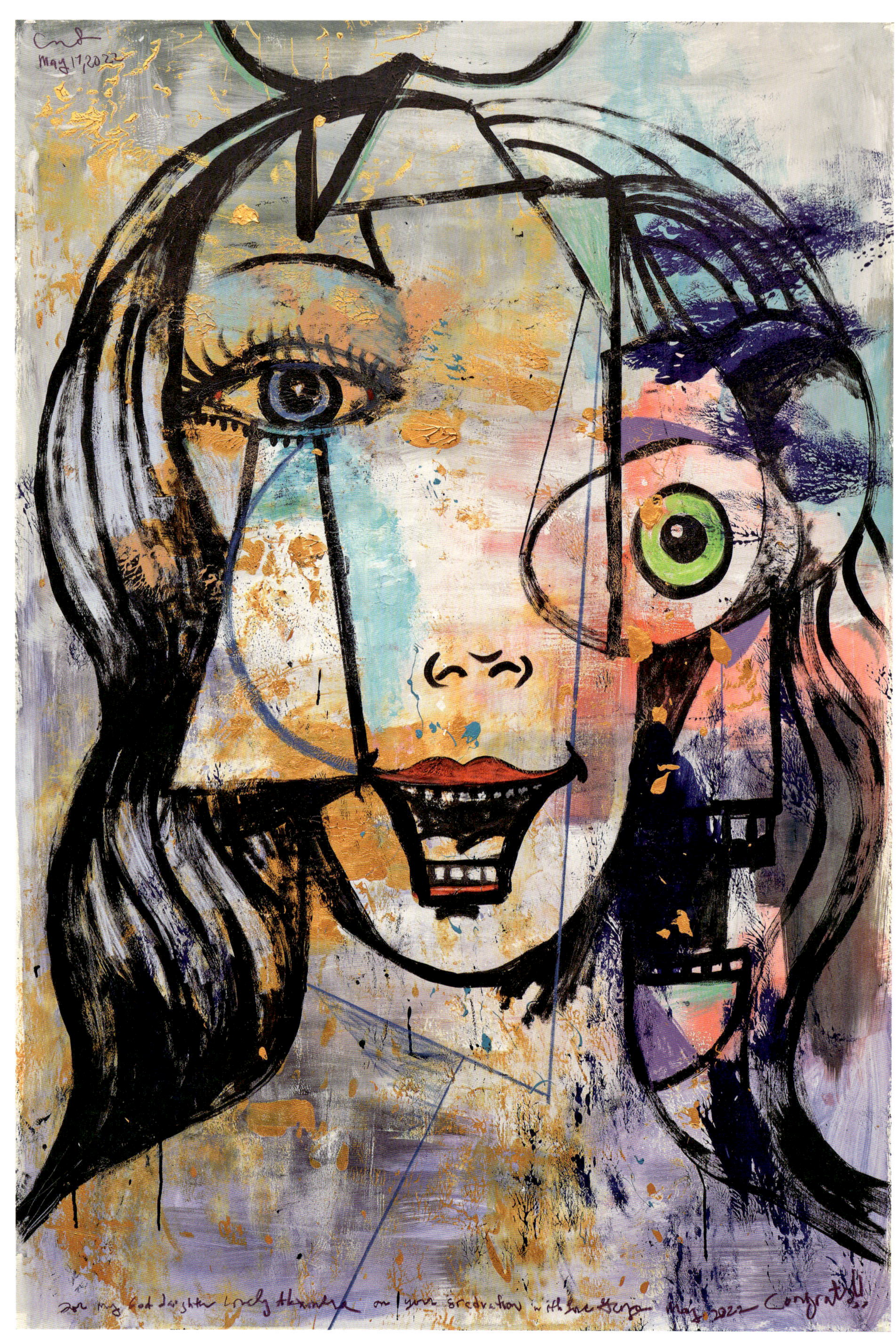

Portrait of a Young Woman, 2022
Acrylic, oil stick, metallic paint, and wax crayon on paper, 6 ft. 6 in. × 5 ft. (198.1 × 152.4 cm)

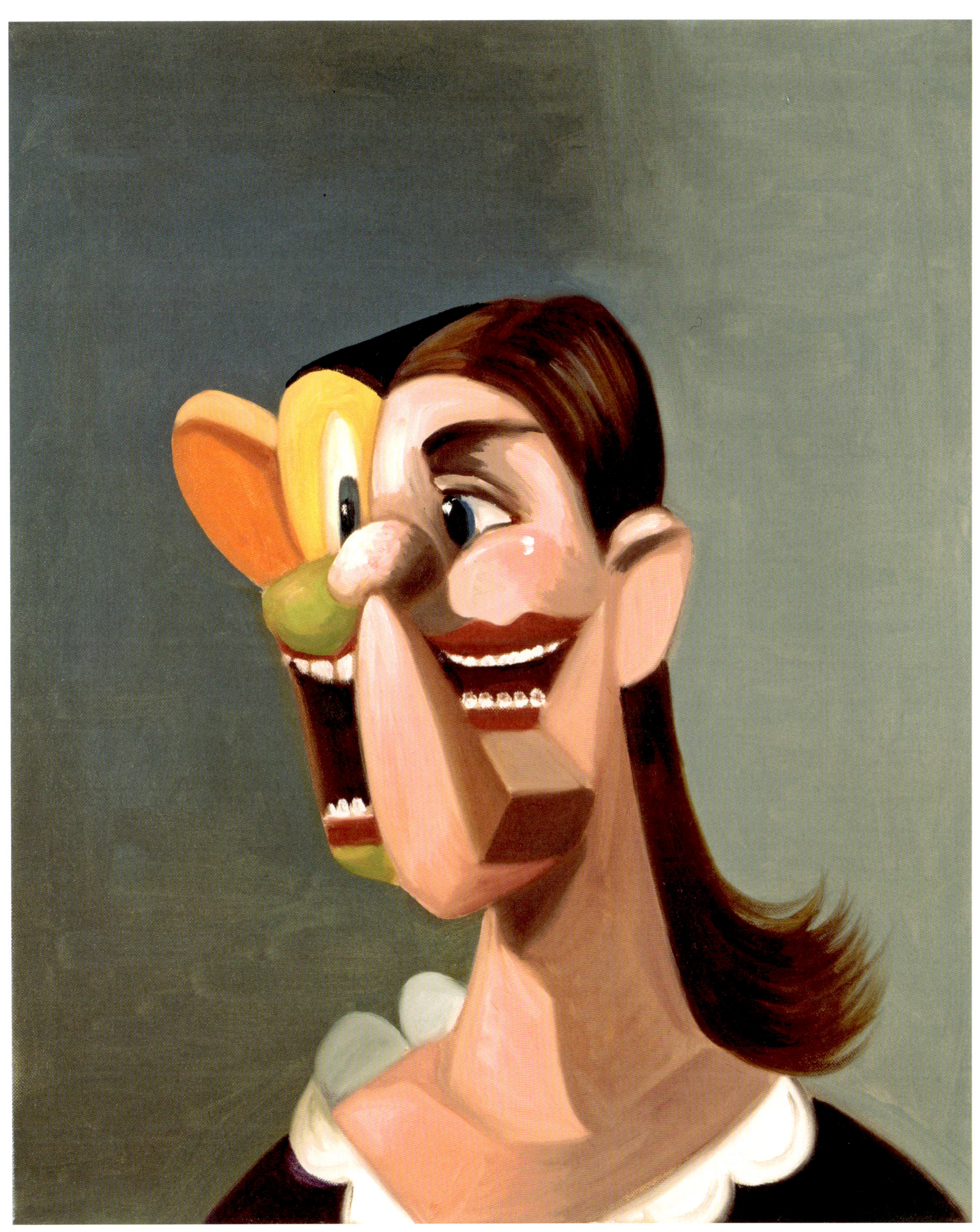

Smiling Girl, 2007
Oil on canvas, 24 × 20 in. (61 × 50.8 cm)

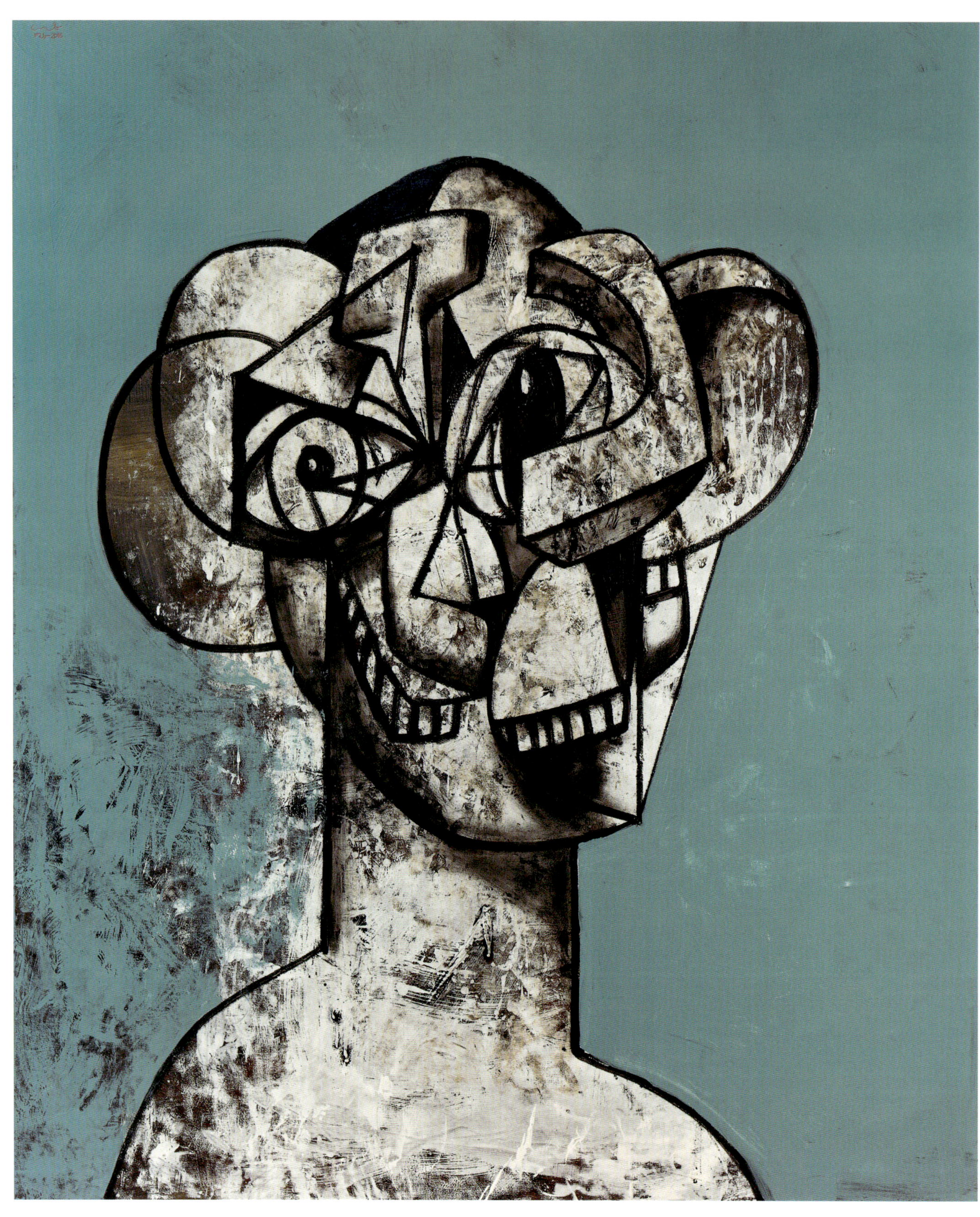

Monolithic Head Composition, 2018
Oil and pigment stick on linen, 7 ft. 9 in. × 6 ft. 7 in. (236.2 × 200.7 cm)

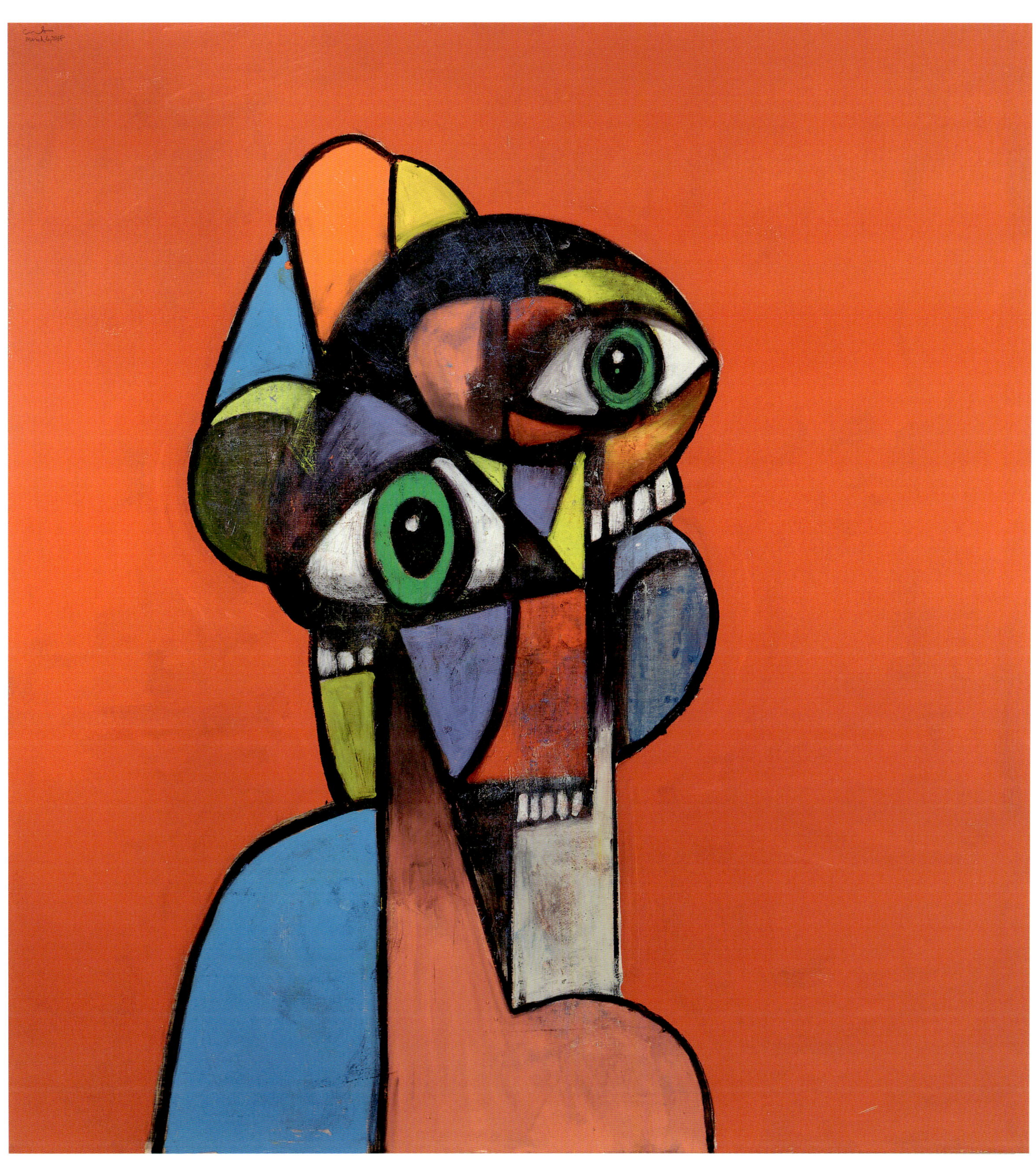

Little Henry, 2019
Acrylic, oil, and pigment stick on linen, 6 ft. 10 in. × 6 ft. 6 in. (208.3 × 198.1 cm)

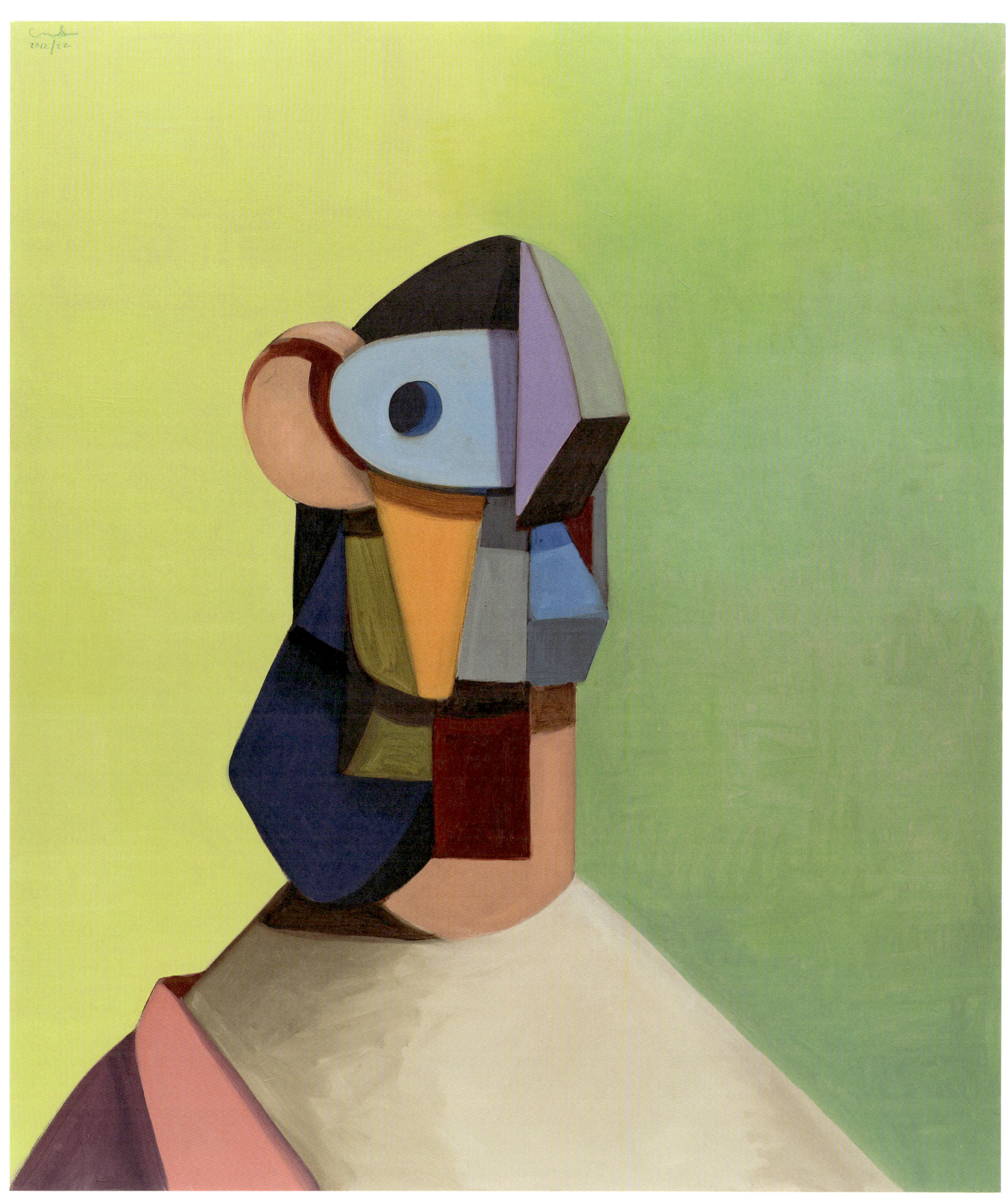

Green Constructed Head, 2012/2022
Acrylic on canvas, 5 ft. 6 in. × 4 ft. 10¼ in. (167.6 × 148 cm)

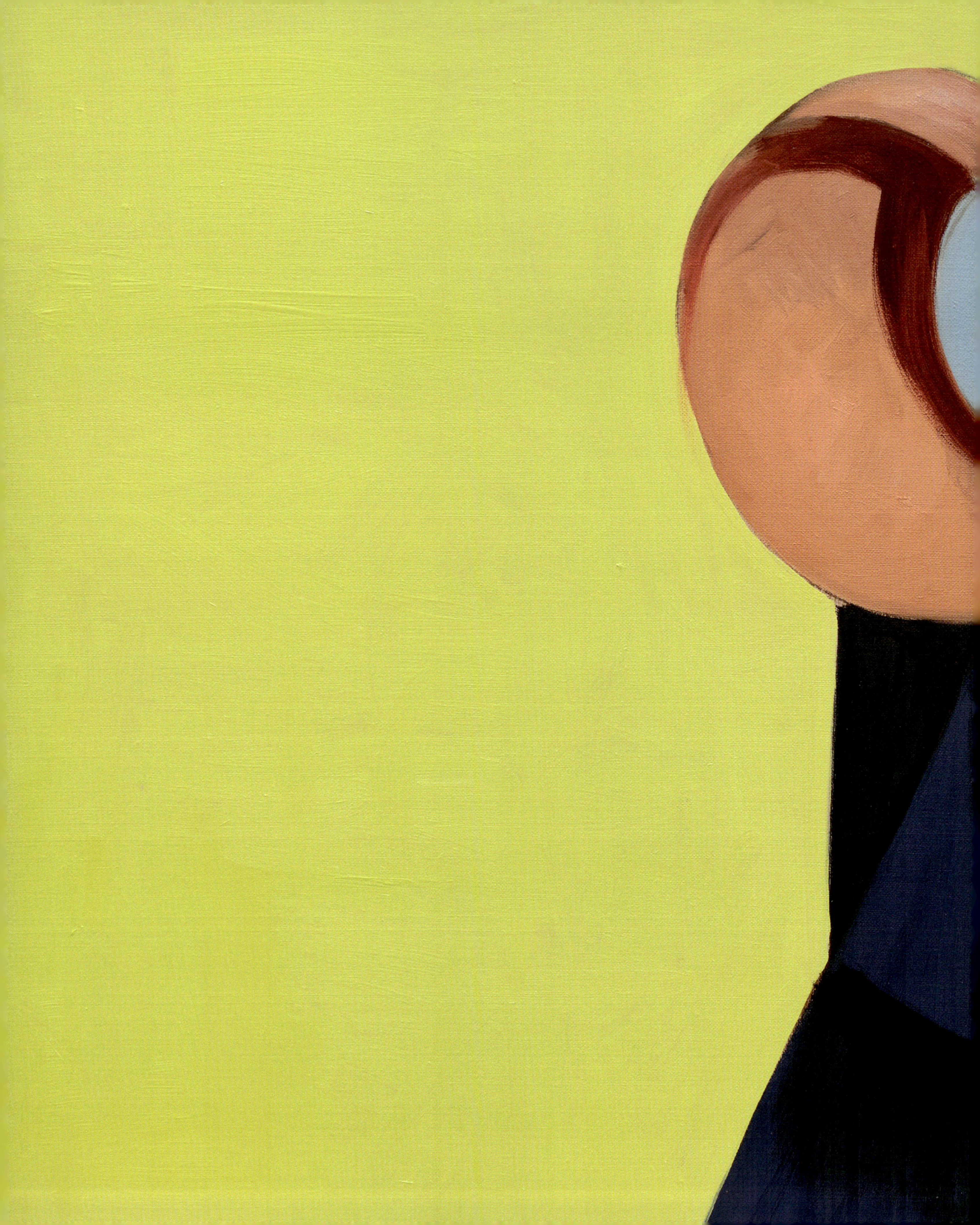

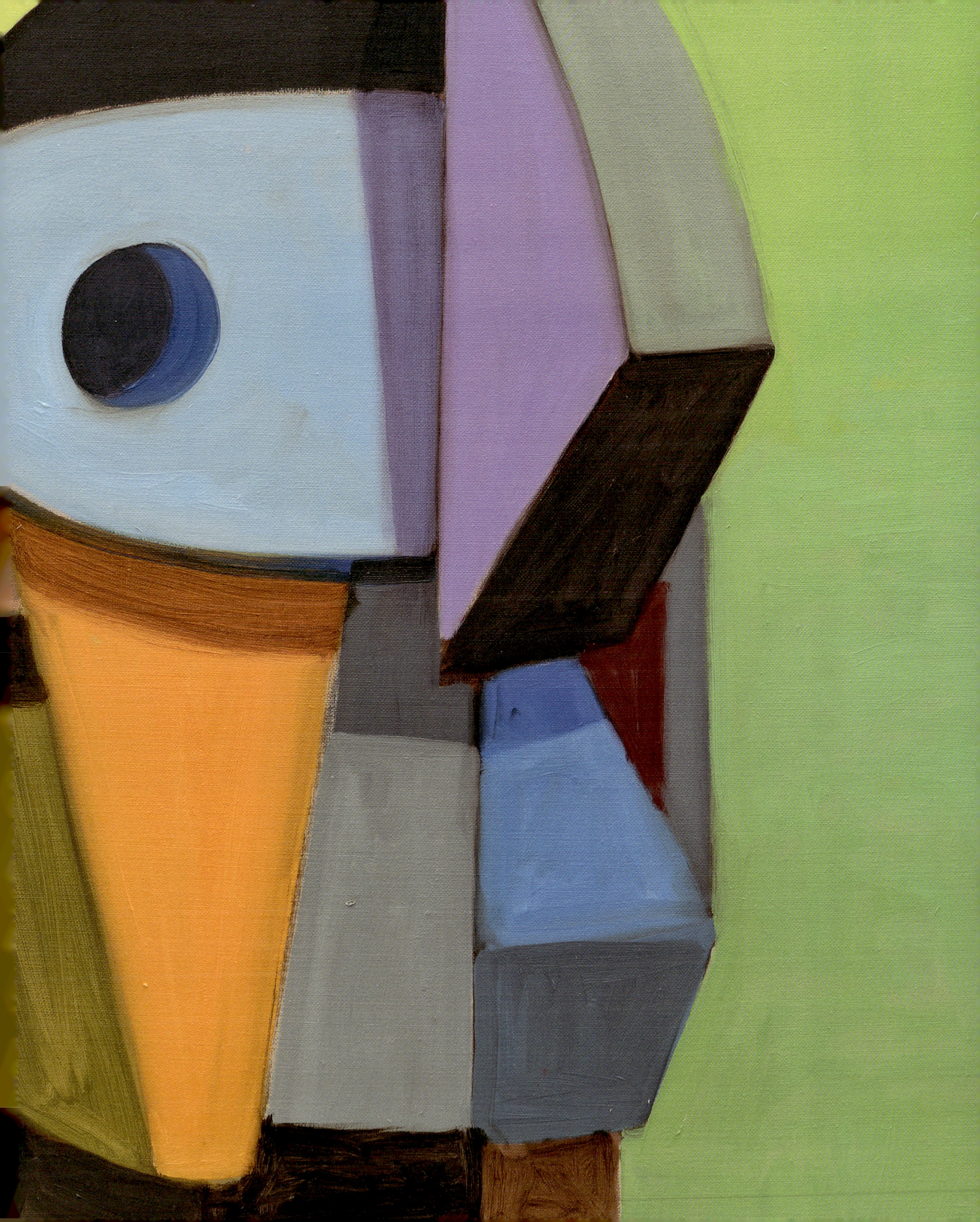

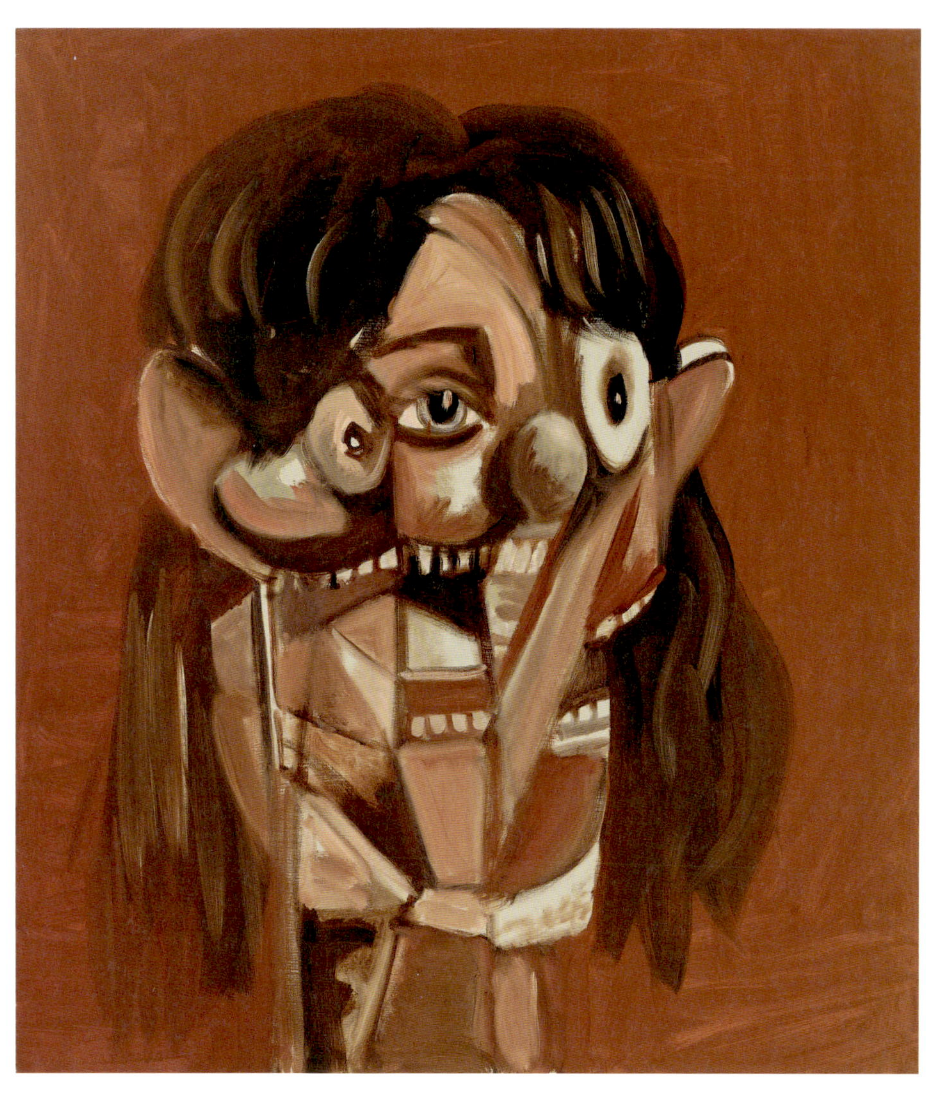

Multifaceted Portrait Composition, 2008
Oil on canvas, 3 ft. 4⅛ in. × 3 ft. ¼ in. (101.9 × 92.1 cm)

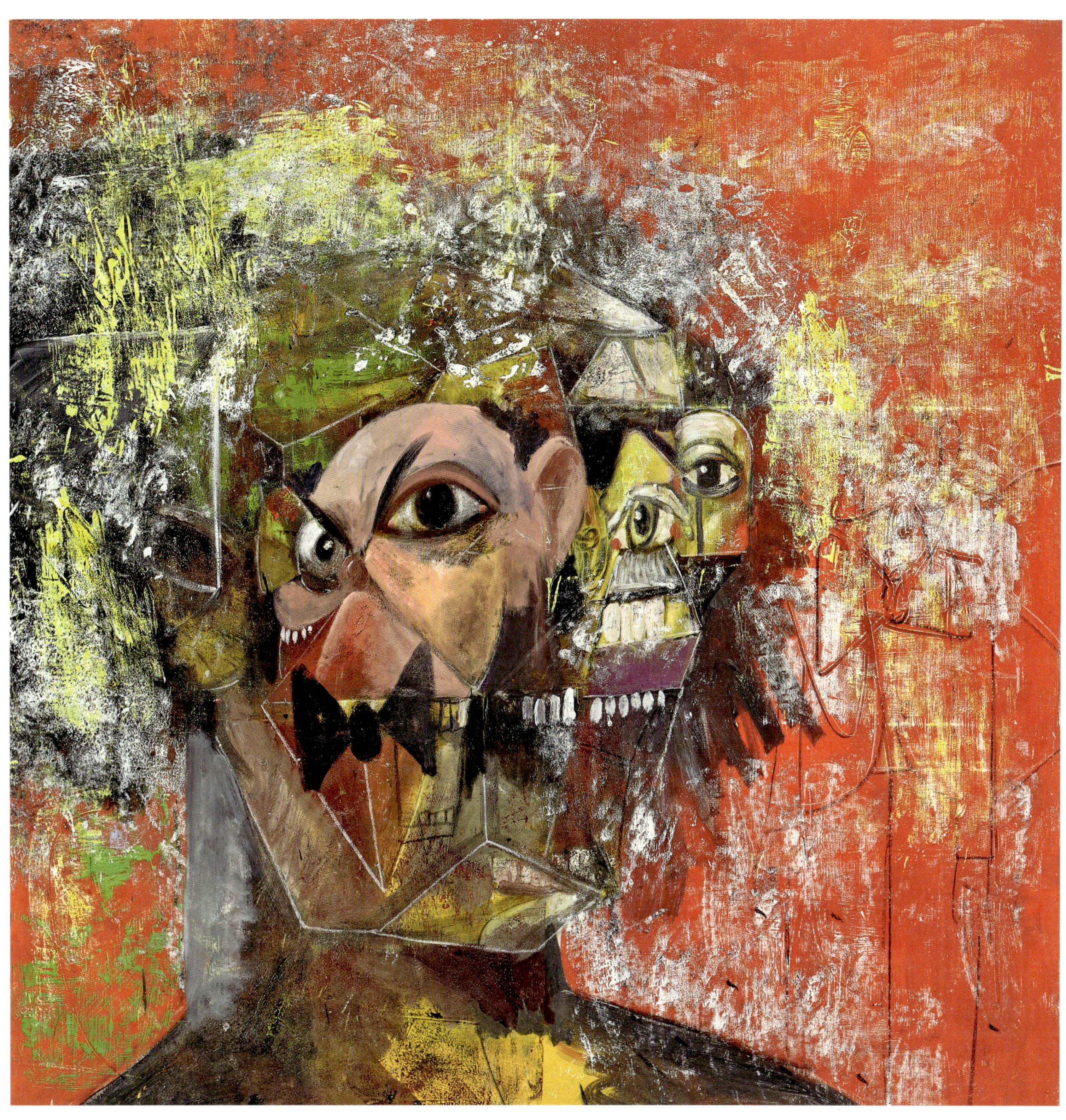

Rodrigo Abstraction, 2009
Oil on canvas, 5 ft. 5⅛ in. × 5 ft. 5¼ in. (165.4 × 165.7 cm)

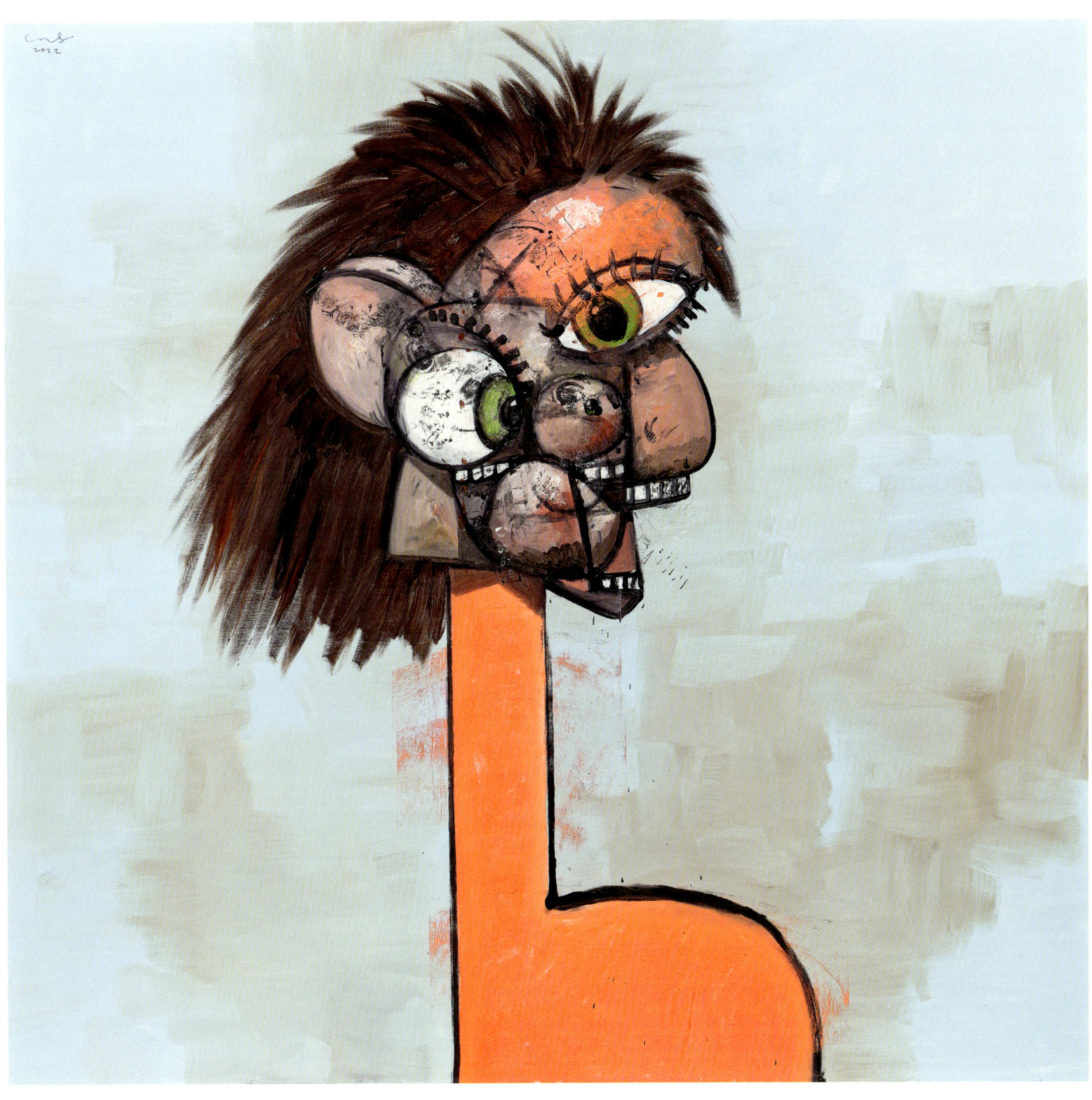

The Last Leg, 2022
Oil on linen, 7 ft. 1 in. × 7 ft. 6 in. (215.9 × 228.6 cm)

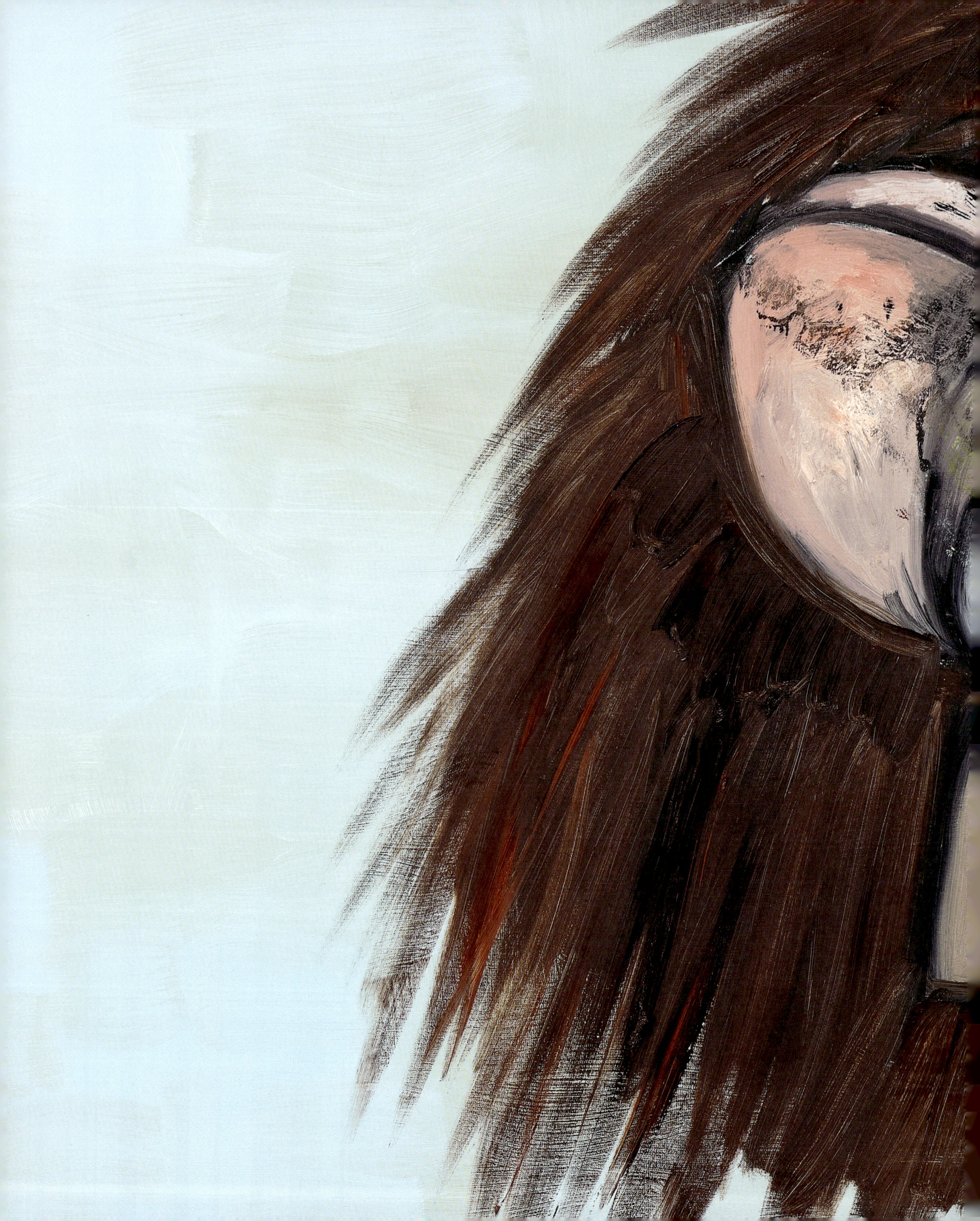

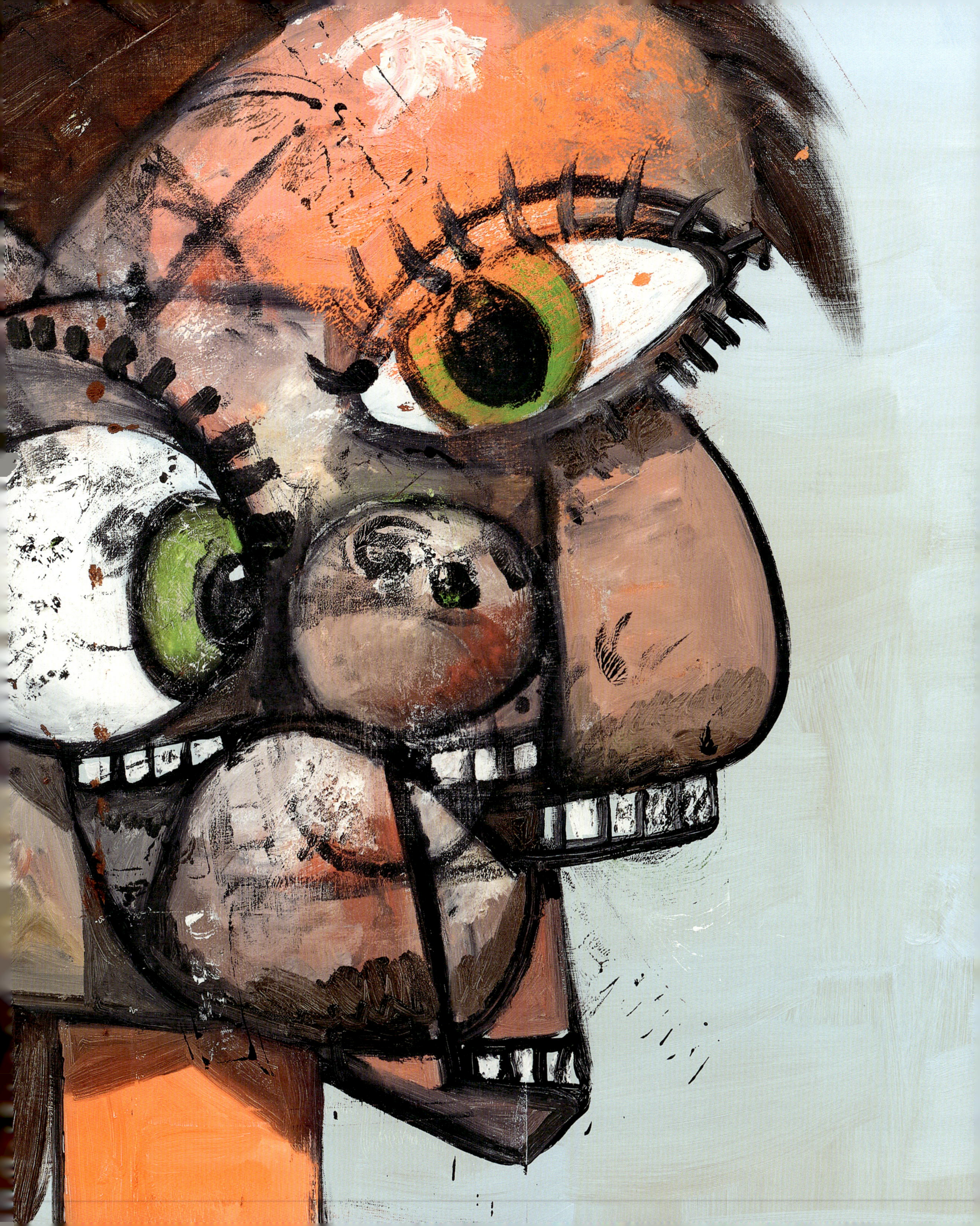

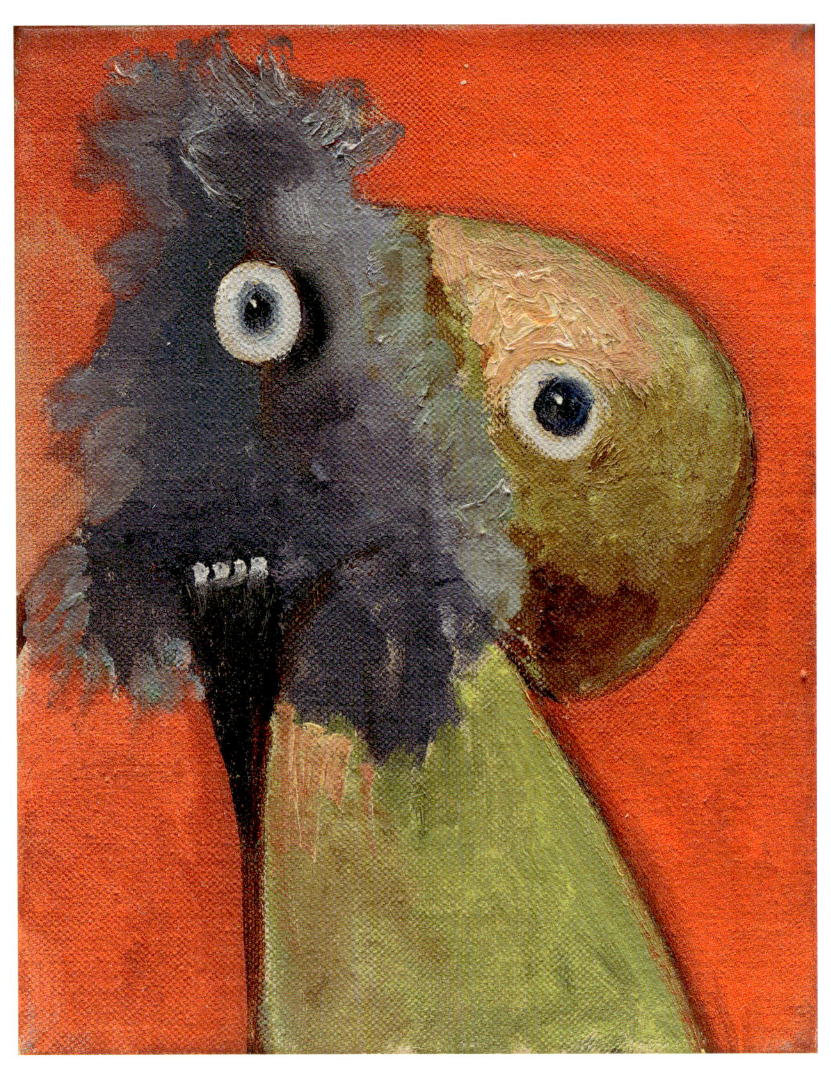

The Cyclops, 2014
Oil on canvas, 10 × 8 in. (25.4 × 20.3 cm)

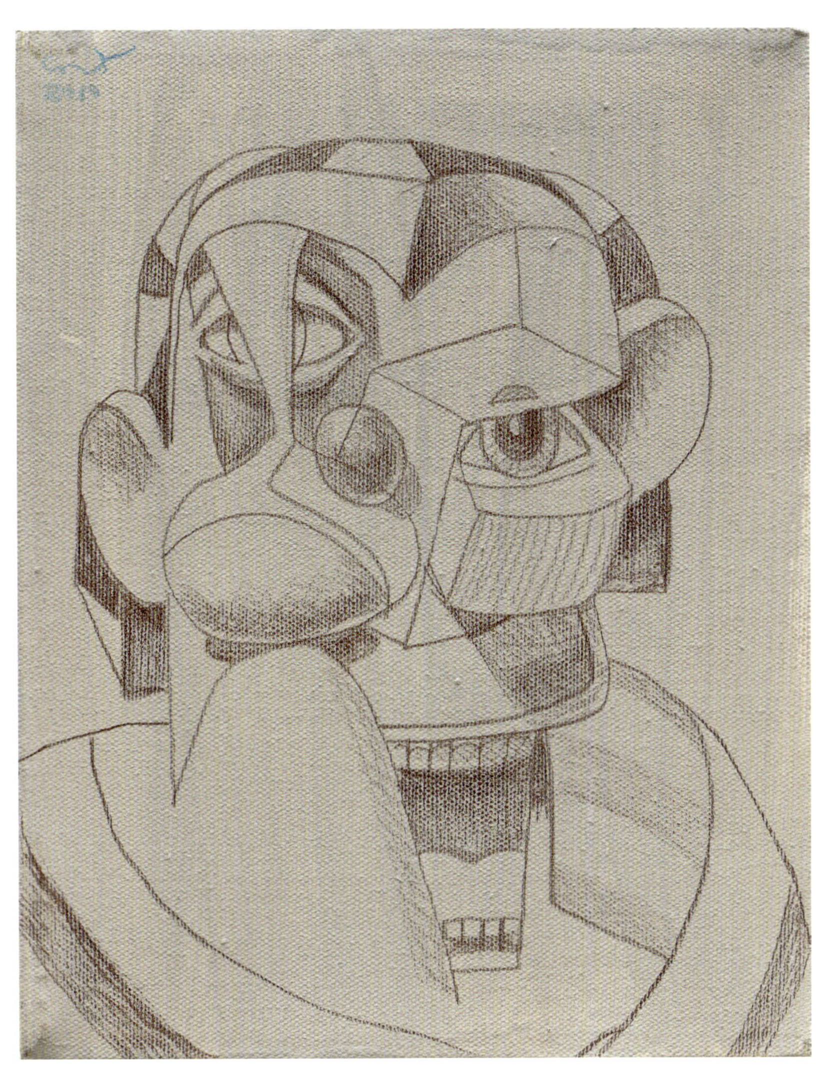

Grisaille Head, 2010
Pencil on canvas, 9¾ × 8 in. (25 × 20.5 cm)

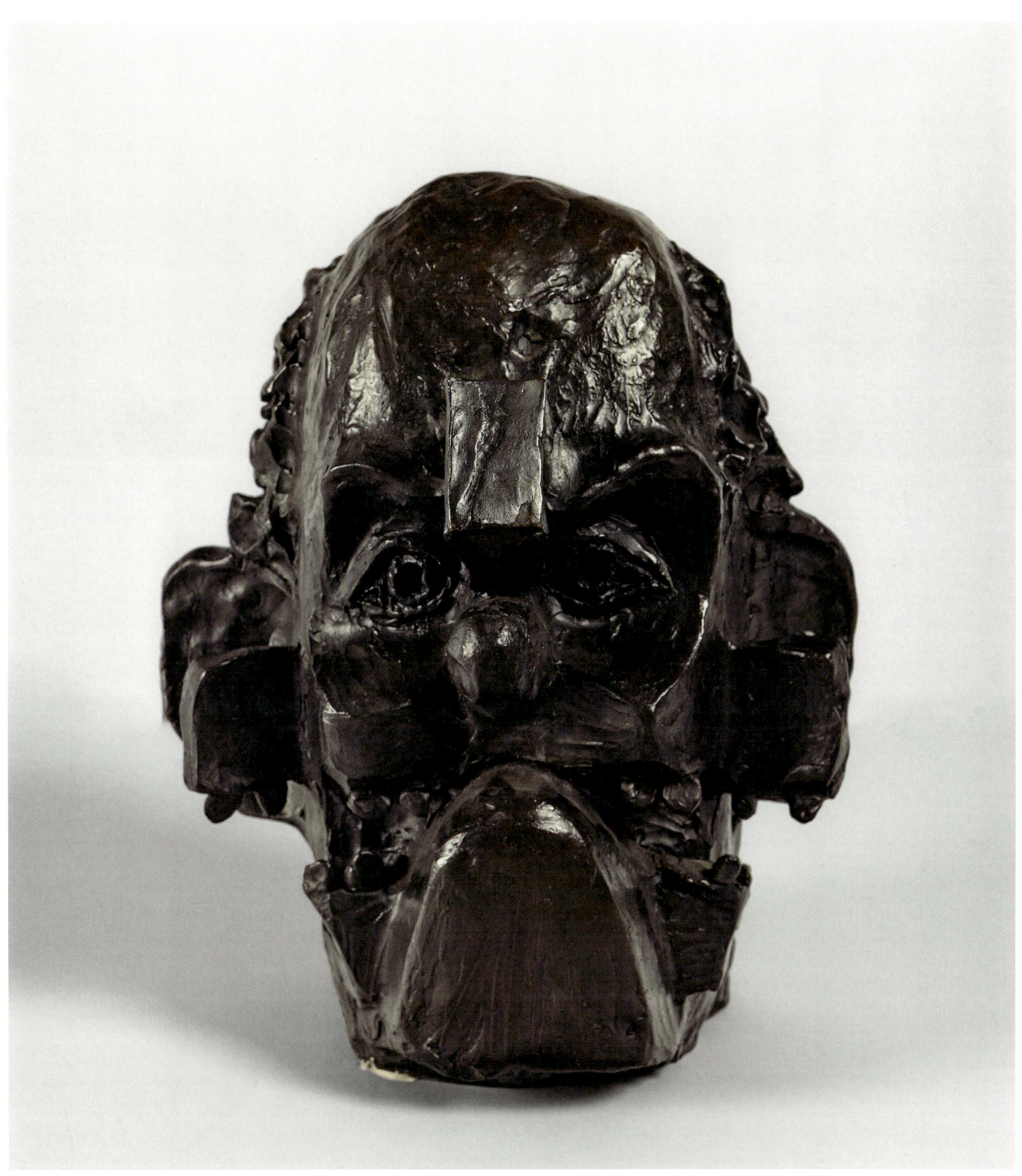

Frankenstein Head, 2012
Patinated bronze, 13 × 10 × 9 in. (33 × 25.4 × 22.9 cm)
Artist's proof, edition of 3 and 1 artist's proof

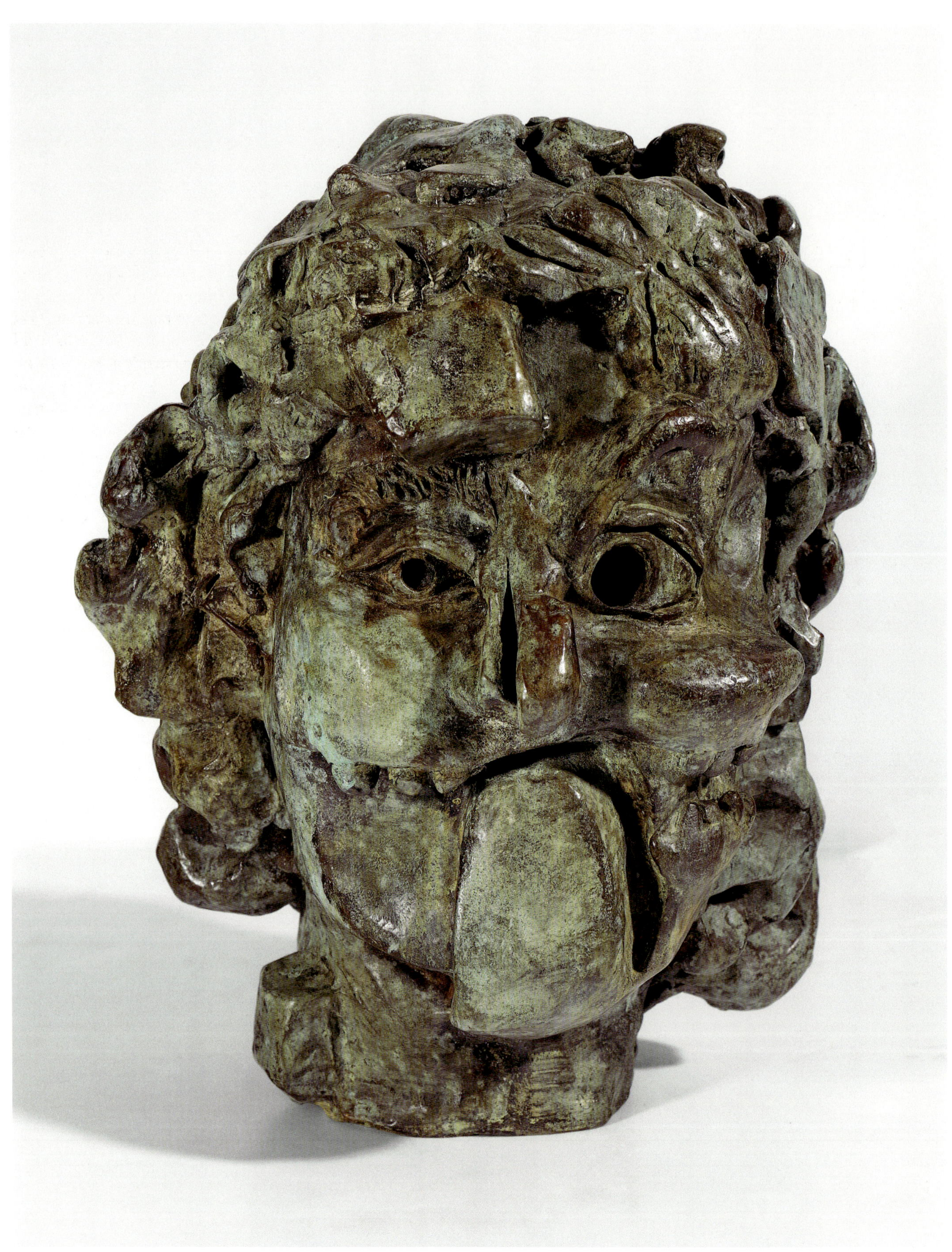

Being, 2009
Patinated bronze, 12 × 10 × 11 in. (30.5 × 25.4 × 27.9 cm)
Artist's proof, edition of 3 and 1 artist's proof

THE QUEST FOR ETERNAL LIFE

There is the external appearance of a person, what they actually look like to the world, and what they look like when reflected in a mirror.… In a cracked mirror they are fragmented but still it is the one who is looking. They cannot see the inside of their own mind by simply looking in the mirror, cracked or not. It's in a moment of reflection in the other sense of the word, when one reflects upon a subject or perhaps one's self that this process takes place.… What do they see? Scenarios or variants of themselves in the process of searching for a solution to reassemble a fragmented vision of what it is they are trying to make whole… the process of identifying the inner self and acting on what they believe to be the correct impulse. This is the thought process.

In painting thought process goes into the decision making process to make something visible, to make this inner reflection or wholeness a solution or a problem visible for the world to see. It's not hiding anymore behind the visage of a human being. It ultimately becomes a Humanoid through this system of analysis and representation. It is to some degree a hybrid form of a human … one whose mind is the outer visage rather than the internal. It's not science fiction, it's psychological portraiture that requires various technical skills to bring to life and remain alive forever that which can never be accessed by one's own self other than in the invisible self-reflective moments … perhaps even in meditation or a dream.… In a painting the dream is made real, it can be analyzed because it is visible. It can be compared with other paintings or portraits or perhaps even sculptures.… The lines that were drawn centuries ago of people are still alive but those who they drew have long been buried. It may be that the only purpose was for those lines to be compared with other lines.… I'm quite sure Ingres wanted his lines to be compared with those of David or Raphael, and I'm quite sure that the lines of Da Vinci were made not only to interpret nature as in his swirling masses of water or hair but to transcend those realities with some form of a vision that was incomprehensible in the real world. The lines of Fragonard and Boucher were certainly designed to outlast their sitters/models.

So the quest for eternal life lies in the ability to be compared not to reality but to other artists, and if one's art is in that beautiful and sublime form it will last. The Humanoid is in fact a form of this quest for eternity.

HUMANOID
ABSTRACTIONS

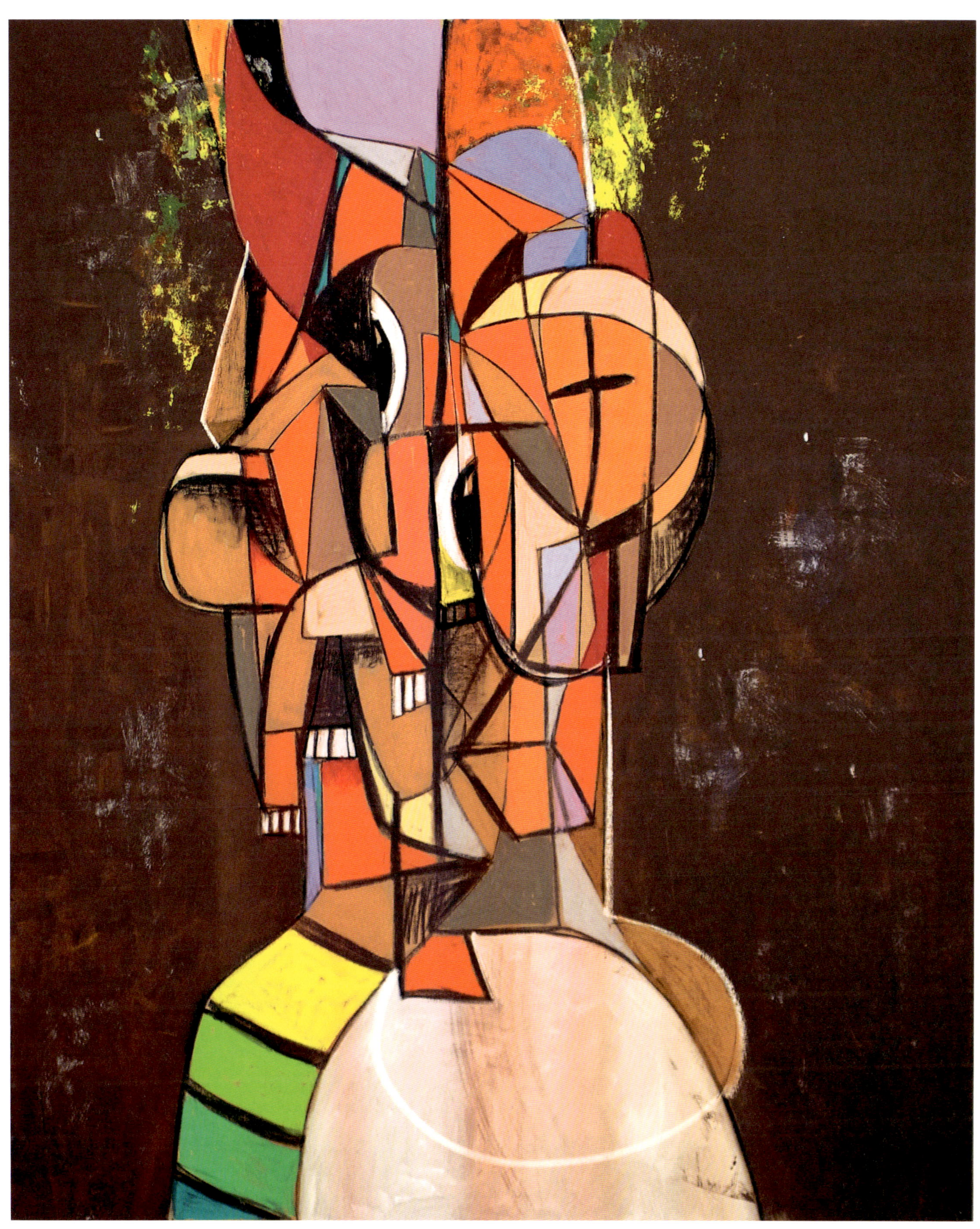

Talking to Steve, 2013
Acrylic, charcoal, and pastel on linen, 5 ft. × 4 ft. 2 in. (152.4 × 127 cm)

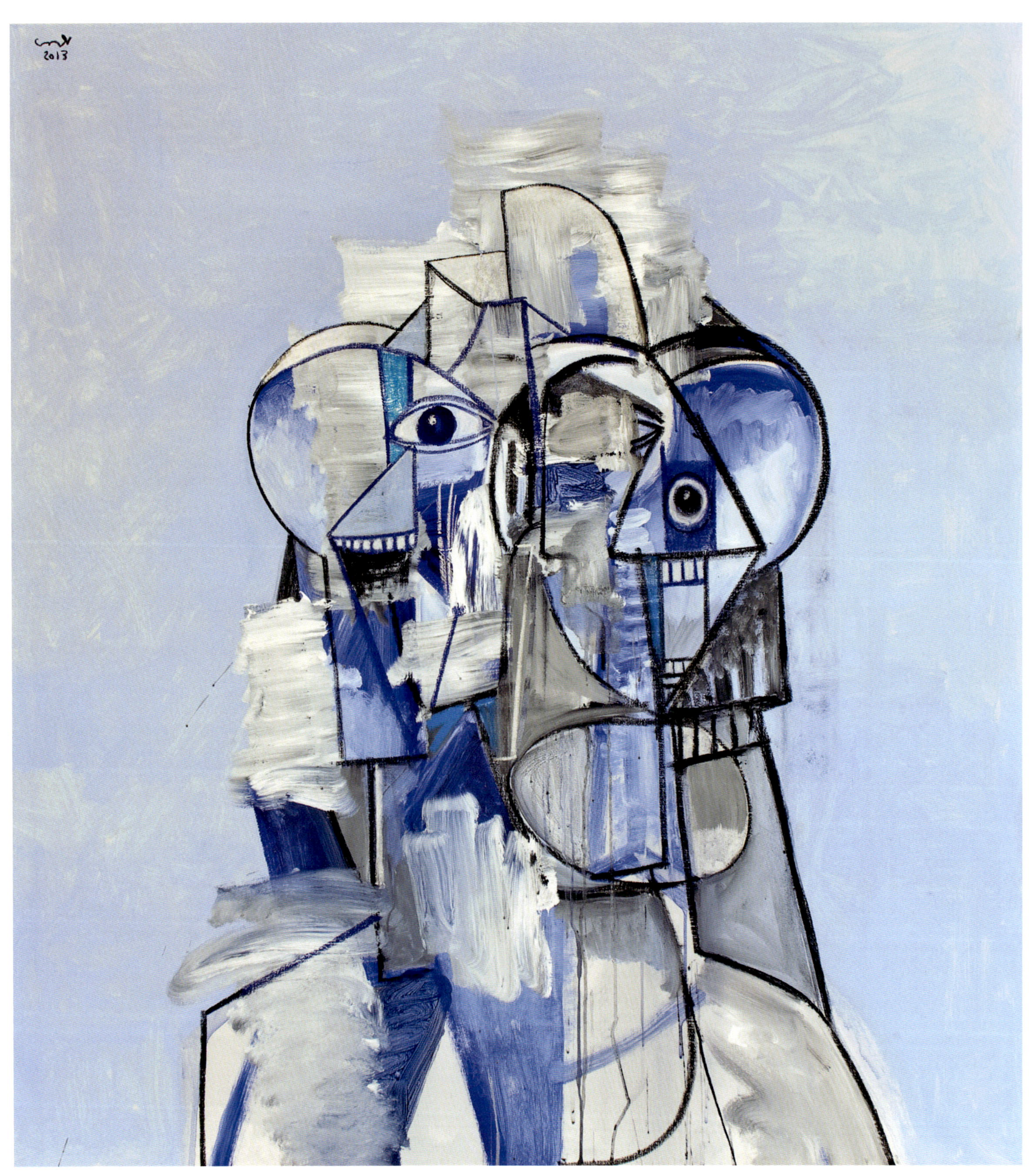

Blue Haze, 2013
Acrylic, charcoal, and pastel on linen, 4 ft. 8½ in. × 4 ft. 4 in. (143.5 × 132.1 cm)

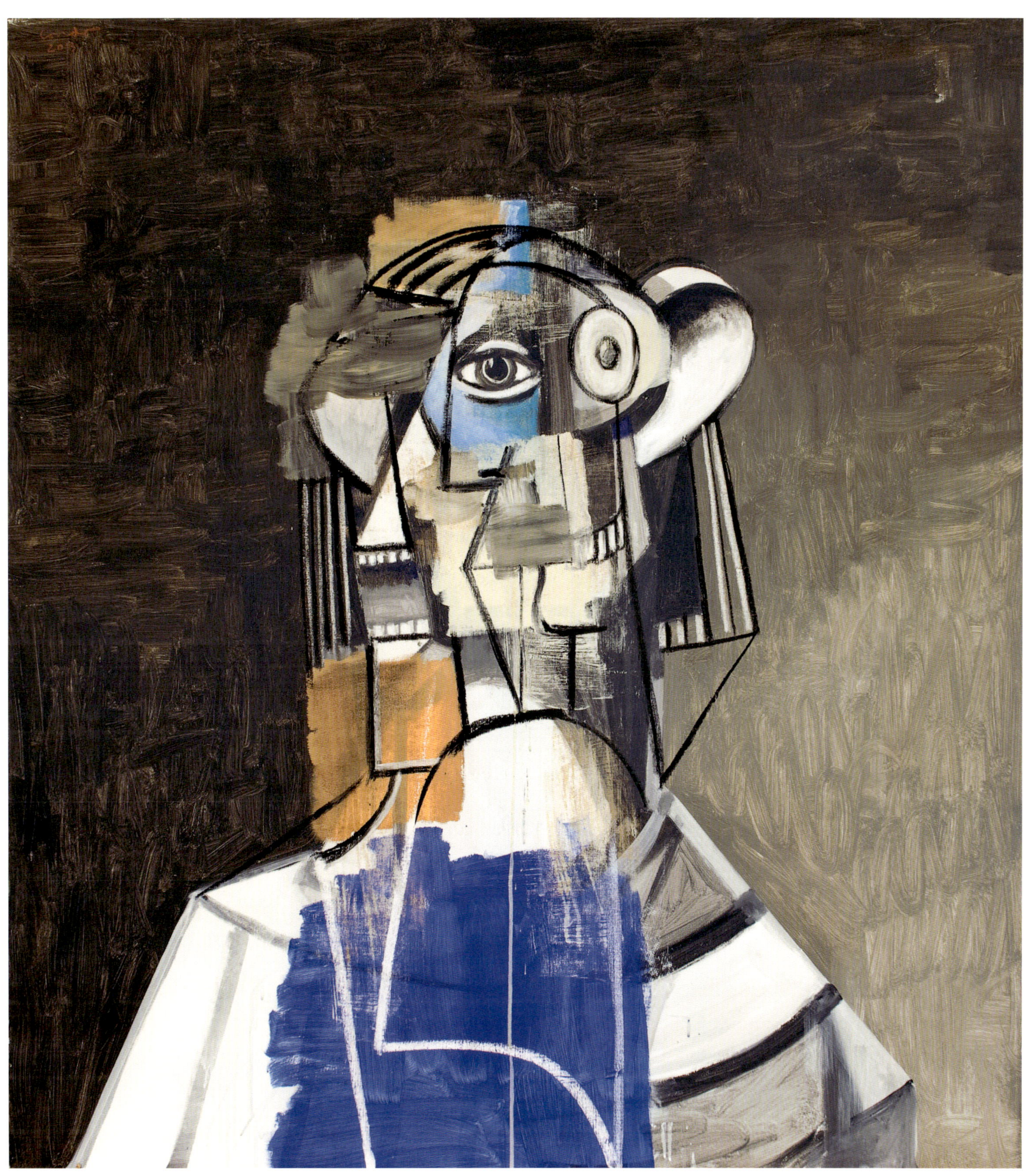

Constructed Head, 2013
Acrylic, charcoal, and pastel on linen, 4 ft. 8½ in. × 4 ft. 4 in. (143.5 × 132.1 cm)

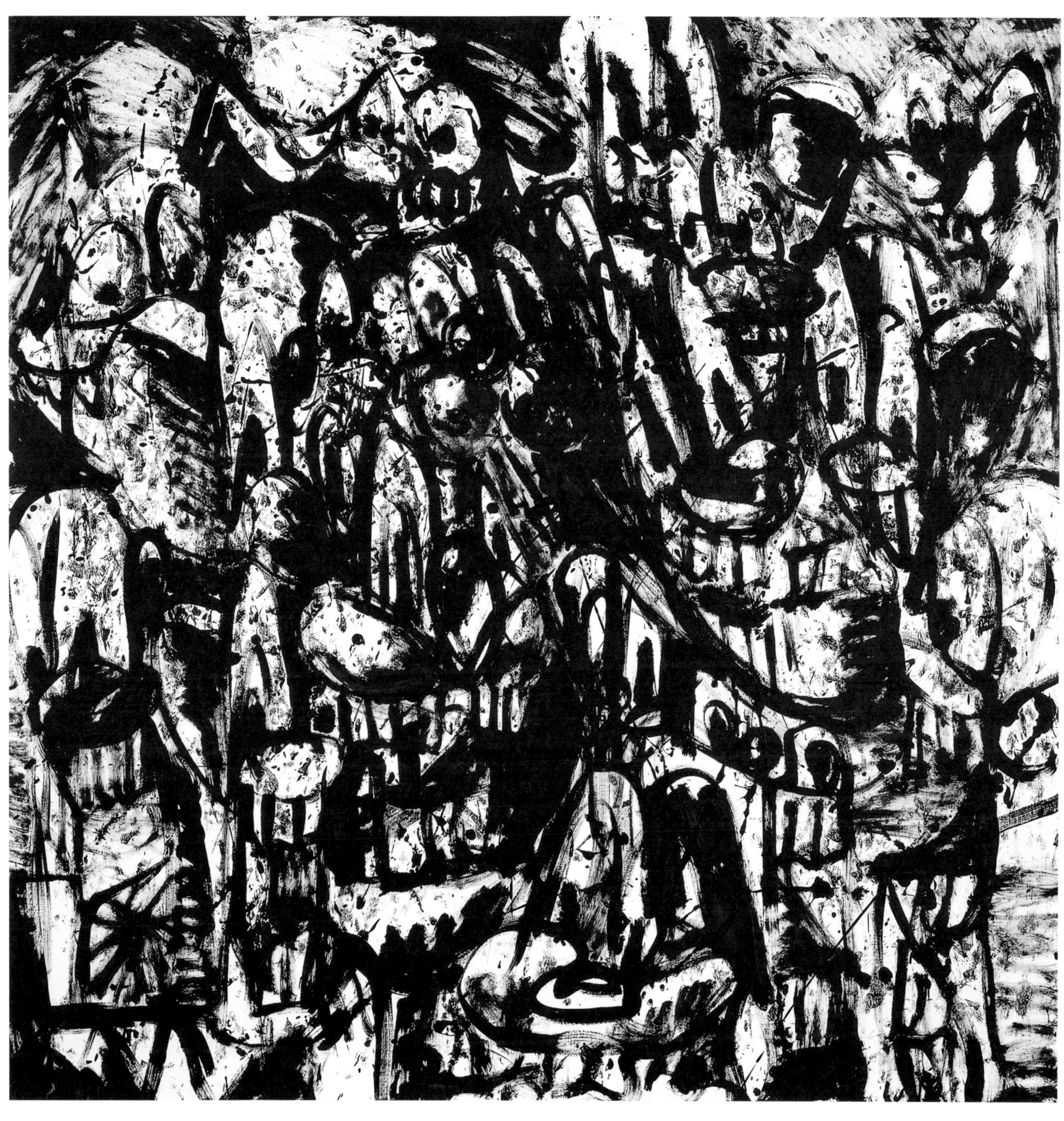

Mental States VII, 2000
Oil on canvas, 5 × 5 ft. (152.4 × 152.4 cm)

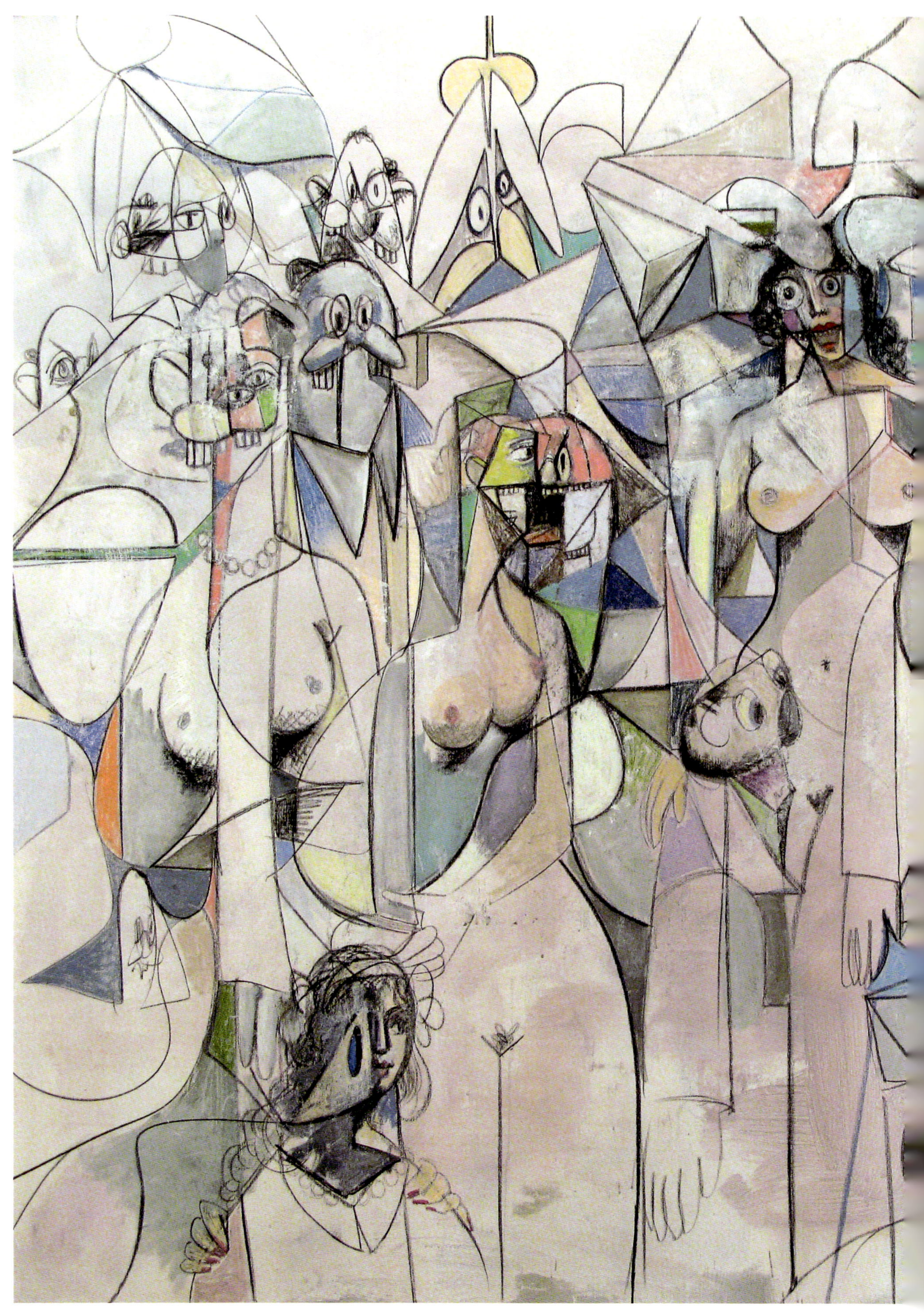

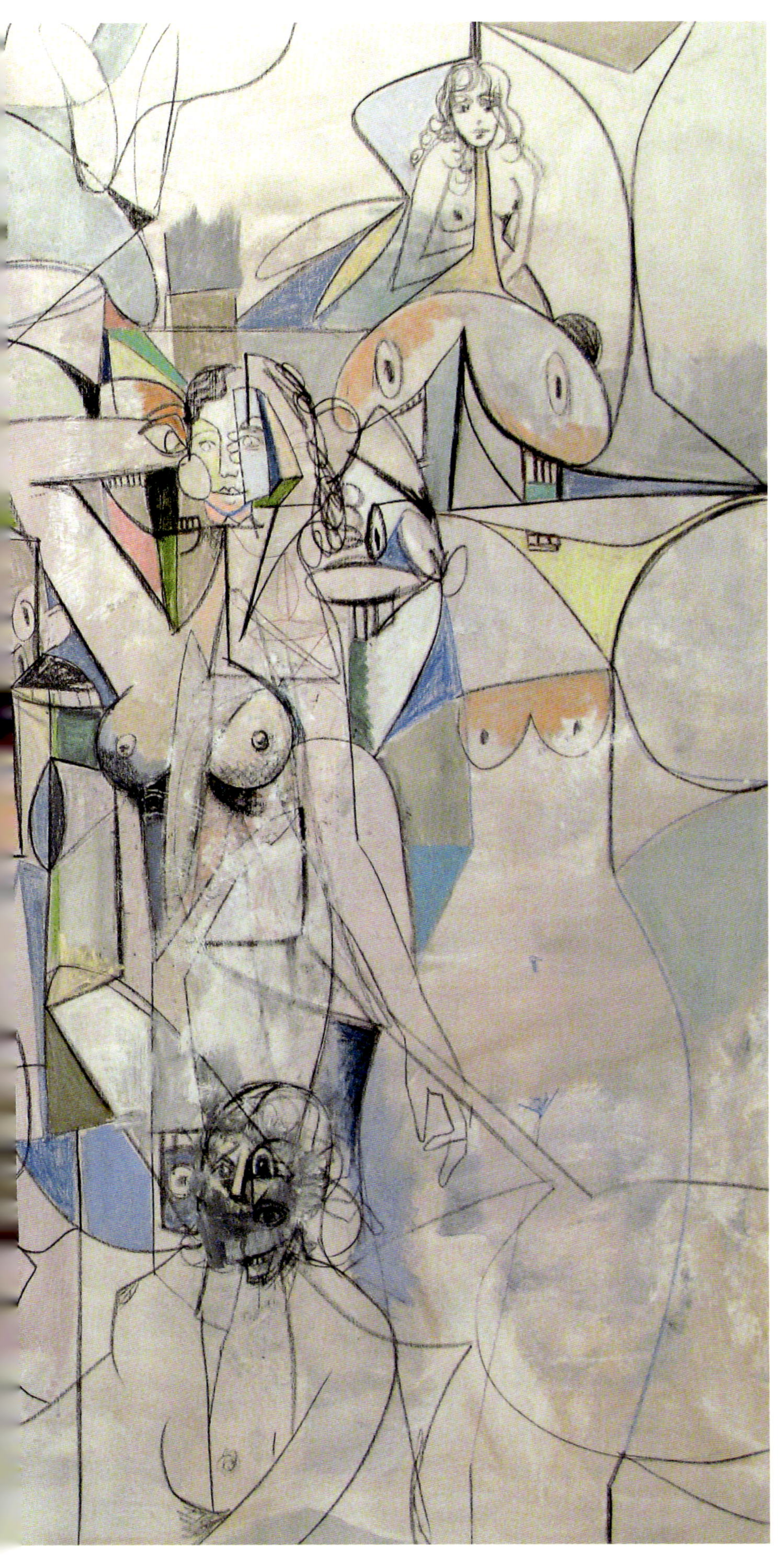

Winter, from *The Four Seasons* series, 2010
Acrylic, charcoal, and pastel on linen, 6 ft. 4 in. × 8 ft. 4 in.
(193 × 254 cm)

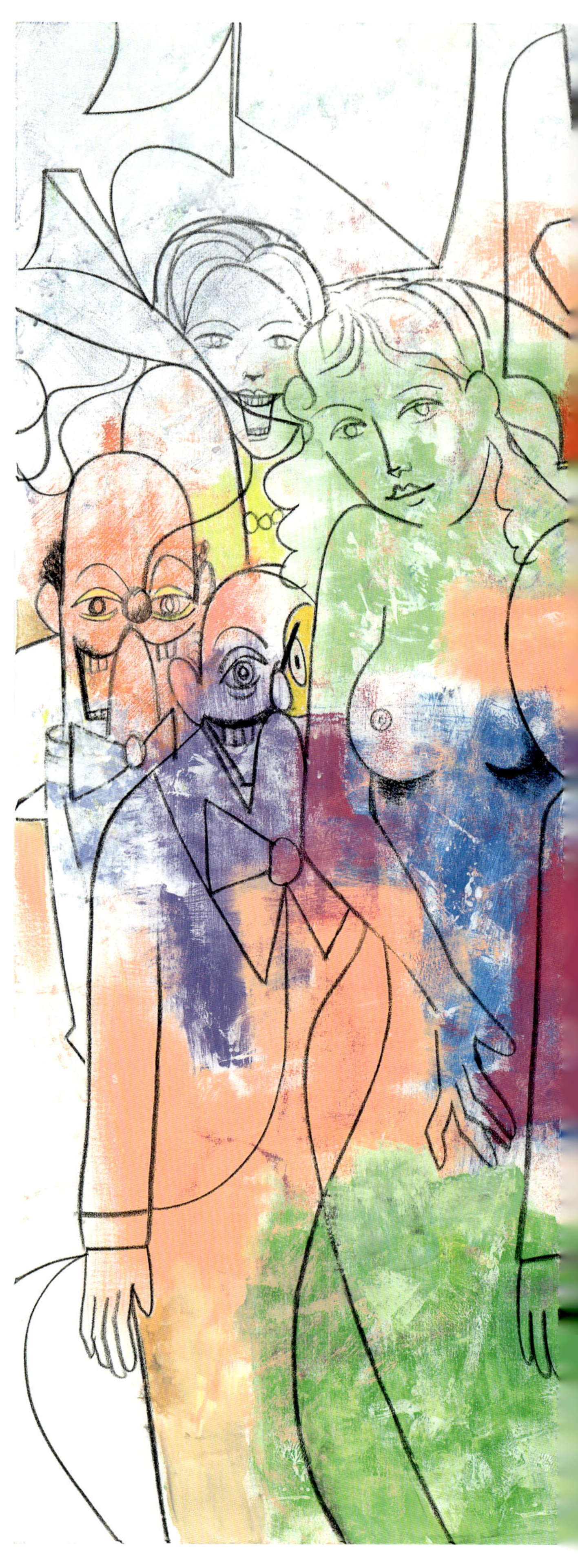

Summer, from *The Four Seasons* series, 2010
Acrylic, charcoal, and pastel on linen, 6 ft. 4 in. × 8 ft. 4 in. (193 × 254 cm)

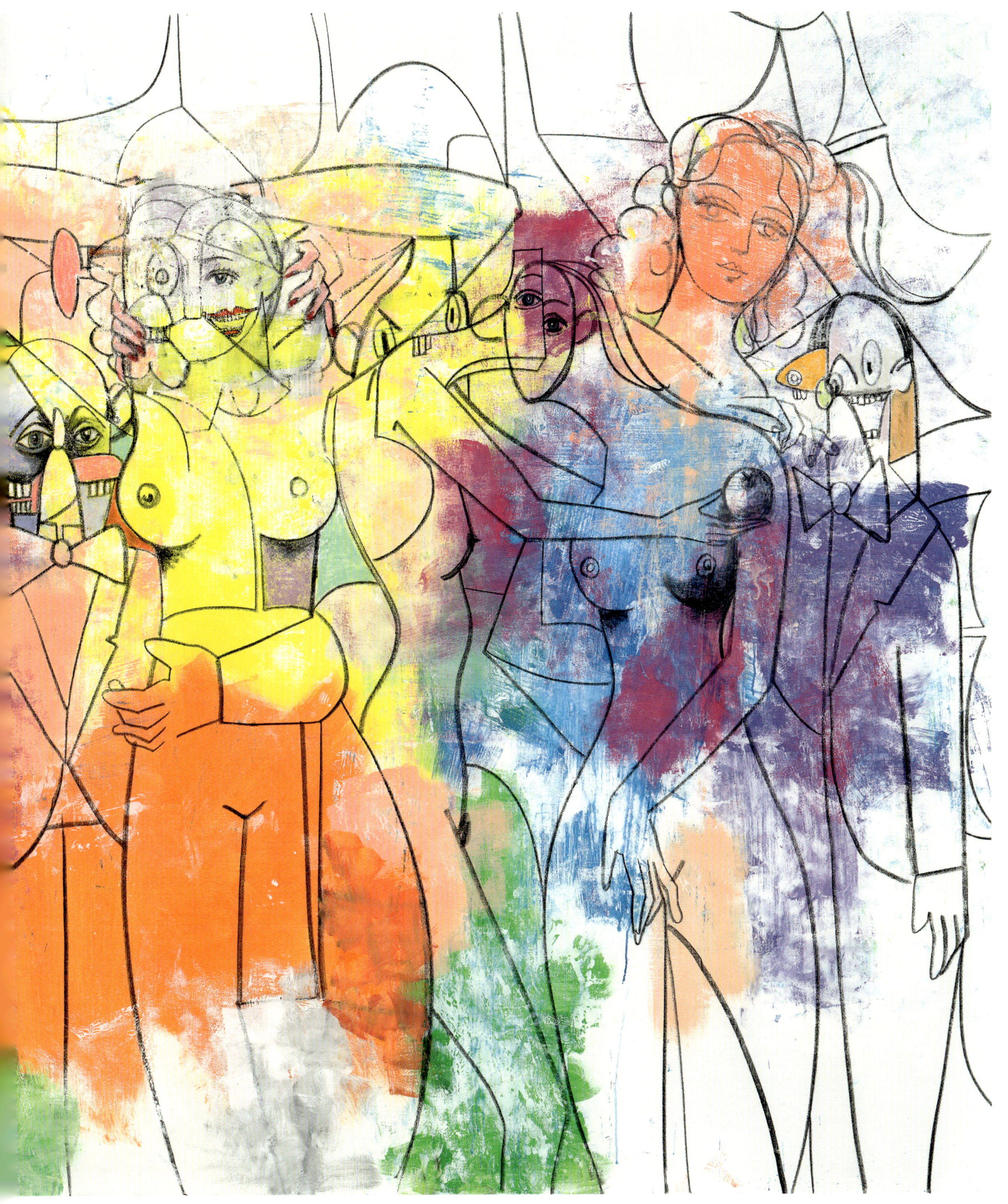

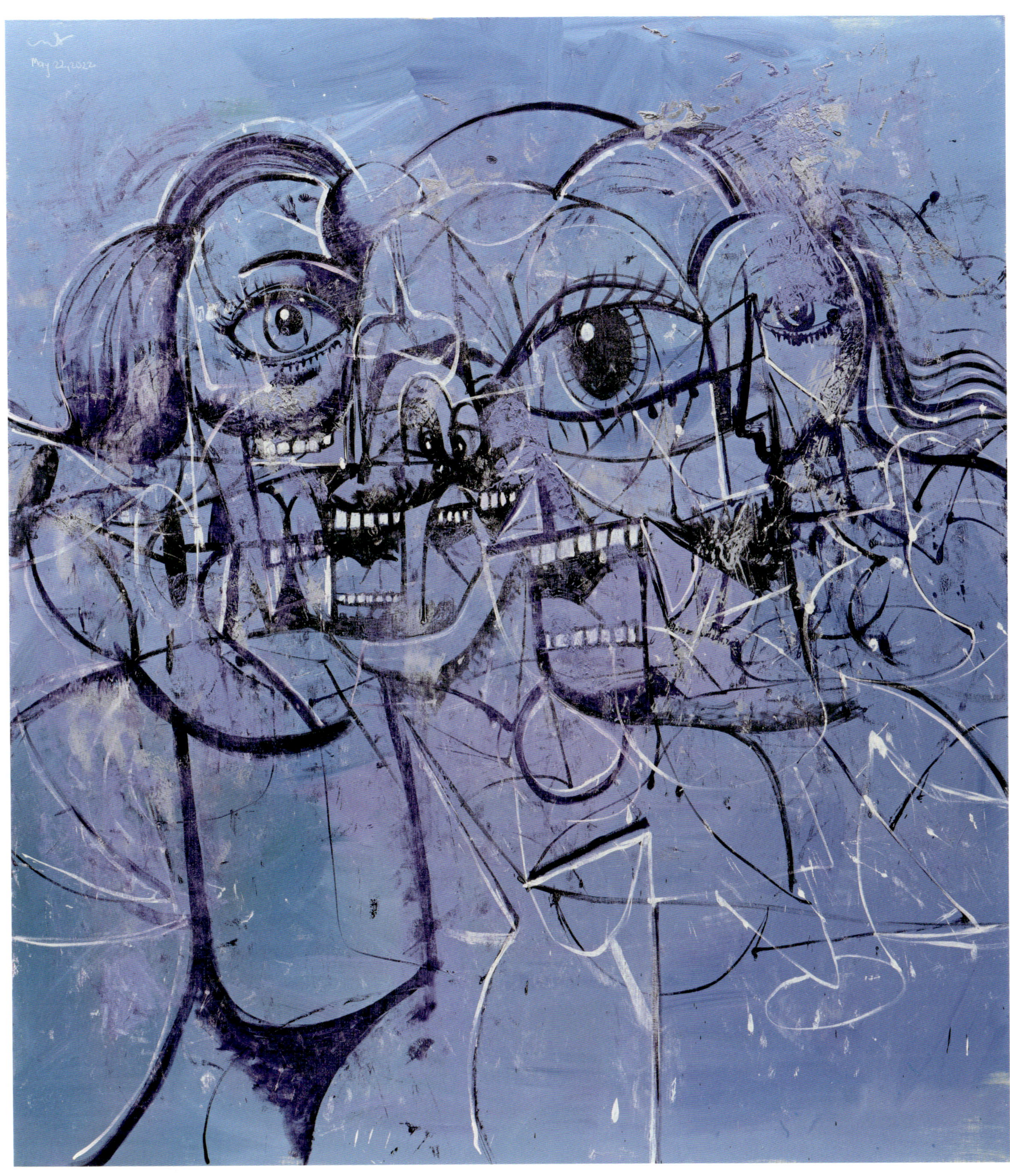

Blues in F Major, 2022
Oil on canvas, 6 ft. × 5 ft. 5 in. (182.9 × 165.1 cm)

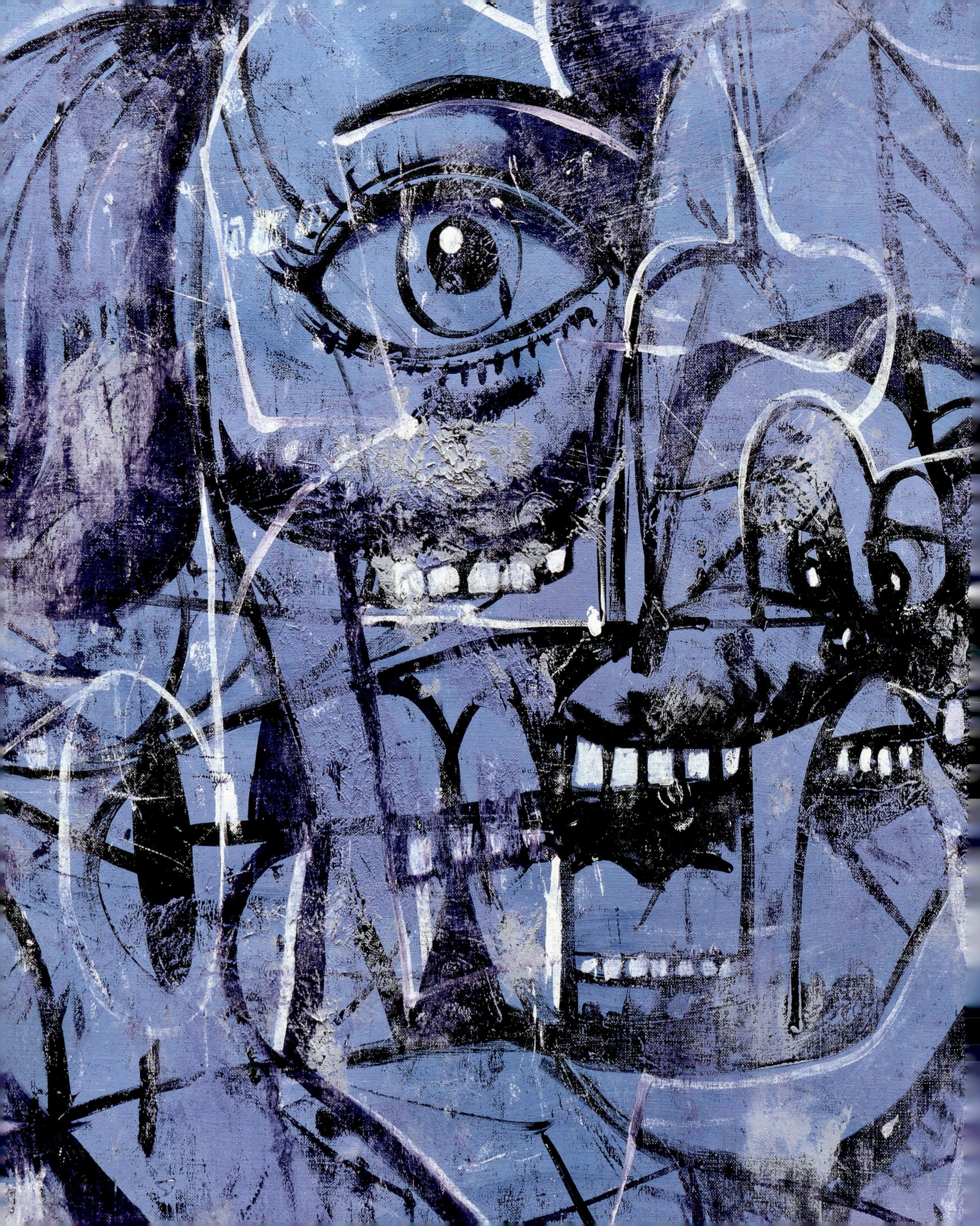

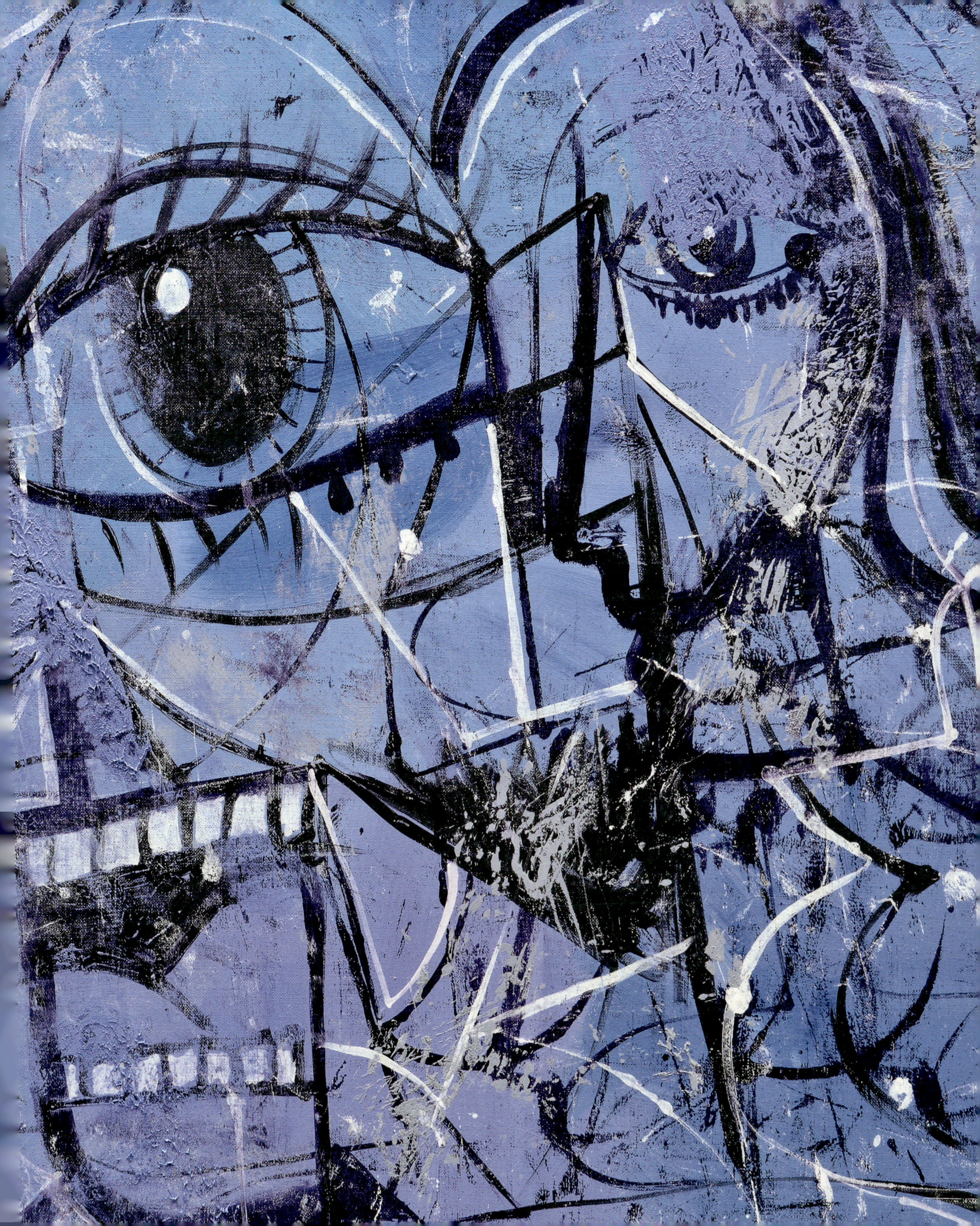

Didier Ottinger

George Condo's Schizo-Frenzy

"Humanoid, n. and adj.
(a creature) resembling
or comparable to a human."

Larousse

The first time he saw *Les Demoiselles d'Avignon*, the critic Félix Fénéon is said to have told Pablo Picasso, "You have a great future as a caricaturist!" Historians of cubism, however, were quick to forget Fénéon's remark, preferring to see Picasso's stylized, schematic rendering of *Les Demoiselles* as the birth of unequivocally abstract, modern art.

In the mid-1980s, George Condo systematically reexamined Picasso's works and found that Fénéon had got it right, and that Picasso had merely used cubism for more "expressionistic" ends.

Through his vast eclecticism—he draws on the Old Masters and on comic strips, on the "heroes" of the television shows he watched as a child and on Picasso—Condo has brought into the world a motley crew of creatures he calls "Humanoids." The word lends a modest, futuristic tone to a project that is in fact a reinvention of *figurative painting*. As Humanoids, his figures assert their fictional nature and lay claim to a "monstrous" genealogy that extends from the golem to Frankenstein and science fiction's "replicant." They belong to an order of reality which is that of painting itself.

High and Low Go Boating…

When George Condo committed to his vocation as an artist, the certitudes upon which modern art had based its authority were teetering on the brink. Like an Energizer bunny whose batteries had run low, the contemporary art of the 1970s faltered and stopped, mallet poised above the drum that kept time for its triumphal march.

And yet it had all begun so well. At the outset of the twentieth century, Pablo Picasso's geometric arrangement of a half-dozen prostitutes in *Les Demoiselles d'Avignon* (1907) had initiated a simplification and "purification" of artistic form that would, in the span of a few decades, cause art to become as light as a soap bubble (filled with "conceptual" air). In the mid-1970s, the momentum that carried Western society to ever-expanding growth faltered under the effects of the oil crisis, and people everywhere remembered

Mikoláš Aleš, *Rabbi Loew and his Golem*, 1899

that the earth and natural resources are finite. Unlimited consumption gradually gave way to energy management and recycling.

Having become a professional artist, George Condo was well-placed to understand the situation and anticipate the changes that lay ahead. For several years, he had been working for a printer who mass-produced Andy Warhol images. Bridging the old and new worlds—half avant-garde and half postmodernist—Warhol seemed to move in step with a merrily industrious age. He had transformed his studio into a "Factory" and established a system of mass-production founded upon Taylorist principles. Condo, who was one of Warhol's workers for a time, couldn't have picked a better school for himself.[1] If Warhol's production methods had one foot in the avant-garde (whose ethos oddly mirrored that of perpetually expanding industrialism), his iconography flourished in the "post"-modern world that had opened up in the 1970s—a world whose values were directly opposed to the individualism, rationality (both technical and scientific), and progress upon which modernism was founded.

Warhol's productivist tendencies made him, unquestionably, a modern artist. But his passion for recycled images, his taste for news photographs and advertisements, and his status as a "supervisor" of works he never touched with his own hands (as Condo's paychecks attested) are all in opposition to the authenticity and inventiveness at the core of the modernist ethos.

Warhol's eclectic iconography undid modernism's sacrosanct hierarchy of high and low, museum and marketplace. Still worse, this iconography had no qualms about incorporating "culture-industry" kitsch, seizing hold of Mickey and other cartoon characters, and taking images from tourist postcards (of Ludwig II's castles, for instance).

Condo first came to the Factory as a kind of court-chronicler, tasked with noting down every least event. After a few days, his knowledge of silkscreen printing led to his being entrusted with

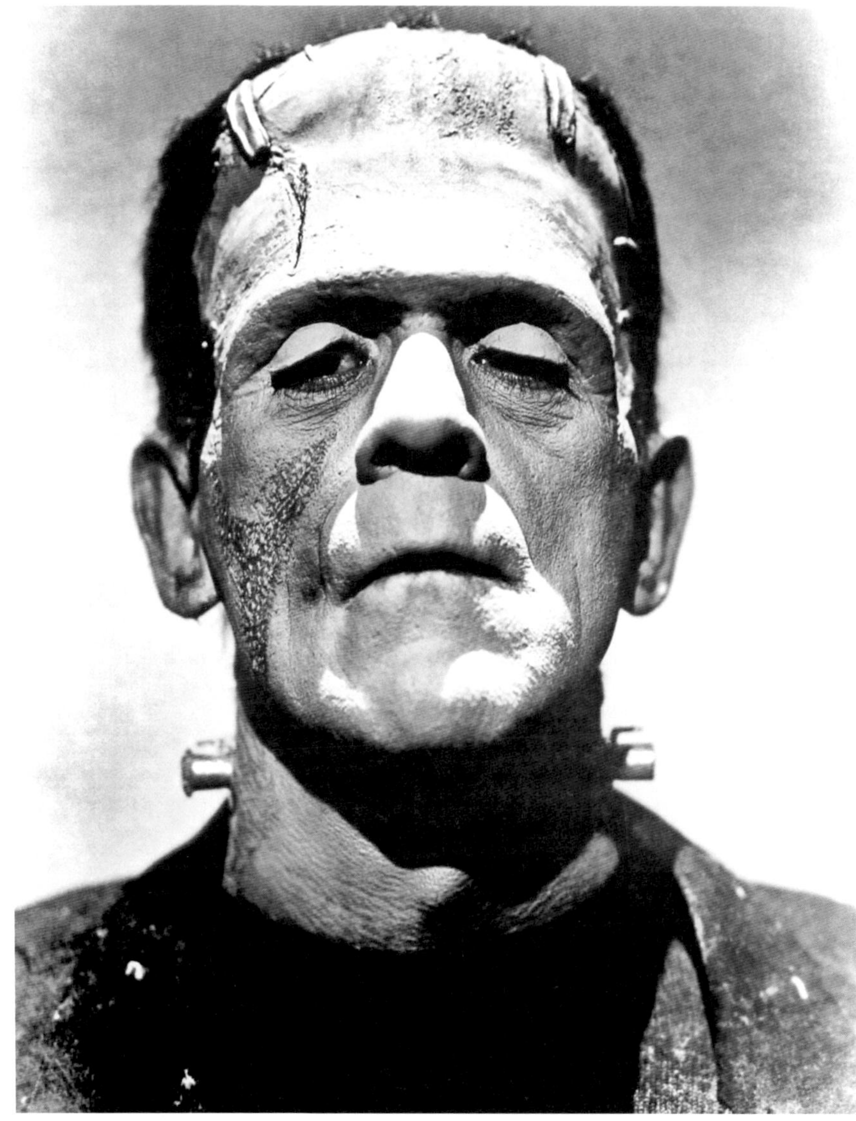

Boris Karloff in James Whale's *The Bride of Frankenstein*, 1935

1. Condo worked on silkscreens for Warhol from 1981.

applying the "diamond dust" to the images of the Myths series. After nine months at the Factory, he left New York for Los Angeles, in the company of the actress Susan Tyrrell.

It was time for Condo to think of his art. Years later, he would say he was looking for "a statement that would stand up against Andy Warhol's soup cans"[2]—not a work that would oppose Warhol, but a work that could formally and conceptually hold its own against him. The project was ambitious; what form it would take remained to be seen. There are many legends illustrating Warhol's knack for debunking the idea of genius and refuting mythologies of inspiration and the muses. One such legend tells of how, during a period of artist's block, he asked his mother, Julia Warhola, "What should I paint?" She is said to have told him to paint what he liked best. Back then, Warhol liked Campbell's soup. The rest is history.... Another anecdote tells of how Warhol confessed a similar difficulty to his gallerist Leo Castelli. Castelli is said to have responded the same way as Warhol's mother. This time, Warhol answered, "Money!" And the Dollar Signs series was born.

In Los Angeles, Condo asked himself what he liked best. His answer—the Old Masters—gave birth to what he considers his first painting, *The Madonna*, a stereotyped image condensing the totality of Virgin Marys he had seen in museums. Having found his theme, he still had to choose his method. Here again, it was a Warhol series that finally offered the technical solution. In his Do It Yourself series, Warhol reproduced children's paint-by-numbers kits: 1=blue, 2=red, etc. (Condo points out that, ironically, these works are precisely ones that only an artist, and not a factory, could make.) Reinterpreting paint-by-numbers, Condo developed a form of craft painting using only the most traditional techniques. Condo's choice of technique was also inspired by the other "good fairy" he sought to invoke at the birth of his vocation as an artist: Picasso. "I wanted to paint everything he had fought against his whole life, using varnishes, glazes and subject matter he had long abandoned," says Condo.[3] And so, under the twofold patronage of Warhol and Picasso, Condo made his first painting, *The Madonna* (1982).

Contrary to Warhol, Condo chose the museum, not the supermarket—a choice prefigured by his incessant wanderings through the halls of the universal museum. His encyclopedic knowledge of art history became the reservoir from which to extract an iconography. While the technique he laid claim to was contrary to Warhol's "detachment" or Picasso's *fa presto*, Condo was nevertheless far from seeing himself as a new Giorgio de Chirico. The latter had rediscovered the Old Masters in the collections of the Villa Borghese, after his "metaphysical" period that marked him out as one of the most innovative

2. George Condo. Interview by Calvin Tomkins. "Portraits of Imaginary People." *The New Yorker*, January 17, 2011.
3. George Condo, email message to author.

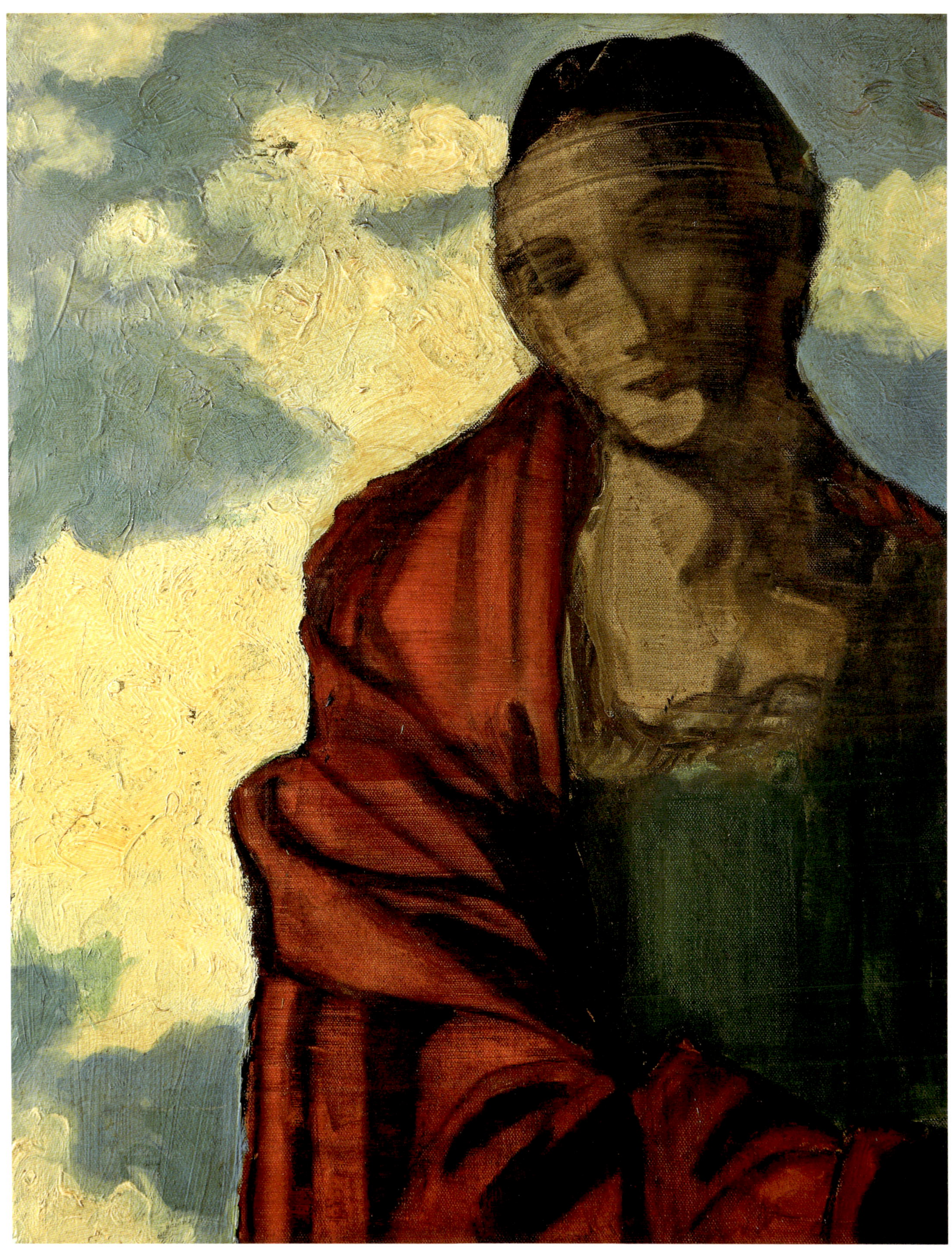

George Condo, *The Madonna*, 1982. Oil on canvas, 20 × 16 in. (50.8 × 40.6 cm)

painters of his generation. De Chirico's reconnection with "great painting" led him to a vitriolic denunciation of modern art. Condo's *Madonna*, however, is no vengeful manifesto. When he was done, he took a ruler and scraped off some of the paint, making the image "sort of blurred, like a Francis Bacon."[4] The act was meant to blot out a face he wasn't happy with. "In doing so it transformed it into something far more modern than I could have imagined," he says.[5] The "modernity" conferred by this gesture (a technique used as early as the 1960s in the blurred images of Gerhard Richter) made the *Madonna* a groundbreaking work. It heralded a contrary movement in painting, a fascination with and aggression towards classical painting—the first incarnation of the "terrible schizophrenia" that Condo recognizes as the main spring of his work.

Over the years, Condo has tried to define the nature of this fundamental schizophrenia more precisely. Shrugging off critics and art historians all-too-ready to speak of Marcel Duchamp and contemporary art, Condo defines this schizophrenia as a conflict between his attachment to classical art on the one hand, and the legacy of a reflexive, critical, "conceptual" modernity on the other. This schizophrenic split would soon become the matrix that gave a second birth to Warhol's comic-book characters, along with all the clowns and fools of the *comédie humaine*.

In Los Angeles, Condo met back up with Jean-Michel Basquiat, whom he had met earlier in New York on the stage of Tier 3, a nightclub where they both had gigs (Condo, at the time, was a bassist for the punk group The Girls). Basquiat was in California preparing a show at the Gagosian. Around him had gathered a group of New Yorkers, with whom Condo would later return to the city.

Surfing the New Wave

In the first days of 1980, Condo left Los Angeles for New York. At the time, the New York cultural scene was in full transition. A period of détente was underway, loosening the dominance of a modernism that had become dogmatic by virtue of universal acceptance. Rejecting modernist asceticism, Condo's generation binged on forms, colors, and stories of all kinds. Nihilism, intentional idiocy, and the "primitiveness" of outsider and "lowbrow" art became the marks of what had now clearly distinguished itself as "postmodernism."

"There was a new wave of figurative art going on in New York then, with Basquiat, and Schnabel, and Keith Haring and a few others," Condo recalls, "but I didn't want to be part of that."[6]

4. George Condo, interview by Calvin Tomkins, "Portraits of Imaginary People."
5. George Condo, email message to author.
6. George Condo, interview by Calvin Tomkins, "Portraits of Imaginary People."

The "new wave of figurative art" in New York wasn't merely a "return to painting." Basquiat and Haring brought their images to the city walls. Condo's quest was similar to that of Basquiat, who looked to outsider art—the legacy of Jean Dubuffet—and to non-European roots—his Haitian family traditions—to find artforms that would call into question the art of his elders, withered by its excess of theory, its pathological fear of bad taste. Along with Keith Haring, Condo pursued the idea of a politics of art anchored in society, a form of popular painting revitalized with graffiti and comic strips. In 1979 at the Mary Boone Gallery, Julian Schnabel, soon to become the figurehead of American "Bad Painting", exhibited works in which he swapped his brushes for shards of pottery, a technique he had brought back from a stay in Catalonia where he learned the lessons of Gaudí. Seeking a revitalized art, Condo looked to the vehement "stupidity" of Bad Painting and took a page from the most scandalous moments in the history of modern art, from Francis Picabia to Magritte's "Vache" period.

In the States, postmodernism took the form of the postconceptual art of Sherrie Levine and Elaine Sturtevant, proud proponents of appropriation. Their reproductions of works by Jackson Pollock, Kazimir Malevich, and Walker Evans undermined the fundamental principles of modern art: originality, innovation, and disregard for the past.

From New York's postmodernist moment, Condo learned that quotation and plagiarism were no longer taboo—a lesson rubber-stamped by the most "advanced" critical thought. Further, he could now lay claim to an art that wasn't forced to look to the future, but could make free use of the past, and even learn from the Old Masters. The new cultural context led him to believe that his *Madonna* was exactly what the age demanded—that it was "totally new … because it 'looked' so old."[7]

No matter how "new" his idea of "retro" painting might be, Condo was aware that the art he wanted to make was subject to lingering suspicion in America. The most influential critics, holding sway in universities and in the pages of *October*, irrevocably condemned the wave of paintings sweeping through the SoHo galleries.

In 1981, Benjamin H. D. Buchloh became the self-appointed spokesperson of avant-garde opposition to postmodern tendencies. In a vindictive essay, he dismissed the revival of painting on political grounds, calling it a reactionary, philistine movement, and contrasting it with the entirely "conceptual" form of postmodernism practiced by Sherrie Levine: "At the very historical moment when a reactionary middle class struggles to expand its

7. George Condo, email message to author.

privileges, buttressing an oligarchic hegemony searching for cultural legitimation, and when hundreds of minor talents in painting obediently provide gestures of free expression, Levine's work subverts this spectacle of a mythical individuality."[8]

The journal *October* became modernism's Fort Alamo, holding out against a horde of shaggy brushmen. Douglas Crimp published an article with the peremptory title "The End of Painting." Adopting the terms of Buchloh's invective, Crimp wrote that the "rhetoric which accompanies this resurrection of painting is almost exclusively reactionary."[9] Like Molière's Monsieur Diafoirus at the bedside of a dying art, he proclaimed that "during the 1960s, painting's terminal condition finally seemed impossible to ignore."[10] After delivering this diagnosis, Crimp suggests that the only remaining option for those who persist in believing in the survival of painting is a pilgrimage to Lourdes, since "only a miracle can prevent it from coming to an end."[11] If it would take a miracle to save his art, Condo had done well to paint *The Madonna*.

Picture Germany

From New York, artists looked to Germany as the center of the new figurative painting. Since the 1960s, Germany had fostered a new painting whose relationship to tradition became a form of collective catharsis. American museums kept an eye on the unique German scene. As Thomas Krens would later write: "By virtue of its lateral and chronological reach, the new German painting enjoyed a reputation for authenticity exempting it from the ontological anxiety that came with various postmodern 'strategies' trapped in the highly self-conscious context of art-making in New York in the 1970s."[12]

Since the early 1960s, far from the diktats of the New York "bolsheviks," Georg Baselitz had taken up his brushes again to create a programmatically figurative, painterly body of work. In 1962, the artists Markus Lüpertz, Karl Horst Hödicke, and Bernd Koberling founded the gallery Großgörschen 35, which soon became a platform for the new Berlin figurative painting. A decade later, another generation of artists emerged from Berlin's Academy of Arts (Rainer Fetting, Helmut Middendorf, Salomé, and others), practitioners of a "wild painting"[13] plugged into the rising punk music scene. In 1982, the new figurative painting held prominent place at *Zeitgeist*, a vast exhibition at the Martin-Gropius-Bau that showcased the vitality of contemporary German art.

8. Benjamin H. D. Buchloh. "Figures of Authority, Ciphers of Regression: Notes on the Return of Representation in European Painting." *October* 16 (1981): 39–68.
9. Douglas Crimp. "The End of Painting." *October* 16 (1981): 69–86.
10. Douglas Crimp, "The End of Painting."
11. Douglas Crimp, "The End of Painting."
12. Thomas Krens, in *Refigured Painting. The German Image 1960-88*. New York: Guggenheim Museum; Munich: Prestel, 1989: 14.
13. "Heftige Malerei" in German.

A year earlier, the Royal Academy in London had shown *A New Spirit in Painting*, an exhibition that demonstrated the European side of the "return to painting." "The current orthodoxies about painting were defined as long ago as the nineteenth fifties by American critics and achieved almost universal acceptance during the following decades. These orthodoxies … aggressively proclaimed the work that was produced in and around New York to be virtually the only universally acceptable art—anything else was at best provincial," the curators wrote in the exhibition catalog.[14]

In New York, Condo shared an apartment with the Czech painter Milan Kunc. Kunc had been a student of Joseph Beuys and Gerhard Richter at the Kunstakademie Düsseldorf, and he associated the legacy of Czech surrealism with the communism he lived under as a child behind the Iron Curtain. Condo was brought face-to-face with completely uninhibited paintings that favored humor over theoretical diktats. In vaguely surrealist compositions, Kunc combined forms from Arcimboldo, comics, pop culture, and Soviet propaganda painting. "Europeans will have a better understanding of his painting than Americans," Jiří Georg Dokoupil had said to Condo, cutting short any last hesitations.[15] With money from the sale of a painting, Condo bought a plane ticket for Amsterdam and, from there, a train ticket to Cologne.

The Ancient Ramparts of Europe

Through contact with Europe and its artists, Condo found confirmation that the path he had chosen was more than a delusive dead end. It was Dokoupil who had suggested Cologne as the first stop in Condo's move to the Old Continent. At Cooper Union in New York, Jiří Georg Dokoupil had been a student of Hans Haacke, who incarnated at the time a form of late conceptualism mixed with political activism—Haacke's most famous works denounce real-estate speculation in underprivileged New York neighborhoods. As Dokoupil later described, "In the late 70s there was nothing dumber than painting. The painters were the dorks, especially for the so-called conceptual artists. Hans Haacke—who became the most important teacher for me—at that time, was not interested in the continuation of painting. But I'd come to realize that the conceptual artists had become liars. What they had promised us was salvation, art without form. I'd go into a gallery and there would be nothing to see, and it would be for a lot of money—that just couldn't be it."[16]

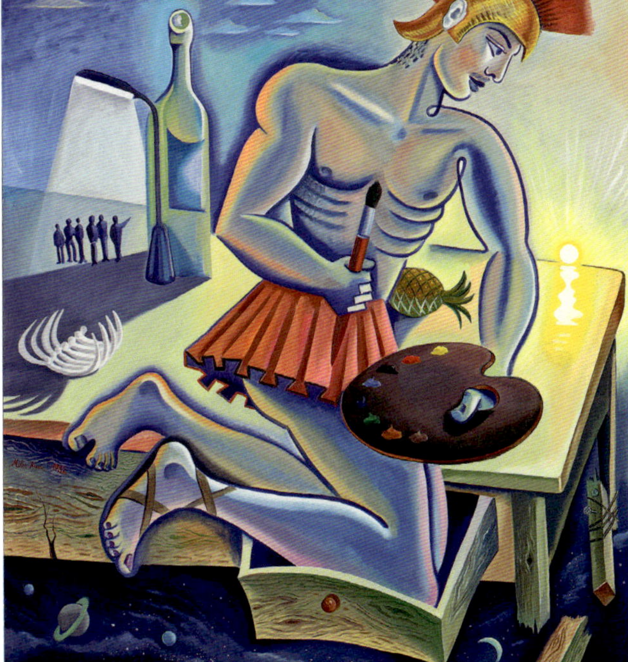

Milan Kunc, *Der wahre Avantgardist versucht vergebens in die Schublade zu passen*, 1982. Acrylic on canvas, 6 ft. 4¾ in. × 5 ft. 9 in. (195 × 175 cm). Groninger Museum, Netherlands

14. Christos M. Joachimides, Norman Rosenthal, and Nicholas Serota. *A New Spirit in Painting*. London: Royal Academy of Arts; New York: Rizzoli, 1981: 12.

15. George Condo, email message to author.

16. Jiří Georg Dokoupil. Interview by Cornelius Tittel. *032c*, August 22, 2012.

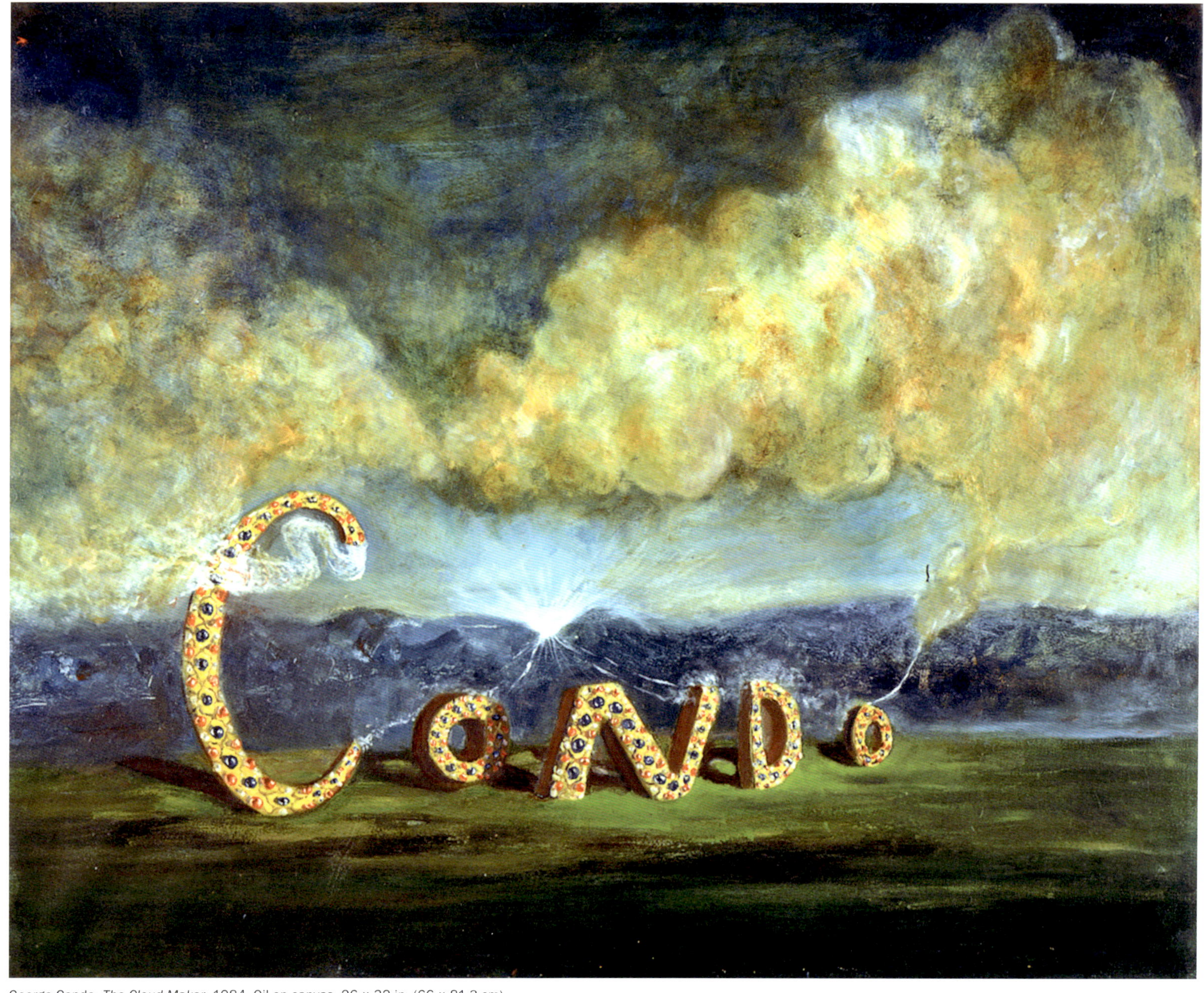

George Condo, *The Cloud Maker*, 1984. Oil on canvas, 26 × 32 in. (66 × 81.3 cm)

In Cologne, Dokoupil and others had founded Mülheimer Freiheit in 1979, more a studio collective than an avant-garde movement. In the absence of a manifesto, Gerhard Naschberger, Hans Peter Adamski, Gerard Kever, Peter Bömmels, and Walter Dahn shared, at least, a way of painting and a taste for equally "wild" rock.[17]

The paintings Dokoupil exhibited in New York had been the subject of an article by Rainer Crone, who analyzed the stakes of the work in the pages of *Artforum*. "This question of a 'personal style,'" wrote Crone, "seems all the more critical when one considers the latest developments in painting; developments which, be they abstract or figurative, follow the years of minimal and conceptual art. Many of today's artists appear to have an aversion toward a normative stylistic integration, displaying instead an outright rejection which leads even to a negation of 'personal style' and to the elimination of such supposedly conflicting terms as 'abstract' and 'figurative.' This negation applies particularly to the young artist under discussion here, Jiří Georg Dokoupil."[18]

Two years after his show at the Mary Boone Gallery—the most prominent gallery in New York—Dokoupil exhibited his work at the prestigious Leo Castelli Gallery. This exhibition confirmed the place not only of his own work but also of the new European painting as a whole, soon leading to a show at the Leo Castelli Gallery for Gérard Garouste as well.

Clown World

Condo's arrival in Cologne reads like the script of a B-movie thriller: "I went and arrived there on the day of the carnival. Even the driver of the train was wearing a mask. It was wild."[19] This carnival welcome was a fitting introduction to the art scene he was about to discover. From Martin Kippenberger to Dokoupil, from Walter Dahn to Werner Büttner, Condo was surprised to find that the work of overtly humorous, resolutely outrageous painters could be taken seriously by critics and the art market alike. No need, here, to claim the alibi of "conceptual art" to gain acceptance for the levity of one's paintings.

In the 1980s, Cologne was the site of a punk reincarnation of dada. As far as the music was concerned, Condo wasn't on unfamiliar ground. In Boston, during his early years, the success of his band The Girls had almost led him astray from painting. Armed with a solid musical background, Condo had had no trouble picking up an electric bass and thumping out the simple

17. Their unbridled art earned them the nickname the "*Neue Wilden*" (the New Fauves).
18. Rainer Crone. "Jiří Georg Dokoupil: The Imprisoned Brain." *Artforum*, Vol. 21, No. 7, March 1983.
19. George Condo. Interview by Olivier Zahm. *Purple Magazine*, No. 23, 2015.

rhythms of the band's songs. At the height of their fame, they shared a spot with Devo on a television show.

Is it as easy to become a painter as it is to become a musician? Yes, according to Dokoupil and his Mülheimer Freiheit friends: "What we were doing in this situation was analogous to punk; they couldn't play three notes, we couldn't paint. But there was energy there, and it led the way back to painting."[20]

From November 1983 to May 1984, Condo shared a studio with Walter Dahn. Between Sex Pistols songs, they listened over and over to a recording of William Burroughs reading his poems.

Capable of more as a painter, Condo temporarily contented himself with less, and made the iconography of the Cologne painters his own. As Dokoupil put it, "Since we had focused on the dumbest of mediums, we also selected the dumbest of subjects—the dumber, the better."[21] (This was after *October* had, on several occasions, criticized the "dumbness" of painting). The most "idiotic" subject Condo could find was clowns, the images that had welcomed him to the city. Of course, this idiocy was only on the surface. Years later, he would confess he couldn't help painting his clowns "like Rembrandts."[22]

How do you translate punk into painting, beyond the simplistic formula of "Bad Painting"? How do you transpose Dionysian frenzy into the domain of the imagination? Surrealism—as practiced by Kunc—appeared to Condo as the visual idiom best suited to transposing the irrationality and narrative excess of Dokoupil and his friends. Condo now explored, quoted, and parodied de Chirico and his metaphysical environments, Yves Tanguy and his genetic spaces, Salvador Dalí and his paranoid mash-ups. As Henry Geldzahler would later point out, surrealism was the avant-garde "of reference" for Condo and his generation.

To give an account of surrealism's return to contemporary painting, the Museum Folkwang in Essen gathered works by Andreas Schulze, Salvo, Milan Kunc, David Bowes, Dieter Teusch, and Condo in 1985 in an exhibition titled *Künstliche Paradiese* (Artificial paradise). In the exhibition catalog, Wilfried Dickhoff, citing the "the irreal constellation of realistic details" in their work, compared these painters (as well as Dokoupil and Albert Oehlen) to the surrealists, particularly to "Dalí and the late de Chirico."[23] Defining the surrealism of this new

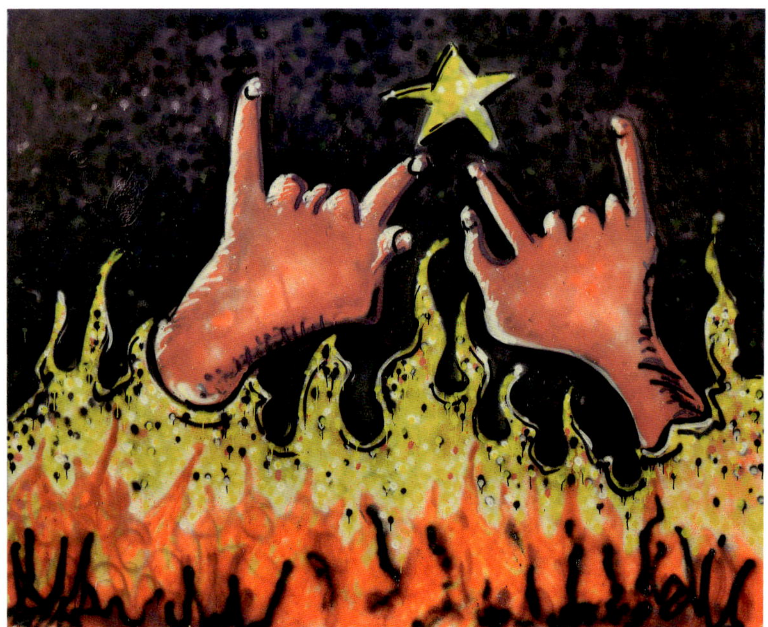

Walter Dahn, *Untitled*, 1984. Spray on canvas, 6 ft. 6¾ in. × 8 ft. 2½ in. (200 × 250 cm)

20. Jiří Georg Dokoupil, interview by Cornelius Tittel.
21. Jiří Georg Dokoupil, interview by Cornelius Tittel.
22. George Condo, interview by Calvin Tomkins, "Portraits of Imaginary People."
23. Wilfried Dickhoff in *Künstliche Paradiese*. Essen: Museum Folkwang; Munich: München Kunstverein, 1985.

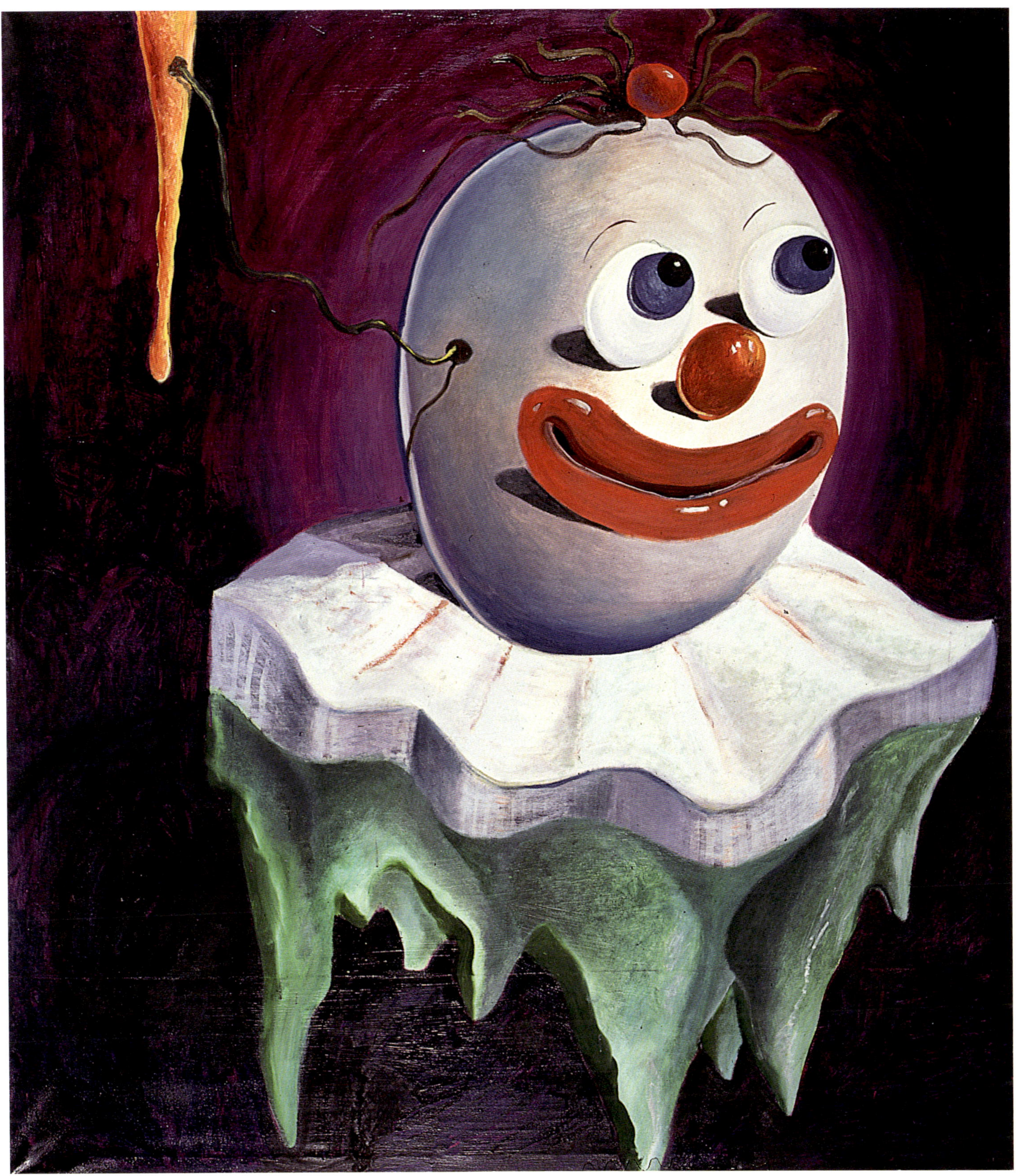

George Condo, *In Order to Think*, 1983–84. Oil on canvas, 6 ft. 6¾ in. × 5 ft. 3 in. (200 × 160 cm)

generation of painters, Dickhoff wrote that it did not stem from automatism or the "paranoiac-critical method," but from Magritte and his "conceptual" approach to the image.

For Condo, revisiting surrealism seemed the most apt way of channeling the flood of images released by postmodernism. As Félix Guattari would write a few years later in an essay on Condo's work: "The excess of formalism and its extreme manifestation in conceptualism have brought us, for want of a better language than self-destructive negativism, to a sort of generalized anorexia. To make up for this, the orgiastic bulimia of the various rehashings of Transavanguardia and post-modernism will, in the last analysis, have been nothing but an inverted duplication of this anorexia."[24]

Surrealism—long cast aside by a modernism whose aesthetics were based on Bauhaus technicism—was now finally able to come out of the closet in which the modern museum had locked it. After decades of a formalist reduction and "purification" of art, the 1970s eagerly dove into the troubled waters of the surrealist imagination.

Georg Baselitz, Anselm Kiefer, and the new German fauvists churned up national cultural memories without regard for hierarchy. In Italy, the Transavanguardia mixed images together, from Russian constructivism to *Valori plastici* neoclassicism. Impeccably classical forms stood side-by-side with fanzines, Malevich danced arm in arm with Dalí, de Chirico embraced Henri Rousseau.

Condo, arranging this tumult according to the laws of William Burroughs' cut-up method or the logic of the Comte de Lautréamont's poems, brought together a carrot and an ancient bust, a guillotine and a stripper. His paintings became rebuses, intricate plays on words and images. Nevertheless, he fairly quickly tired of these riddles and nonsense games and returned to his oldest obsession: the portrait. He swapped surrealism for cubism. Just as his musical background had made him get tired of the meagerness of extremely simplified music, his love of the Old Masters left him bored with the painterly babbling of the artists in Cologne.

A proposed Parisian exhibition at the Galerie Nancy Gillespie, along with his readings of Proust and Céline, made Condo look toward Paris. As he says, "The cold German weather, the dark rainy days could only be alleviated

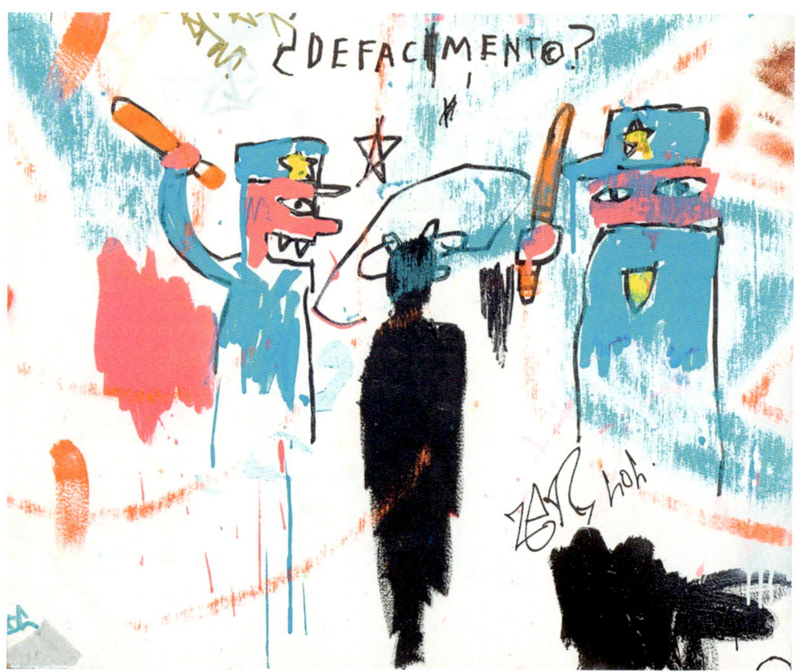

Jean-Michel Basquiat, *Untitled*, 1983. Acrylic and marker on wood, 25 × 30½ in. (63.5 × 77.5 cm)

24. Félix Guattari. "Introduction (Paris 1990)," in *George Condo. The Lost Civilization*. Paris: Gallimard/Musée Maillol, 2009: 18.

140

by making art and being drunk every day with my friends and fellow artists."[25]

Like the time he left New York for Los Angeles, a love affair set things in motion: on a trip to the Canary Islands with Dokoupil, he met a *Parisienne*.

In Paris, Condo stayed briefly at the Hôtel de Crillon, then took up longer-term lodgings (for nearly a year) at the Le Lotti hotel on Rue de Castiglione. He then moved into an apartment on Rue de Condé, which quickly transformed into a studio. The Parisian air, along with French cuisine and wine, seemed to suit Condo well. During the first few years of his stay, he made more than four hundred paintings and hundreds of drawings.

From Surrealism to Psychedelia

Outraged Figuration; Figuration Unbound

In 1983, the young Black artist Michael Stewart was arrested for spraying graffiti in an East Village subway station, and died at Bellevue Hospital from police brutality inflicted during his arrest. Outrage swept through the New York art community. Condo met up with Jean-Michel Basquiat to respond to the artist's death. On a wall of Keith Haring's studio, Basquiat painted the death of Michael Stewart. Condo made a portrait of the murdered young man. Many artists took up the theme. Warhol made a screen-printed "headline" painting in 1983 using a *New York Daily News* article that reported Stewart's death. Two years later, Haring painted *Michael Stewart—USA for Africa*. In 1986, David Hammons made an edition of stenciled prints, *The Man Nobody Killed*, after the police officers responsible for Stewart's death were acquitted. Stewart's death would later inspire a scene in Spike

25. George Condo, email message to author.

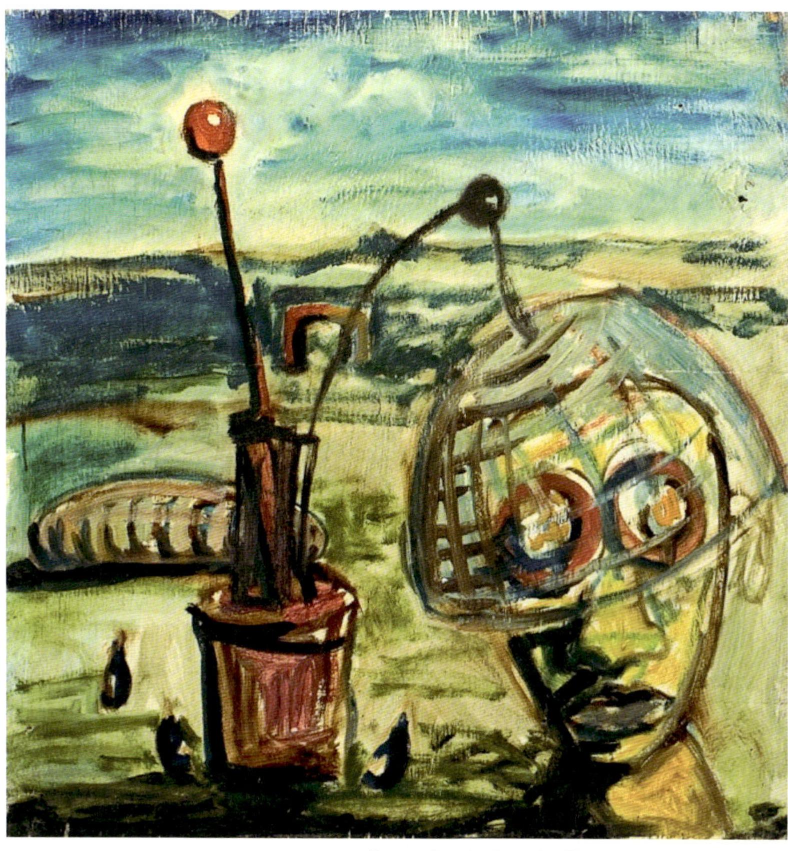

George Condo, *Portrait of Michael Stewart*, 1983. Oil on panel, 24 × 24 in. (61 × 61 cm)

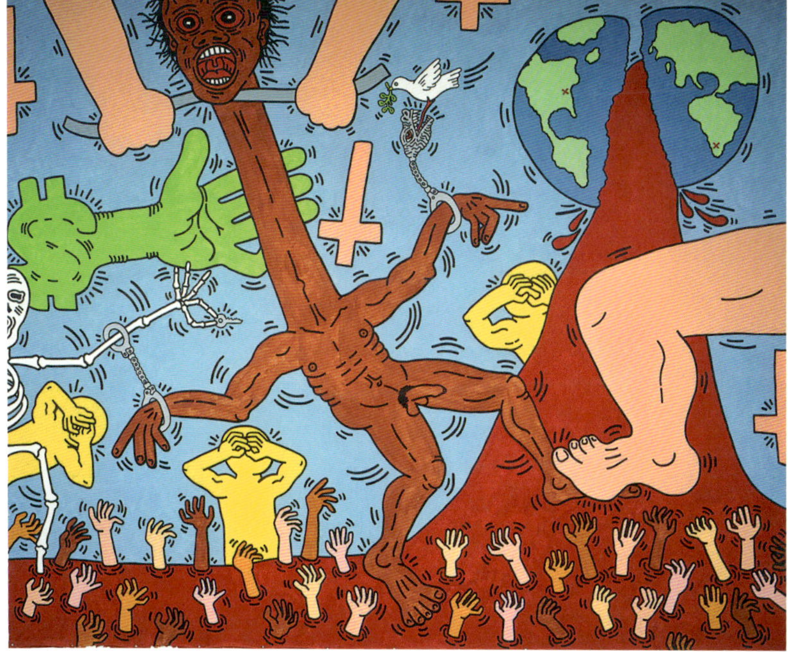

Keith Haring, *Michael Stewart—USA for Africa*, 1985. Enamel and acrylic on canvas, 9 ft. 8¼ in. × 12 ft. ½ in. (295 × 367 cm)

Lee's 1989 film *Do The Right Thing*, along with the Lou Reed song "Hold On," of the same year.

In 1985, Condo made several trips to New York, staying at a studio Keith Haring lent him in the East Village. With Europe far away, the history of American painting loomed large again. A big blank canvas 9 ft. 2 in. × 11 ft. 6 in. (280 × 350 cm) in Haring's studio seemed to summon Condo to reconnect with the founding fathers of modern American painting. In the footsteps of Jackson Pollock and Arshile Gorky, Condo painted *Dancing to Miles*, the second of his "expanding canvases." A year earlier, during a stay in Italy, he had painted *Diaries of Milan* (1984), a kind of illustrated journal where, for the first time, he covered the canvas with signs and images, close to Haring's "all-over" compositions.

Dancing to Miles (1985) inaugurated an uninterrupted series of paintings, generally large-format, in which Condo escaped the influence of the Old Masters, left portraiture behind, and developed a more resolutely abstract art. By its biomorphic elements (a heap of "organic" forms), *Dancing to Miles* is stylistically close to the surrealist periods of Arshile Gorky, Wifredo Lam, or even André Masson. By its monumentality and all-over composition, however, it aligns with the heroic period of abstract expressionism.

Once Condo was back in Europe, the walls of his Paris studio began to fill with imaginary portraits. The comedy and uncanniness of these works stem not so much from surrealism—the legacy of Arcimboldo and the free associations of *Maldoror*—as from the reimagining of models lifted from comic books and recollections of works seen in museums. The portraits signaled a shift in method that would lead Condo from an unbridled exploration of the imagination to an inquiry into style and construction: from surrealism to cubism, from Arcimboldo to Picasso.

Painting on the Beat

And yet Condo wasn't done with surrealism, which soon caught up with him in form of the Beat poets, the "cosmonauts of inner space." The encounter took place through Keith Haring. Whenever Haring came to Paris, he would make a point of stopping in to see Condo.

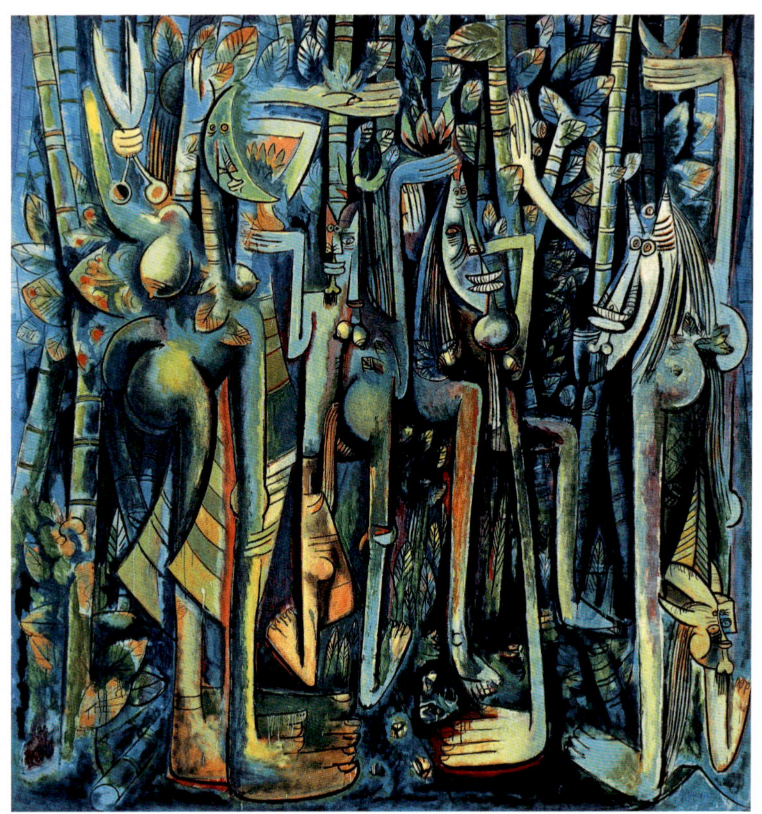

Wifredo Lam, *The Jungle*, 1943. Oil and gouache on paper on canvas, 7 ft. 10¼ in. × 7 ft. 6½ in. (239.4 × 229.9 cm). The Museum of Modern Art, New York

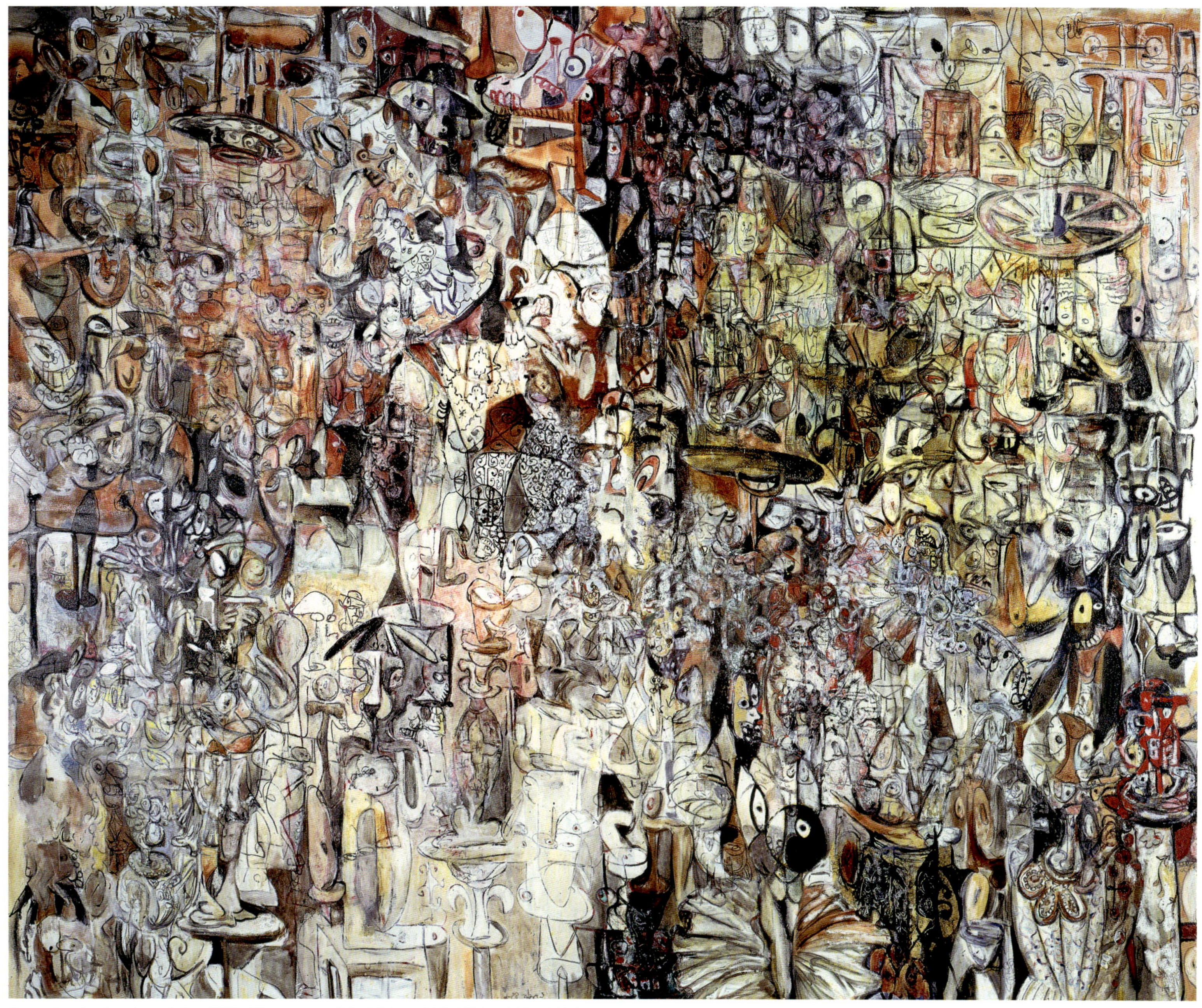

George Condo, *Dancing to Miles*, 1985. Oil on canvas, 9 ft. 2¼ in. × 11 ft. 5¾ in. (280 × 349.9 cm)
The Broad Art Foundation, Los Angeles

Haring's admiration for his friend's work had even led him to consider buying one of the paintings he saw at the studio. Once, after leaving an exhibition by a Figuration Libre artist, Haring wrote in his journal, "Basquiat and Condo are the only ones I think are really good."[26]

Haring introduced Condo to Brion Gysin, who lived in Paris. Gysin had invented a drawing practice akin to calligraphy, between poetry and image. On July 19, 1985, learning that he had been hospitalized, Haring and Condo stayed up all night and, fueled by a bottle of 1975 Mouton Rothschild, painted two "conjuratory" paintings meant to keep the poet alive.

Condo would later write the preface to *Brion Gysin, Calligraffiti of Fire*, the exhibition Gysin presented at the Galerie Samy Kinge in Paris in the spring of 1986.

Later, when the Whitney Museum invited Condo to suggest an author with whom to pair up for a new commissions program, Condo immediately replied, "William Burroughs." As Condo says, "I think William [Burroughs], when he did the cut-ups in his writing, when he started to rearrange the sentences in the paragraphs so he would write a paragraph and then just cut the words out and put them in different places, in a way, I kind of did that with art history."[27]

Burroughs invited Condo to come to Kansas. Their collaboration *Ghost of Chance* was published in 1991.[28] The subject was a previously unpublished Burroughs short story, retracing the origins of human evil in a tale of seventeenth-century piracy and twenty-first century devastation. The text was published by James Grauerholz, Burroughs' long-time assistant. Condo illustrated the work with three original etchings printed by Aldo Crommelynck, twelve offset lithographs of paintings, and calligraphic illuminations.

Between 1986 and 1996, Burroughs and Condo made a series of paintings that would be exhibited in 1997 at the Pat Hearn Gallery in New York. For an exhibition of Condo's works at the Pace Gallery in 1994, Burroughs wrote a preface that endows Condo's invented figures with actual existence, transforming them into "golems," creatures able to interact with their viewers: "To put it apple pie simple, artists are trying to create life, what else?"[29]

To shore up his animist conception of art, Burroughs invoked Stendhal syndrome, the capacity of artworks to take possession of their viewers. Burroughs even made this capacity a criterion of artistic judgment: "In the future it seems inevitable that artists will be judged on their Stendhal rating," he wrote.[30]

26. Keith Haring. *Keith Haring Journals.* April 30, 1987 entry. New York: Penguin Classics, 2010.
27. George Condo, interview by Olivier Zahm.
28. William Burroughs and George Condo. *Ghost of Chance.* New York: The Library Fellows of the Whitney Museum of American Art, 1991.
29. William Burroughs in *George Condo. Recent Paintings.* New York: PaceWildenstein, 1994.
30. William Burroughs. *George Condo. Recent Paintings.*

To complete his acquaintance with the Beats, Condo only had to look to Allen Ginsberg and Jack Kerouac.

A portrait of Ginsberg appears in a 1994 photo of Condo in his studio. The portrait would later grace the cover of a poetry collection Ginsberg published in 1996.[31]

Ten years later, writing the introduction to a book that collected Jack Kerouac's verbal sketches, Condo finally had occasion to pay tribute to the writer whose works had first sparked his interest in the Beats. This encounter with Kerouac was a singular example of "objective chance," as André Breton would call it. In his youth, Condo had gone to college in Lowell, Kerouac's hometown. As he recounts in his preface, "I learned a lot from Jack, and I can say all this not being a writer. At the age of fourteen he was the first radical I ever heard of. When I first became aware that he wrote his novel *The Subterraneans* in one long stretch, unrevised straight out of his head in three days, and he had a 'steel trap' memory—it was the combination of these two very important factors that inspired a new way of painting for me. From then on I combined memory, speed, and spontaneity to create most of my work."[32]

In 2000, John McNaughton's film on the painter's work, *Condo Painting*, offered another occasion to summon up the Beats. Both Ginsberg and Burroughs appear in the film. They offer their poetic accord to a body of work inspired by the exploration of the unconscious under the influence of psychedelics, as described by Aldous Huxley.

Condo made Burroughs' and Ginsberg's cosmos-dreams his own. From Burroughs, Condo retained a passion for science fiction; from Ginsberg, a sense of "interconnection with the universe" that would soon lead him to summon up his "antipodal beings." One day, Ginsberg had thought he heard the voice of God, which he later interpreted as the voice of William Blake, or "the voice of the ancient of days."

In Condo's eyes, the Beat poets "psychedelicized" surrealism, remaking for their own times the (now "chemical") exploration of the unconscious.

As objective chance would have it, Condo's downstairs neighbor in his Parisian apartment was the psychoanalyst Félix Guattari. In 1990, Guattari wrote an essay on the works of the painter whose comings-and-goings wove the rhythm of his nights. For Guattari, Condo's imagery intertwines the expression of various phases of the development of the self. The paintings give form to a complex of drives and feelings characteristic of a personality during infant development. Writing his essay as an open letter to Condo,

31. Allen Ginsberg. *Selected Poems 1947-1995*. New York: HarperCollins, 1996.
32. George Condo. "Introduction: Thoughts about Jack Kerouac," in Jack Kerouac, *Book of Sketches*. London: Penguin Books, 2006: IX.

Guattari defined him as a surrealist in the strict sense: "Yours is not a 'paranoiac knowledge' such as Dalí and the other Surrealists describe, because with them, interpretation is always under control, always centered around a cognitive sphere. With you, on the other hand, the dive into a paranoid universe is authentic and takes on perceptive, emotional and fantastic dimensions."[33]

Translated into aesthetic terms, Guattari's analysis links Condo's art to a primal surrealism. Detaching the "genetic space" of these paintings from any form of cognition, Guattari describes Condo's art as the product of "spontaneous generation," an emanation from a poetic "athanor," or the alchemist's furnace whose myth was familiar to the surrealist painters and poets from the works of André Breton. One version of the athanor myth was the model of the "Mothers"—primordial crucibles from which all life forms emanate— that Breton took from the pages of Goethe's *Faust II*, and that he made use of to account for the paintings of Yves Tanguy. Victor Brauner would later reinterpret the myth in his series "Mythologie et Fêtes des Mères" (1965).

The "genetic space" of the athanor is found in other writings as well. Borges once dreamed of it as the Aleph. Plato, in the *Timaeus*, described it as the *chôra* whose meaning is accessible only to the dreamer. Breton, in the *Second Manifesto of Surrealism*, wrote of the athanor as the most sacred point in the poetic surrealist quest: the point at which "life and death, the real and the imagined, past and future, the communicable and the incommunicable, high and low, cease to be perceived as contradictions."[34]

By associating the genetic space of Condo's images with the athanor, Guattari accounts for the transformations that shatter the coherence of these "amorphous" images, as he calls them. He explains the temporal aberrations that allow for the representation of successive, contradictory mind-states in Condo's characters—an unfurling in space and time that Condo will name "psychological cubism."

Picassomania

In Paris, Condo's principal genre became the portrait. Here again, the figure of Picasso was near at hand. Condo's surrealism ceased to be projective and became maieutic, an inward eliciting of ideas. As he explains: "Picasso painted a violin from four different perspectives at one moment. I do the same with psychological states. Four of them can occur simultaneously. Like glimpsing a bus with one passenger howling over a joke they're hearing down the phone, someone else asleep, someone else crying—I'll put them all in one face."[35]

33. Félix Guattari. "Introduction (Paris 1990)", 16.
34. André Breton. "The Second Manifesto of Surrealism (1930)," in *Manifestos of Surrealism*, trans. Richard Seaver and Helen R. Lane. Ann Arbor: University of Michigan, 1969: 123.
35. George Condo. "George Condo: I was delirious. Nearly died." Interview by Stuart Jeffries, *The Guardian*, February 10, 2014.

By naming this operation "psychological cubism," Condo defined the method that would soon constitute the irreducible originality of his art, a singularity that Guattari described as an exploration of "the precariousness of the signified form in relation to the strong unconscious forces that seethe within it."[36]

Methodically dissecting Picasso's art, Condo finally objectified the influence it had exerted upon his formative years. Looking back at this in 1987, Condo said he spent two years understanding Picasso's work "from within." Leaving no period of the master's work unstudied, Condo revisited the *Las Meninas* series, grappled with the *The Musketeers*. During a visit to the Museum of Fine Arts in Boston, he had been struck by Picasso's reinterpretation of Jacques-Louis David's *The Intervention of the Sabine Women*. And with good reason. Everything about the *Sabines* prefigures Condo's oeuvre: the energy and confidence of the rendering, the apparent lack of deference towards the source, the imaginative caricatures, the eroticism. Condo's *Spanish Head Composition* (1988) carried admiration into identification. After a span of ten years, the work assembles on a single canvas the pages of a notebook in which Condo interpreted approximately forty head studies after Picasso.

Spanish Head Composition was followed by a series of nude studies, again inspired by Picasso's own. Condo analyzes their principles of construction, reinterprets their organic curves and their geometric synthesis.

In a small painting titled *Études* (1920), Picasso, prefiguring the stylistic eclecticism of postmodernism, blithely skipped from one style to the next. He set his cubist forms from the late 1910s side by side with his neoclassical figures from the same period. In 1989–90, Condo explicitly placed his own plurality of forms under the sign of Picasso. *Crazy Cat Combination* juxtaposes "photographically" rendered portraits with a head inspired by Picasso's works from the early 1930s. From one portrait to the next, we witness the sudden transformations of characters turned into burlesque creatures through lessons learned from Picasso. At the center of this "killing game" appears a character straight out of a comic strip.

By bringing together images born of vastly different styles and subjects, *Crazy Cat Combination* calls into question the stylistic coherence and identity that artists are expected to uphold. The *Crazy Cat Combination* polyptych becomes the image of a creative process that demonstrates its own versatility, privileging the flux of inspiration over the fetishism of icons. Here again, Condo was following in Picasso's footsteps.

36. Félix Guattari. "Introduction (Paris 1990)", 18.

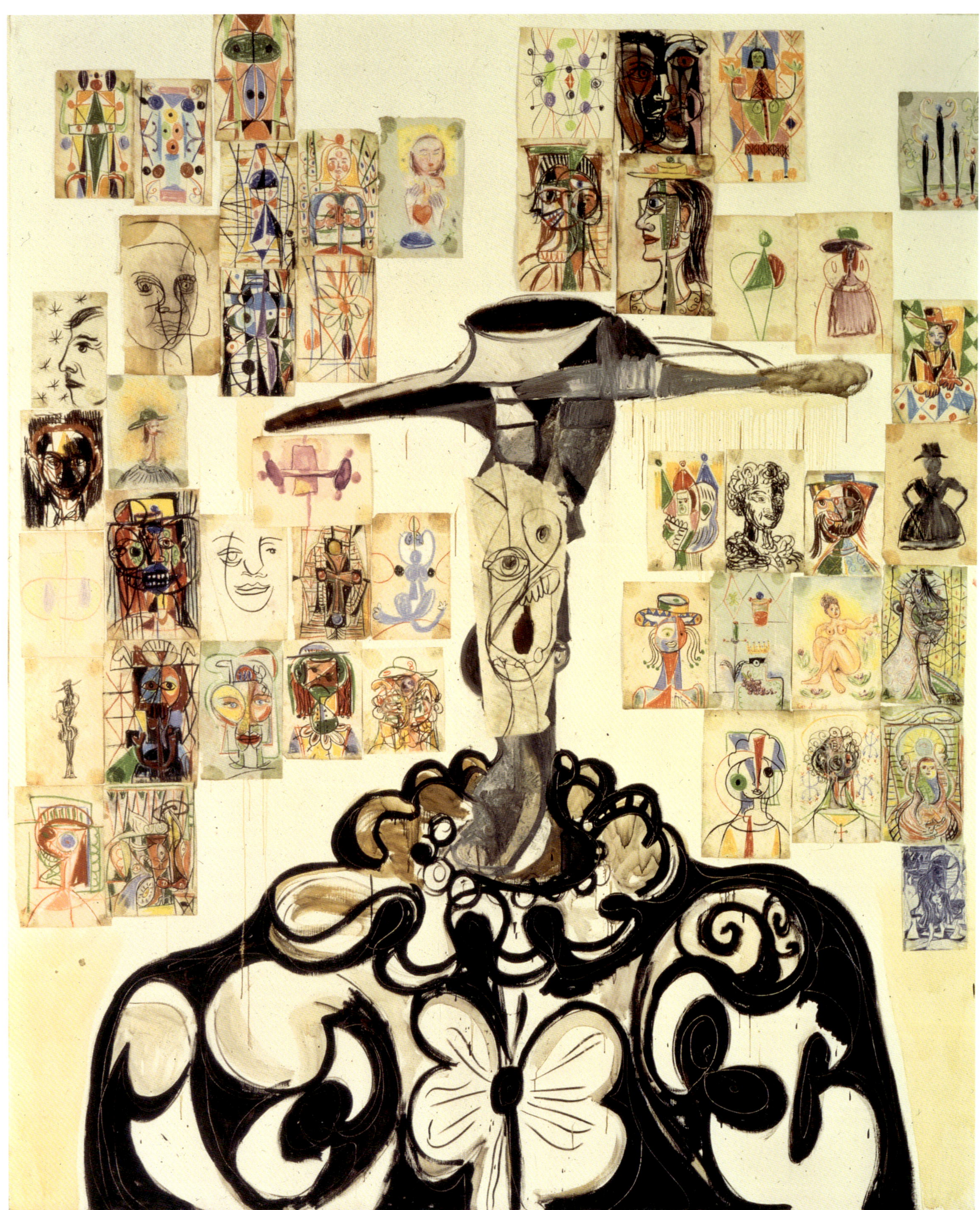

George Condo, *Spanish Head Composition*, 1988. Oil and collage on paper mounted on canvas, 9 ft. 10 in. × 8 ft. 2 in. (299.7 × 248.9 cm). The Museum of Modern Art, New York

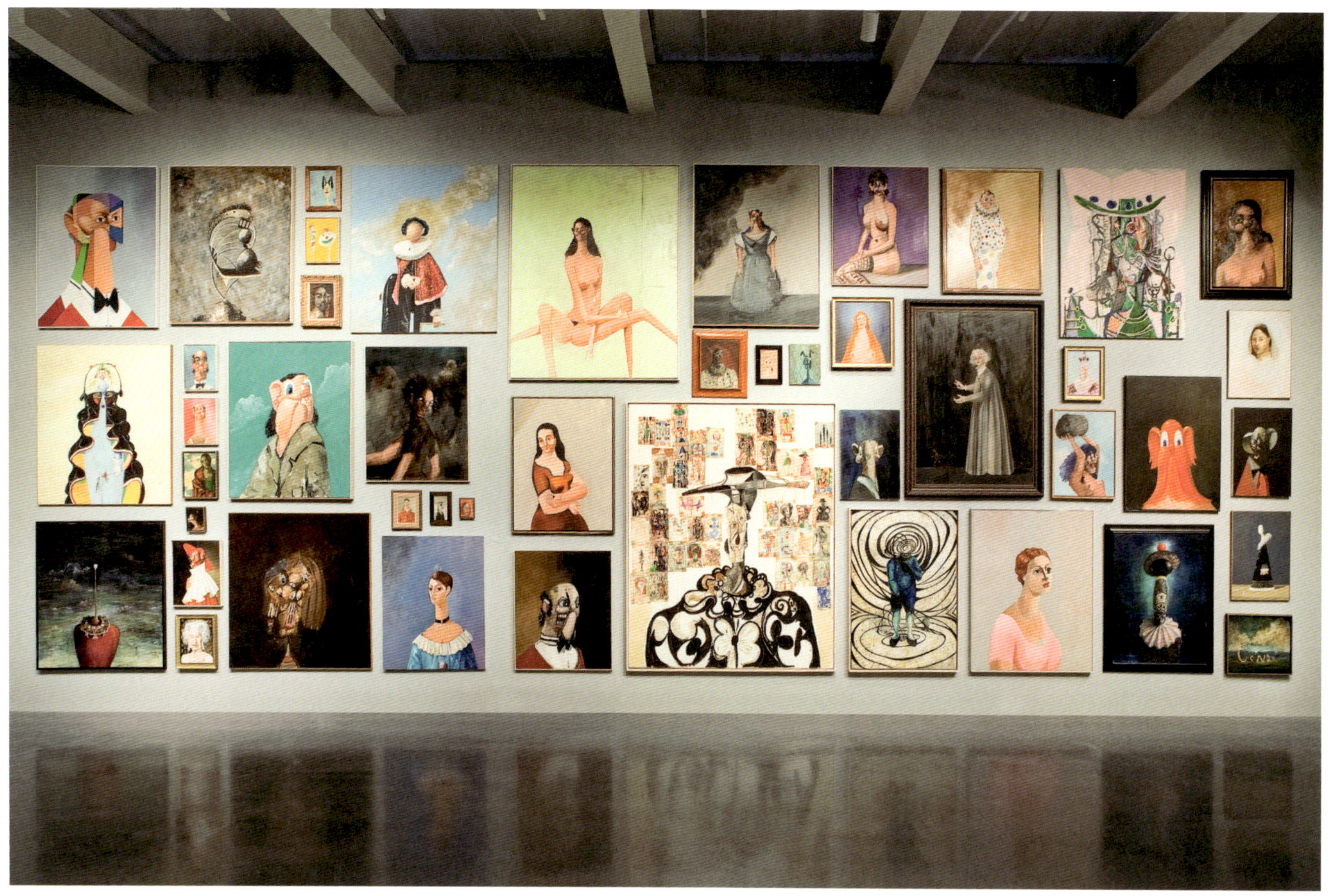

In 1970 and 1973, for his late-paintings exhibitions at the Palais des Papes in Avignon, Picasso had devised a wall-to-wall hanging that placed his works side by side from ground to ceiling. This arrangement allowed a reading comparable to the one Henri-Georges Clouzot presented in his 1956 film *The Mystery of Picasso*. One of Picasso's constant preoccupations was the metamorphosis, the movement that links one form to the next. This is reflected in Picasso's precise dating of his works that meticulously reconstitutes their genealogy. Condo possesses a similar obsession. In 1985, for his exhibition at the Galerie Bruno Bischofberger in Zurich, he decided to cover the entire walls of the gallery without leaving aside a single recent painting: "I said to Bruno, 'I don't feel comfortable editing the work. I would rather show every single thing I've done, … even if it's bad for the art business.' So we showed roughly 345 paintings and about 400-500 drawings: the walls were just plastered, floor-to-ceiling."[37]

37. George Condo quoted by Simon Baker,
George Condo. Painting Reconfigured. 2015.
London: Thames & Hudson, 2022: 45.

Condo reprised this type of hanging for his exhibition *Mental States* at the New Museum in New York in January 2011. There, he set up a wall on which he juxtaposed his paintings from every period, mashing-up all varieties of subjects. Five years later, for the *Picasso.mania* exhibition at the Grand Palais in Paris, he again set up a large wall, this time summarizing the various moments of his dialogue with Picasso in a single vast composition.

Crazy Cat Combination laid down the principles of the work to come—highbrow meets lowbrow, the purest beauty rubs elbows with lewd, degrading farce. This artistic program, which Condo placed under the sign of Picasso, confirms the Spanish painter as Condo's principal model. For Condo, Picasso gave license to shuffle between past and present, and validated a carnivalesque reading of the universal museum (just as Picasso himself had seized upon Delacroix, Manet, Velázquez, and so many others). As Apollinaire wrote of Picasso in 1905, "Everything delights him, and his undeniable talent seems to be at the service of an imagination that specifically combines the exquisite and the horrible, the abject and the delicate."[38]

Raphaël or Bust

Though Condo's late-1980s work demonstrates his mastery of a vast formal vocabulary, his pictoral technique was still marked by relics of Bad Painting (those "errors" he would try to make "correct," as he describes it). To eliminate all trace of crudeness, he decided to invite into his studio a Raphael copyist he met in the halls of the Louvre. This copyist taught Condo all his secrets, the knack of his technique. The experience gave Condo's works a newfound precision, monumentality, and depth of form. Backed by this knowledge, Condo now peopled his paintings with figures inspired by the Old Masters.

Condo's paintings became a theatre filled with figures from the *comédie humaine.* "Characters, all created carefully," he says. His actors composed a motley, comical troupe. "It's quite a crew: Indian chiefs, cavemen, office bosses, the nun, two-bit hustlers, low-life criminals, people with one tooth, one eye, protruding chins, enlarged facial features."[39]

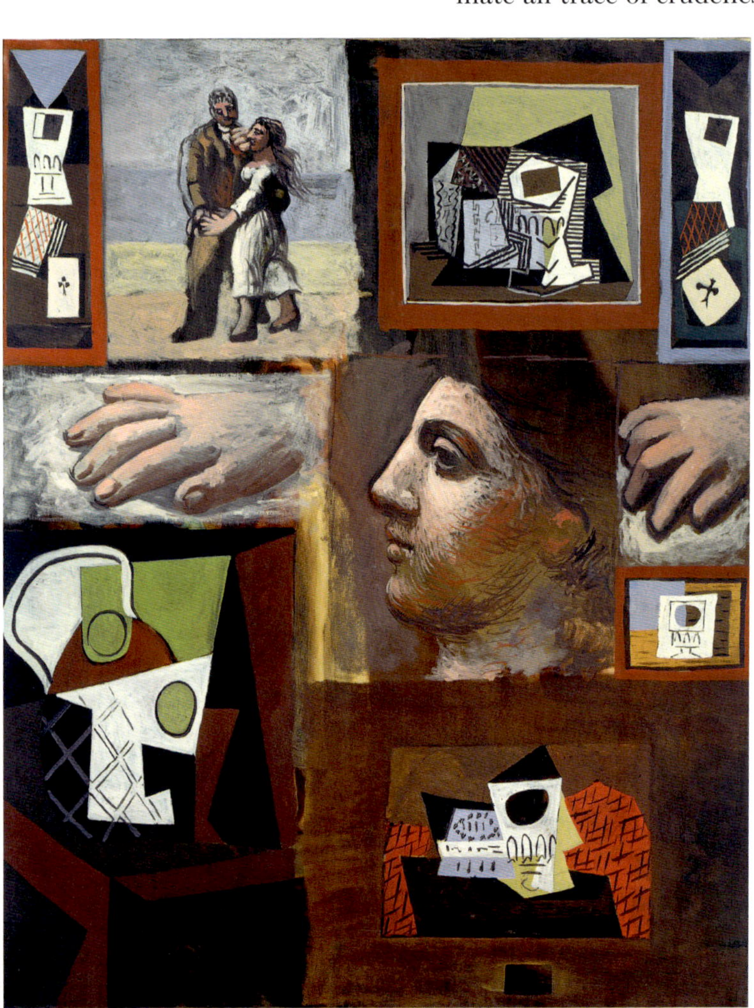

Pablo Picasso, *Études*, 1920. Oil on canvas, 3 ft. 3¼ in. × 2 ft. 8 in. (100 × 81 cm). Musée Picasso, Paris

38. Guillaume Apollinaire. "Picasso, Peintre et dessinateur," *La Revue Immoraliste*, April 1905: 39.

39. George Condo. "George Condo by Anney Bonney." Interview by Anney Bonney. *BOMB*, No. 40, July 1, 1992.

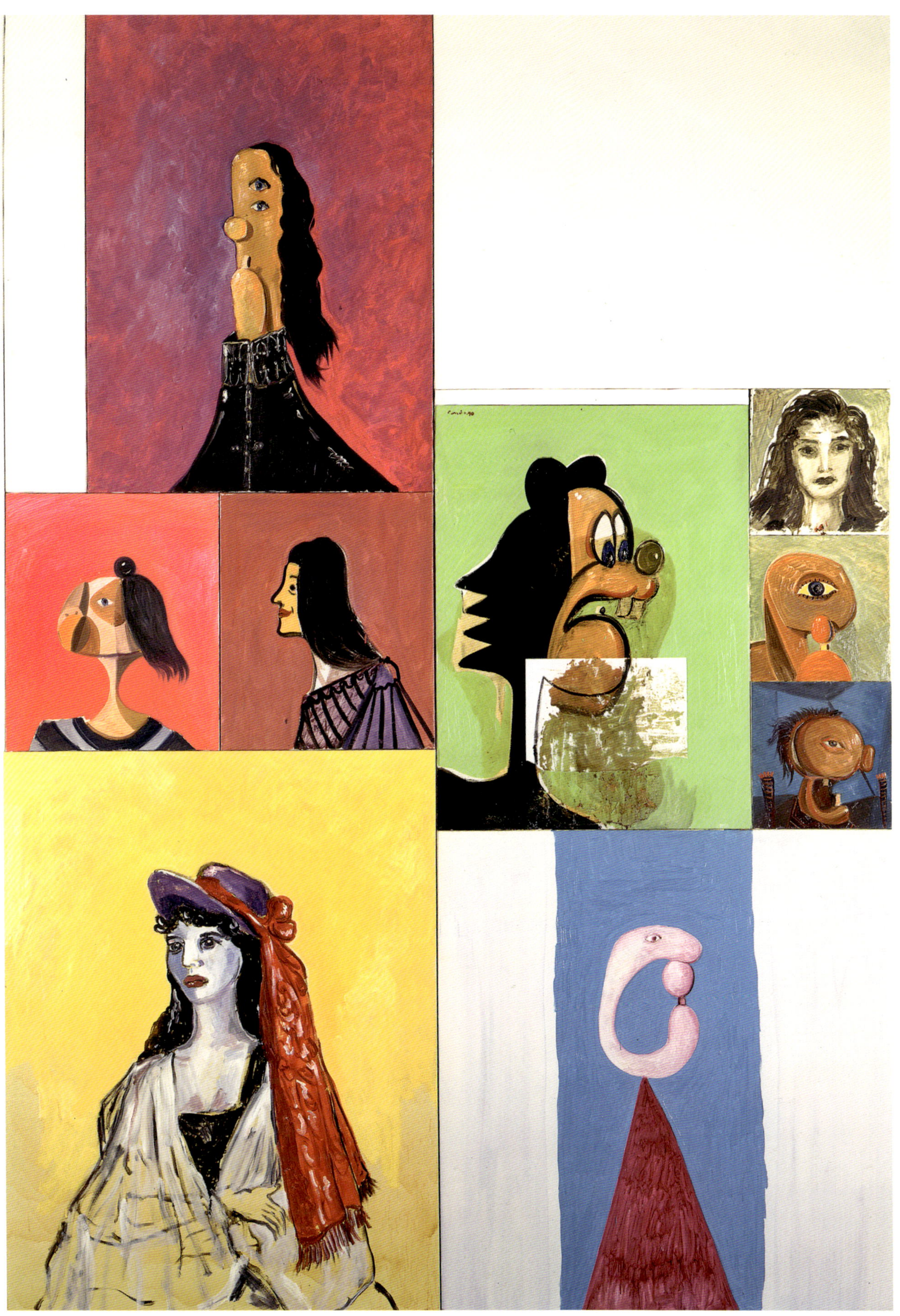

George Condo, *Crazy Cat Combination*, 1989–90. Oil, paper, and charcoal on canvas, 11 ft. 3 in. × 8 ft. 3¼ in. (342.9 × 252.1 cm)

With the Big Bosses and Indian Chiefs waiting in the wings, the "Imaginary Portraits" were the first to step on stage. In this first series, the figure's ruffs and brocade gowns link them to classical painting; sometimes they have a featureless balloon instead of a head.

Distant cousins of Malevich's figures from the 1930s, the Imaginary Portraits embody an impossible presence. Malevich's figures expressed the tension that he was living under at the time, attempting to reconcile his (formalist, abstract) supremadist ideal with the decrees of an ideology that forced him towards realism. Emerging from imprisonment at the hands of the Soviet political police, Malevich needed to invent a way of painting that could be understood by the masses. The solution he found was to skip over the history of modern art and reconnect with the Renaissance. In 1933, Malevich formalized this anachronism with a portrait of himself as a fourteenth-century painter.… The only other modern painter to have risked such a transformation is Giorgio de Chirico. The latter, asserting the irony of his position and the ridiculousness of his anachronism, painted himself as a nobleman and as a Roman emperor.

If the anonymity of the faces that Malevich gave to his figures expresses the dehumanization of life in Stalinist Russia, it also expresses the impossibility of cutting the contemporary world off from the heritage of the old order, even aesthetically. In a similar vein, Condo, to avoid plagiarism and ward off ridicule, gave his figures carnival balloons for heads.

When he emerged from the Louvre (after having "digested" Raphael) Condo faced the same dilemma as Malevich and de Chirico: How does one create a modern painting while remaining connected to the lessons of the Old Masters?

By the mid-1990s, Condo had found the method of his art, its technical means of expression. Having filled his mind with the museums of Europe, he no longer needed to stay in France. The past, the Old Masters, weren't useful to him anymore.

Back in the United States, he went to his hometown, Chelmsford, Massachusetts: "It's the oldest town in America, consecrated in 1656. I really wanted to abandon my admiration for European aesthetics and European things. I realized that, ironically,

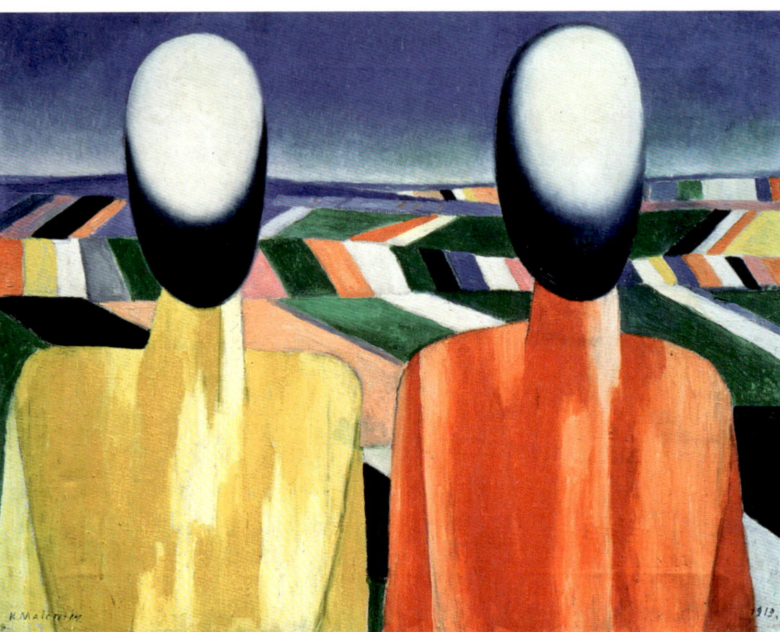

Kazimir Malevich, *Peasants*, c. 1930. Oil on canvas, 20¾ × 27½ in. (53 × 70 cm). State Russian Museum, Saint Petersburg

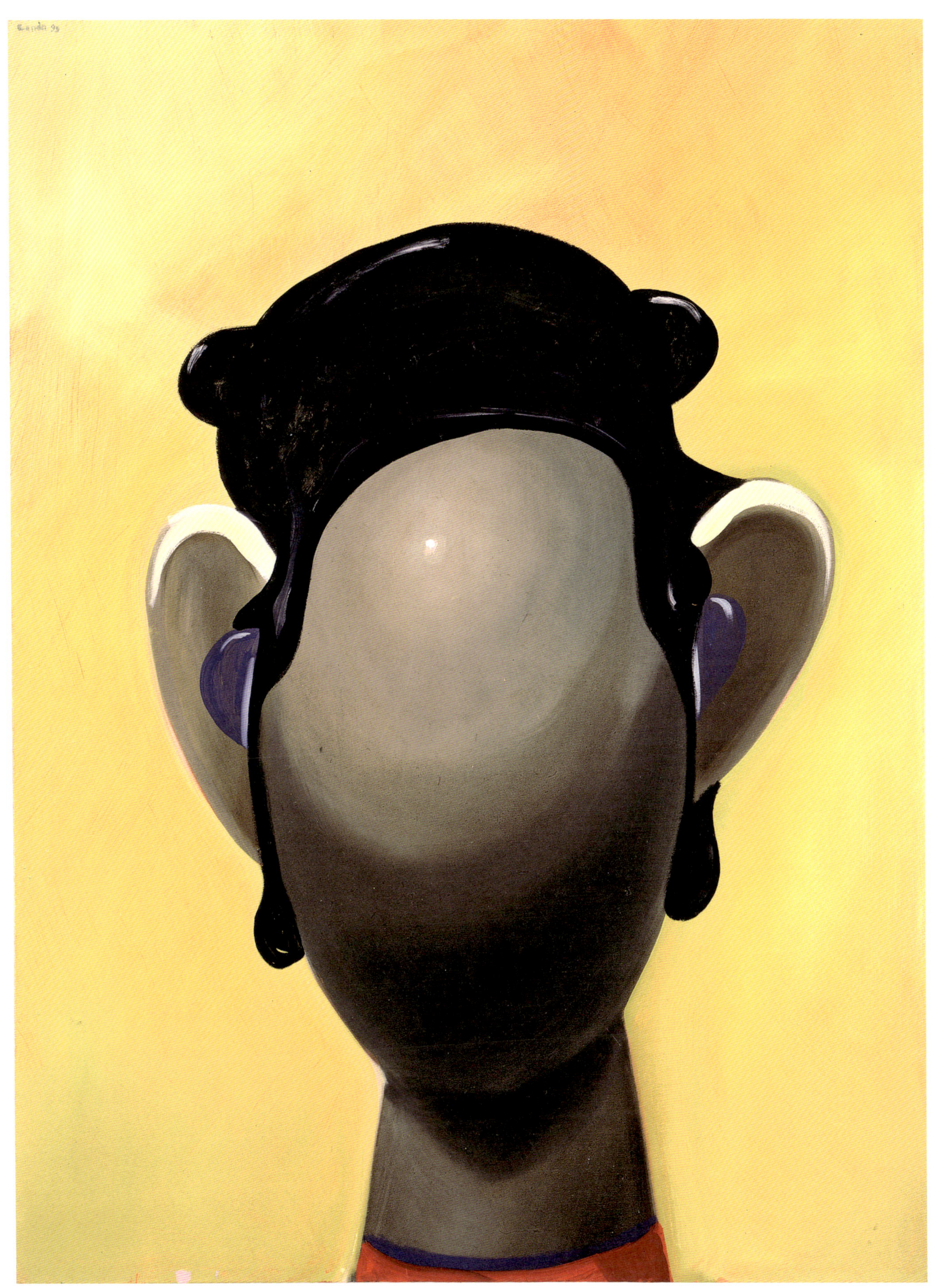

George Condo, *The Unknown*, 1995. Oil on linen, 3 ft. 4 in. × 2 ft. 6 in. (101.6 × 76.2 cm)
Work put on display during the "Humanoids" exhibition

Chelmsford was older than some sections of Paris. I was tired of the pretension some Europeans have about being older and wiser, when, in fact, a lot of them came later, if they came at all. So I was entwined in this happiness of being home, in the States, in Chelmsford, and I had just found this beautiful color of paint down at the hardware store. I was happy not to go to the Lefebvre-Foinet where they ground pigment in special recipes for Bonnard, Léger and Vlaminck. I went to a real American paint store and I picked up this charcoal gray latex. I came home, put down the canvas, got out some scotch tape and put it on."[40]

Customs and Clamors

Back in the USA

In 1995, Condo was back in New York and looking to forget Raphael and the Louvre. He reconnected with surrealism, as adapted by the Beat poets. Ginsberg's and Burroughs' imaginations, fed with a mixture of speculative fiction and hallucinogenic substances, gave a futuristic, psychedelic twist to the old myths put forth by André Breton. Like the Beats before him, Condo plunged into reading Aldous Huxley, the author who united the futuristic literary imagination of science fiction—in *Brave New World*, for instance—and the exploration of the depths of the unconscious in *The Doors of Perception*.

In keeping with the dialectic between seriousness and farce, reality and fiction, that underlies Condo's work, the first of the "Pods"—those creatures from the "other world"—came from an Old Master's brush.

One painting returned obsessively to Condo's mind: *The Descent from the Cross* by Rogier van der Weyden that he had seen at the Kunsthistorisches Museum in Vienna. "Jesus was lowered into the tomb—into a landscape that exists underground, a mental landscape that we all fear," says Condo. "I realized this was the landscape I was summoned there to paint".[41]

To give shape to his memory, Condo summoned the first of his figures from the "other world": "Without warning I looked up and upon my canvas, the first inhabitant of this mental landscape stood staring at me. 'Red Antipodular Agent'—born from the wings of Van der Weyden's angels. Smiling with insipid eyes that looked like some kind of painted Easter eggs—The First Antipodal Being, a being that was ushered in from the periphery of my consciousness and brought forward to be painted."[42]

40. George Condo. "George Condo by Anney Bonney."

41. George Condo. "Physiognomical Abstraction," *George Condo— Physiognomical Abstraction*. Paris: Galerie Jérôme de Noirmont, 2001: 7.

42. George Condo. "Physiognomical Abstraction."

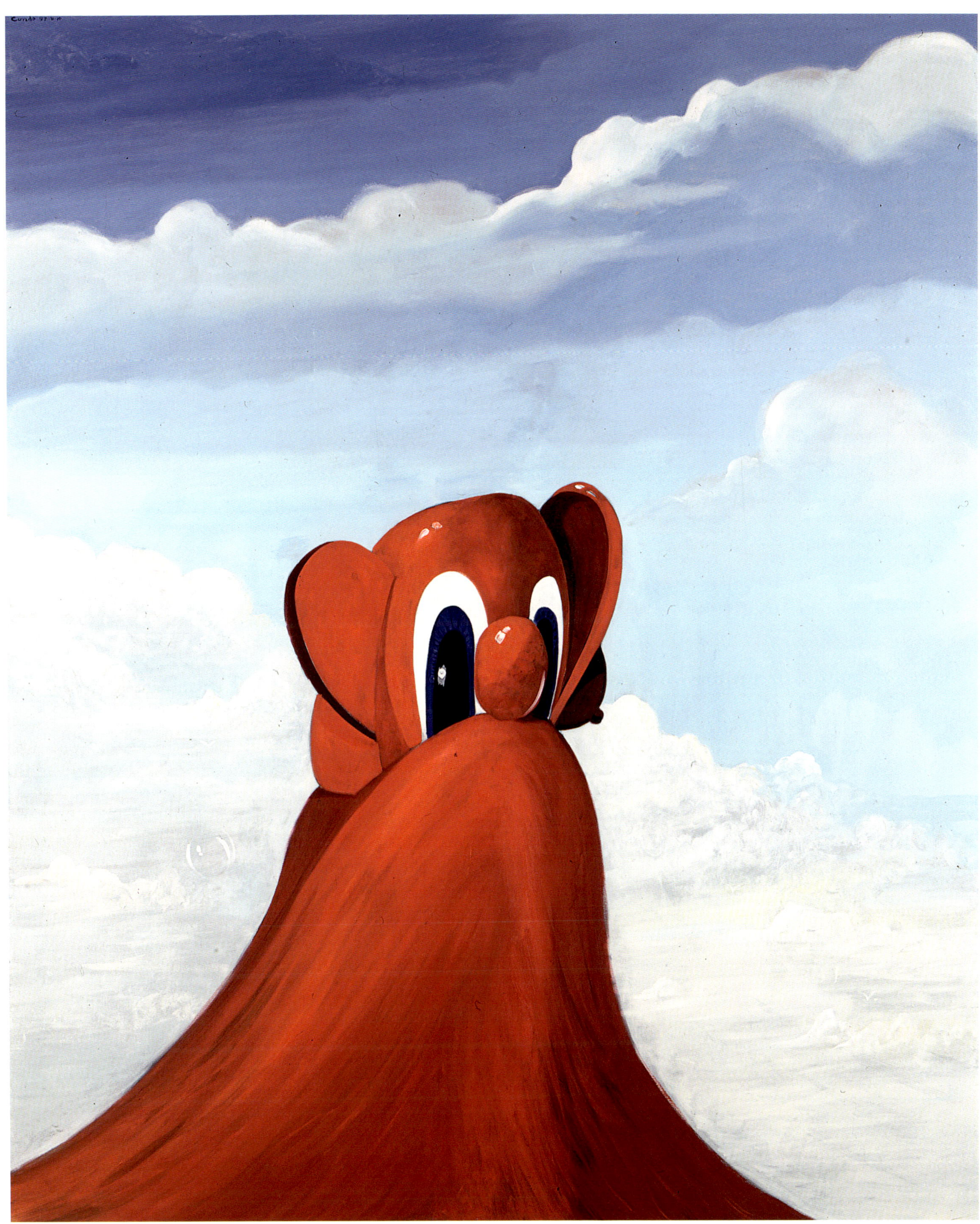

George Condo, *Big Red*, 1997. Oil on canvas, 8 ft. 4 in. × 6 ft. 11½ in. (254 × 212.1 cm)

The existence of these "antipodal creatures" had been first inspired by Condo's reading of Aldous Huxley's *Heaven and Hell*. In that work, Huxley analyzes the various methods—namely, hypnosis and various chemical compounds—by which to open the gates to the "mind's antipodes." These are the gates to the "Far West of the collective unconscious, with its flora of symbols, its tribes of aboriginal archetypes; and, across another, vaster ocean, at the antipodes of everyday consciousness, the world of Visionary Experience."[43] The antipodal world, as described by Huxley, is inhabited by creatures whose absurdity and grotesqueness shatter all forms of rationality: "Like the giraffe and the duck-billed platypus, the creatures inhabiting these remoter regions of the mind are exceedingly improbable."[44] Their lantern jaws are derived from Goya's *Old Women* that Condo remembers seeing at the Palais des Beaux-Arts in Lille.

Rechristened Pods in 1995, these antipodal creatures soon transformed into comic book characters.

During the 1940s, the artists of the New York School had broken free of surrealism by inventing their own mythology. Jackson Pollock took André Masson and Max Ernst's Greco-Roman Ariadne and replaced her with his *Moon Woman* of the Plains tribes. Similarly, the Pods are American counterparts of forms imported from Europe. In the late 1930s, André Breton invented the "Myth of the Great Invisibles," cosmic messengers or travelers from beyond the grave, inspired by Charles Fourier's *ultra-mondains*.[45] The Great Invisibles held prominent place at the 1947 Galerie Maeght exhibition that marked the return of European surrealism after World War II. With the Pods, Condo took the Great Invisibles and brought them into the age of comic books and heroic fantasy.

The Pods and the Great Invisibles both come from "parallel worlds." They emerge from the same depths of the psyche, surrounded with the aureole of the same mythic dreams. But Sigmund Freud and Gradiva have given way to Bugs Bunny and LSD…. Several years after the Pods' first appearance, a monograph by Michael Kwakkelstein[46] led Condo to propose a genealogy that traces their origins back to Leonardo da Vinci's physiognomic studies. As Condo writes: "In December 2000 I came across a book written by Michael Kwakkelstein, called 'Leonardo da Vinci as a Physiognomist' which led me to a brief study of the science of physiognomy as it was known during

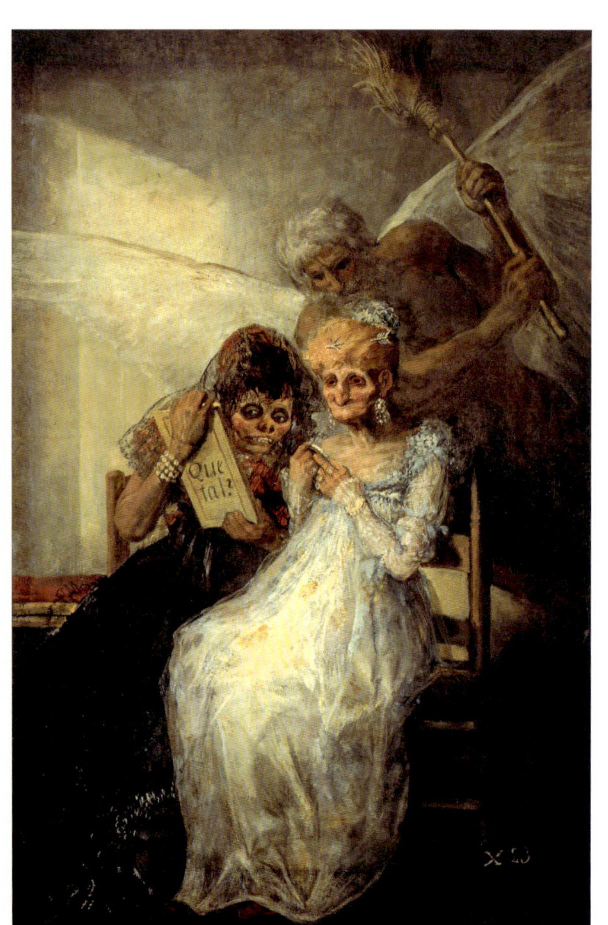

Francisco Goya, *Old Women/Time*, c. 1808–12. Oil on canvas, 5 ft. 11¼ in. × 4 ft. 1¼ in. (181 × 125 cm). Palais des Beaux-Arts, Lille, France

43. Aldous Huxley. *Heaven and Hell* (1956) in *The Doors of Perception and Heaven and Hell*. London: Chatto & Windus, 1960: 74.

44. Aldous Huxley. *The Doors of Perception and Heaven and Hell*: 73.

45. "It appears that Messrs. C— and P— have abandoned their work on magnetism. I would venture that they failed to assert the fundamental principle: that if all things in the universe are connected, a means of communication must exist between the creatures of the other world and those of our own. I do not mean by this a direct communication, but rather a communication of faculties, a temporary and accidental participation in the faculties of the *ultra-mondains* or the dead. This participation cannot occur in a waking state, but only in an intermediate state, like sleep. Have the magnetists discovered this state? Not that I am aware of—but, in principle, I know it must exist." Charles Fourier quoted in Charles Pellarin, *Charles Fourier. Sa vie et sa théorie* [1843]. Paris: Hachette Livre/BnF, 2012.

46. Michael Kwakkelstein. *Leonardo da Vinci as a Physiognomist. Theory and Drawing Practice*. Leiden: Primavera, 1994.

the time of the Renaissance in Italy. It shed some interesting light on the potential of explaining the 'Antipodal Beings' as physiognomical variants on the study of human expression. The inner mental state expressed by outward appearance.... This led me to the concept of 'Physiognomical Abstraction,' where the mental state or physical representation of the inner consciousness (that of the antipodal beings) and the appearance of the being, which is in effect a collage of memory and experience, can be expressed as the material form that 'gives out' consciousness, in order to 'send back' consciousness into its non-material appearance, and represent the material consciousness of an imaginary being."[47]

It is vital to Condo that his Pods do not repudiate the Old Masters. This is a prerequisite of his artistic "schizophrenia," constantly oscillating his art between the bazaar and the museum. In the film *Condo Painting*, we see one of Condo's favorite works: an art history textbook where he has replaced the heads of figures from classical paintings with the comic heroes of the television shows he watched as a child.

The figure of his great-great-uncle Salvatore Albano, a late-nineteenth century Calabrian neoclassical sculptor, is never far from Condo's memory.

Postmodern Tribe

In December 1998, for an exhibition at the Sandra Gering Gallery in New York, Condo temporarily left painting aside and returned to the silkscreen printing he once practiced in Warhol's studios. The series of works that Condo now exhibited stand as his personal tribute to postmodernism. They testify to a new plunge into the 1950s and 1960s pop culture that shaped his imagination. His technique was collage, or nearly cinematic montage.

Postmodernism, before it extended to the domain of the visual arts, flourished in the field of architectural theory, particularly within La Tendenza, the Italian movement that arose in the late 1960s, led by Aldo Rossi. In 1976, a collective artwork, *La Città analoga*, presented at the Venice Biennale by Aldo Rossi, Eraldo Consolascio, Bruno Reichlin, and Fabio Reinhart, crystalized the movement's theoretical position. *La Città analoga* is a vast collage. It pays homage to the "analogical Venice" imagined by Canaletto in the eighteenth century, as he made a cityscape out of historical Italian buildings and

47. George Condo. "Physiognomical Abstraction."

Jacques Hérold, *Le Grand Transparent*, 1947/1964. Plaster, mirror, quartz crystals, and dried thistle, 6 ft. × 3 ft. ¼ in. × 1 ft. 8¾ in. (183 × 92 × 53 cm). Musée National d'Art Moderne, Paris

imaginary edifices in his painting *Capriccio with Palladian Buildings*. Rossi's *La Città analoga* broadens the historical range of Canaletto's city, combining buildings from the Italian renaissance (Palladian palaces) and modern architecture (Le Corbusier's Ronchamp chapel) with contemporary pieces (fragments of Rossi's own projects), all inserted into Vitruvius' vision of the ideal city.

La Città analoga, through its accumulation of references, its mashed-up temporalities, and its collage aesthetic, became the first postmodern manifesto. The work's formal and theoretical principles—its dismantling of a directed chronology, or the "teleology" characteristic of modernism—would later be implemented by the postmodern artists of the early 1980s who established the ostensible norms of pictorial postmodernism.

In 1994, Janet Malcolm would write of the new aesthetics that had "made a kind of mockery of art history, treating the canon of world art as if it were a gigantic, dog-eared catalogue crammed with tempting buys and equipped with a helpful twenty-four-hour-a-day 800 number."[48]

For Condo, Warhol had shown the way once again. Condo's eclectic iconography—riding roughshod over chronologies and hierarchies, gorging on references—took him back to the Factory days. The composite images of the Televised Silkscreens series arose from an art of quotation and reference that the theorist Charles Jencks described in 1977 as postmodernism's "most potent metaphorical level of meaning."[49] Ten years later, the French philosopher Jean-François Lyotard would likewise consider "the high frequency of quotations of elements from previous styles or periods" a defining characteristic of postmodernism.[50]

Condo associates the origin of Televised Silkscreens with the film *Condo Painting*. He began to wonder, back then, about the comparative efficacy of television images and images from the history of painting. If the television icons of his childhood (Granny, Andy Griffith, Ed Sullivan) faced off against his artistic heroes (Frans Hals, Rembrandt, Van Gogh), who would win?

The Televised Silkscreens are not only an homage to Warhol but also a meditation on the historical moment of

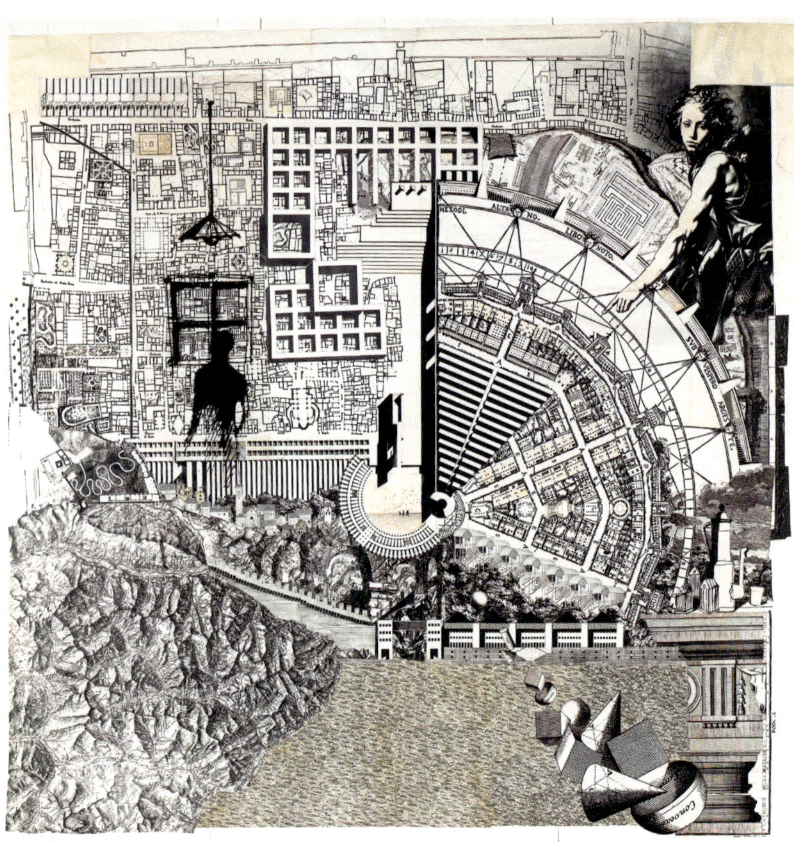

Aldo Rossi, Eraldo Consolascio, Bruno Reichlin, and Fabio Reinhart, *La Città analoga*, 1976.
Collage, felt, India ink, gouache, and synthetic film on paper, 7 ft. 6½ in. × 7 ft. 10½ in. (230 × 240 cm).
Musée National d'Art Moderne, Paris

48. Janet Malcolm. "Forty-One False Starts." *The New Yorker*, July 11, 1994.
49. Charles Jencks. *The Language of Post-Modern Architecture*. New York: Rizzoli, 1977: 50.
50. Jean-François Lyotard, "Defining the Postmodern" (1986), in Lisa Appignanesi (ed.), *Postmodernism*, London: ICA Documents, 1989.

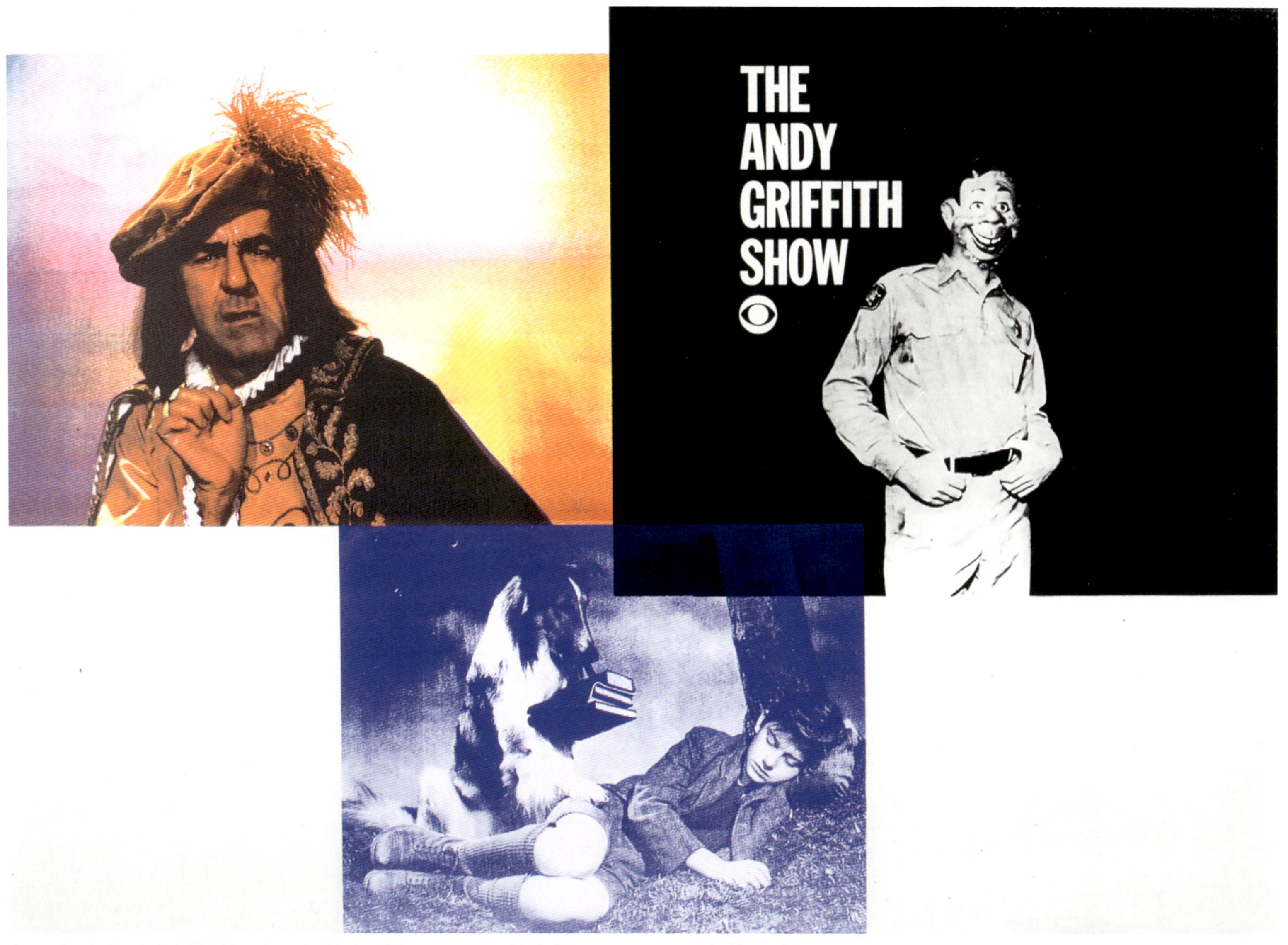

George Condo, *The Andy Griffith Show*, from the *Televised Silkscreens* series, 1998. Silkscreen on canvas, 5 ft. 10 in. × 8 ft. 2 in. (177.8 × 248.9 cm)

entertainment and mass-culture that shaped Condo's imagination. *Get Dumb* (1998) assembles, in a single image, the characters from the television shows of his youth. From *The Beverly Hillbillies* to *Gilligan's Island,* from *Get Smart* to *Green Acres,* the work composes a portrait gallery of pathetic heroes, of characters whose geographic or social displacement (often inversely mimicking the promise of the American dream) explodes social mores and lays bare the conventions and hypocrisies of American society. The characters in *Green Acres* have given up their elegant, high-society city life to go back to land as farmers; *Get Smart* follows a loser who becomes a secret agent; *Gilligan's Island* tells the story of a group of looney castaways on a desert island; *The Beverly Hillbillies* (a show that never made it across the Atlantic) follows a Texas family's move to upscale Beverly Hills, after they strike oil in their farm's backyard.

In Condo's paintings, the memory of these television characters provoked the apparition of Rodrigo, an unrepentant blunderer, a maverick whose downward mobility explodes the social order.

Enter Rodrigo

"Could I be the court painter for an Alien King?"[51]

After the Pods, new characters, owing nothing to imaginary worlds this time, entered Condo's painting. One of them is Rodrigo. He is the embodiment of moral depravity, the champion of simple-minded mediocrity. His peasant common sense makes him a distant cousin of Sancho Panza: a man whose mere presence exposes the ridiculousness of aristocratic posturing, the empty charades of class and social status. For Condo, this sad clown could only be a down-and-out musician. "A kind of low life," says Condo. "The piano player at a wedding, doing the worst song you've ever heard."[52] Condo's obsessive attachment to this character strongly suggests he might be the painter's alter ego.

As his maker's avatar, Rodrigo stands in judgment upon the world and delivers a verdict that the painter himself cannot express directly—bound as he is by social obligations, caught between the aristocratic muses of old Europe and supermarket swindlers: the admirer of Rembrandt, Velázquez, and Manet, collapsing onto a sofa each night in front of a television that pours forth a flood of idiotic images. Rodrigo is the incarnation of the junkfood crammed artist that Philip Guston gave us in his late self-portraits, the

51. George Condo quoted by Simon Baker, *George Condo. Painting Reconfigured*: 69.
52. George Condo, interview by Calvin Tomkins, "Portraits of Imaginary People."

one who drowns his dreams of pure art in a haze of cigarettes and third-rate liquor. Rodrigo has the artistic soul of a less-than-minor poet, mangling the classical repertoire in the lobby of a seedy hotel. From behind this mask, Condo testifies against a culture that has passed straight from Rothko's mysticism to "commonism," as Warhol called it.

Rodrigo opened the way for a slew of social and political realities to enter Condo's paintings. In his wake, a troupe of characters emerged, sprung not from the abyss of the unconscious but from the spectacle of the world, the most banal reality. *The Secretary* (2002) is the symbolic victim of an office hierarchy transformed into a sadistic William Tell; *The Stockbroker* (2002), a "master of the universe" broken by the 2000–02 stock market crash; *The Executive* (2003), an employee condemned, by ambition or enthusiasm, to become a puppet of his company. And then there is *Yankee Doodle* (2003, see p. 67), the "fragmented composite … of a man who was sold a dream that could never be. He is the American—partially Captain Ahab, who was our first mega tragic hero—and he has been endowed with a blown glass golf club, a bottle, and the inventive spirit of Thomas Edison or Ben Franklin. One could also say that *Yankee Doodle* appears like a hunter 'hunting down' the American dream."[53]

Hogarth on Wall Street

In the first years of the new millennium, Condo became the moralist of a society whose degradation, pretension, and victimization condemned it to constant ridicule.

Condo's paintings of human misery and meanness from this period immediately evoke Goya. "The king looks like an innkeeper, and the queen looks like an usherette … or worse!" Renoir once declared at the Prado. In painting his contemporaries, Condo resolutely opted for the "worse." He stayed true to his method of transforming his figures' outer appearance to fit their inner psychology—a method formerly developed and systematized by the eighteenth-century sculptor Franz Xaver Messerschmidt. Formerly a prominent sculptor to the Austrian court, Messerschmidt broke with the neoclassicism of his time and became instead a sculptor of the soul. Messerchmidt gave this soul, or unconscious, the form of his "character heads."

Goya, Messerchmidt, and William Hogarth were all, in separate ways, "psychologists" who witnessed the uprooting of conventional values caused by the spread of Enlightenment ideas.[54] This dissemination of knowledge

53. George Condo quoted by Peter Fleissig in *George Condo, Memories of Manet and Velázquez.* Paris: Galerie Jérôme de Noirmont, 2004: XVIII.
54. An eighteenth-century English satirist, William Hogarth denounced the habits of British society and condemned political corruption.

toppled the thrones of monarchs, shook established hierarchies, and tarnished the prestige of authority figures.

As the chronicler of a society whose lust for money and power were incarnated by its Wall Street bankers, Condo too became a moralist. His weapon was easy to find: caricatures of the new masters of the universe. But that was only part of it, as Condo says: "What else is it about? You just made me realize that it's also about, believe it or not, the Actors Studio, Lee Strasberg (via Stanislavski) and his acting method of breaking down. Movies written during that time by people like Tennessee Williams were designed for the main characters to really break down, crack up, totally reveal their rudimentary anxiety, desire, fear, etc."[55]

Always keen for a chronological mash-up, Condo associates the Actors Studio method of "breaking down" with Leonard da Vinci's physiognomic studies, in keeping with the writings of Michael Kwakkelstein. As Condo says, "The grotesque figures that Da Vinci drew were from his imagination but required meticulous details based on observations of reality in order to be believable. That is really the key to these new paintings of mine."[56]

Spleen-Bustingly Modern

If the historical context of Condo's work connects it to postmodernism, there is one essential modern principle that it has always upheld: the power of laughter.

Charles Baudelaire formulated the first definition of the modern[57] a few years after writing his essay "On the Essence of Laughter."[58] By the time of the 1865 Paris Salon exhibition, laughter had caught up with the modern. This encounter took place in front of Edouard Manet's *Olympia*. As Georges Bataille once wrote: "Others before [Manet] had roused indignation; the relative unity of classical taste had been all but shattered by romanticism, while Delacroix, Courbet, and even Ingres, for all his classicism, had set the public laughing. But the laughter that lay in wait for *Olympia* was something unprecedented."[59] This "roaring laughter" caught the ear of the public at the 1865 Salon. Ernest Chesneau reported in *Le Constitutionnel*, "Manet provokes quasi-scandalous laughter, drawing crowds of Salon visitors before this comical creature he calls Olympia."[60]

Before the 1865 Salon confirmed the union of laughter and modern art, Baudelaire had already had intimations of their close relationship. This

55. George Condo. "George Condo by Anney Bonney."

56. George Condo. *George Condo. Existential Portraits. Sculpture, Drawings, Paintings 2005/2006*. Interview by Ralph Rugoff. Berlin: Holzwarth Publications; New York, Luhring Augustine, 2006: 12.

57. Charles Baudelaire. "The Painter of Modern Life" (1863). *The Painter of Modern Life and Other Essays*, trans. Jonathan Mayne. London: Phaidon, 1964.

58. Charles Baudelaire. "On the Essence of Laughter" (1855), *The Painter of Modern Life and Other Essays*, trans. Jonathan Mayne. London: Phaidon, 1964.

59. Georges Bataille. *Manet*, trans. Austryn Wainhouse and James Emmons. Geneva: Skira, 1955: 17.

60. Ernest Chesneau. "Salon de 1865," *Le Constitutionnel*, May 16, 1865.

discovery was prompted by a new character he happened upon at a foreign pantomime: "The English Pierrot swept upon us like a hurricane, fell like a sack of coals, and when he laughed, his laughter made the auditorium quake; his laugh was like a joyful clap of thunder."[61] Emphasizing just how different the "English Pierrot" was from his French equivalent, Baudelaire continued, "Where Deburau would just have moistened the tip of his finger with his tongue, he stuck both fists and both feet into his mouth." This modern Pierrot distinguished himself from his pallid French counterpart not only by his crude manners, but also by his outrageous makeup: "Upon his floured face he had stuck, crudely and without transition or gradation, two enormous patches of pure red." A few years earlier, in 1854, Champfleury had known what to call this figure that Baudelaire still referred to as the "English Pierrot": "For every Englishman, Pierrot is above all a clown; they don't even call him Pierrot, they call him a clown."[62] *Clown*, by its etymology, is a descendant of *clod*: a "lump of earth," a "lout" of the worst kind. The name associates the clown with dim-witted peasants. His country bumpkin atavism inclines him toward the meanest values, predisposes him to the most regressive attitudes. Rodrigo, and later a figure named Jean-Louis, are two of his avatars.

The figures Condo invented at the end of the 1990s are resolutely clownish. Like Manet's *Olympia*, which imbued Titian's Venuses with the immodesty of a prostitute, Condo's characters are the geometric site of a mash-up between the "infinite grandeur" of their high cultural heritage—their ancestors in Goya and Leonardo—and the "infinite misery" of their third-rate, miserable selves. As Baudelaire once wrote, "It is from the perpetual collision of these two infinites that laughter is struck."[63]

After Manet, modern artists laid claim to the most degraded values and forms. Giorgio Agamben has situated the historical moment when this turn toward depraved taste took hold: "[As] the balance of the man of taste becomes widespread in European society, the artist enters a dimension of imbalance and eccentricity."[64] The battle between the artist and the "man of taste" caused the artist to side with the "clodhoppers," adopting values contrary to the established codes of elegance. The clown, figure of the working class, soon took art by storm. Guillaume Apollinaire accompanied Picasso, Max Jacob, and Kees van Dongen to the Cirque Medrano and dreamed of a "circus-theatre, more violent, more burlesque than the other—simpler too."[65] It is no coincidence that Carl Einstein chose to set his novel *Bebuquin* in a circus, as he applied to literature the narrative and syntactical

61. Charles Baudelaire. "On the Essence of Laughter," 160.

62. Champfleury, "Souvenirs des funambules," in *Contes d'automne*. Paris: Victor Lecou, 1854; reprinted Geneva: Slatkine, 1971: 164.

63. Baudelaire. "On the Essence of Laughter."

64. Giorgio Agamben. *The Man Without Content*, trans. Georgia Albert. Stanford: Stanford University Press, 1999: 16.

65. Guillaume Apollinaire. "Les Tendances Nouvelles," interview published in *SIC (Sons, Idées, Couleurs, Formes)*, August 1916, quoted in Giorgio Agamben, *The Man Without Content.*

deconstructions he learned from cubism. Philip Guston, for his part, would later slip into a clown costume to express his works' comings-and-goings between "beast-like intuition" and "childlike naiveté." In the late 1960s, Guston had abandoned abstract painting, his mode of work since the early post–World War II period, and developed a deliberately grotesque figurative painting, a form he considered better able to express the pitiful state of the world as America tore itself apart over the Vietnam War and segregation.

Back to the Museum

At the Metropolitan Museum of Art in 2003, George Condo found the energy he needed to lift himself out of a period of painter's block. "I hadn't painted anything for a good month or so," he writes, "mostly just sketched and had been lamenting my lack of travel to see different paintings but I knew just up the street two blocks away The Met was showing the 'Manet Velázquez' show—finally I went to see it—I was astonished to see that Manet had been more than slightly inspired by the big V he had taken it upon himself to 'learn' from this inspiration yet he was able to maintain in his transformation, a kind of nerve that is always felt in his work a constant pushing towards the patheticism of contemporary life in comparison to the supernatural (that which Baudelaire found) and brought these elements together. I saw the exhibit about four more times began painting one full standing figure after the next combining all that I saw until I had exhausted the concept which was to reassemble (much like the Burroughs manuscript) what I liked and what I learned."[66]

At the *Manet/Velázquez* exhibition, Condo once again saw how the painters he admires constantly borrowed themes from the artists in their imaginary museums, the members of their spiritual family. In keeping with the pendulum-swings of his imagination, after the antipodal creatures and the archetypes of the *comédie humaine*, Condo returned to the Old Masters. Out of Manet, Velázquez, and Rembrandt came Condo's "Imaginary Portraits," which Donald Kuspit has described as "the latest generation of metaphysical mannequins." Kuspit writes, "They belong to the modern family of quasi-human figures that first made their appearance in the painting of de Chirico. But they may have already been on the scene, in embryo form, in Picasso's analytic Cubist portraits.... Condo's *fin de siècle* metaphysical mannequins are inevitably more decadent—which means also more precious, and above all bitterly ironic—than those made earlier in the century.... They embody the emotional decadence with which this century, which began so hopefully, is ending."[67]

66. George Condo quoted by Peter Fleissig in *Memories of Manet and Velázquez*: IV.

67. Donald Kuspit. "George Condo: Artifices of the Visionary," *George Condo. Paintings and Drawings*. New York: PaceWildenstein, 1995: 7.

In 2020, responding to a question about what he reads, Condo named Nietzsche's *The Birth of Tragedy* as the book that had most influenced him: "It had so much to do with Greek mythology, which I had always found fascinating as a child and believed in to a certain extent. But I could not connect it to art. Of course, there are examples of great masterpieces depicting figures by artists such as Titian and Bernini, and many others, but somehow this book crystalised the difference between that which was Apollonian and of the sun and that which was Dionysian. Which state of mind or power were these forces derived from? In any case, as a result I began to read endlessly about philosophy, from the early Greeks to the most recent, and have always loved it."[68]

The Birth of Tragedy inspired Condo to make a series of sculptures. These allowed him to give free reign to the "schizophrenia" that he identifies as the mainspring of his art. Here, he reinterpreted this schizophrenia in light of the Apollonian and Dionysian principles that Nietzsche analyzes: contradiction, complementarity, dialogue between antagonistic drives and forces. On the one hand, there is pure form and analytical synthesis; on the other hand, the irrational power of the unconscious and the abandoning of oneself to eroticism and violence. From his reading of Nietzsche, Condo retained the power of the work of art to conciliate these opposing forces, to become a space for what Duchamp called the "cointelligence of contraries."

The Becoming-Burlesque of the World

"Superman thinks he can fly, but what happens is eventually he jumps off a building and is found dead in the parking lot. Right when he is about to jump, during that paranoid moment looking out the window, dressed in his costume…. The expression on his face—that's the one I want to capture."[69]

The geopolitical events that marked the opening years of the new millennium led Condo to become a "history painter." Neocons ruled the Capitol. The right-wing hawks among them orchestrated a military build-up that led to the invasion of Iraq in late March 2003. Looking back at this period, Condo recalls Jacques-Louis David, painter of the French Revolution: "It was the spirit of the revolution that propelled David. The use of such terminology 'radical conservatism' came on the eve of my exhibition at the Carpenter Center in Cambridge, Mass in October 2003. It appears that in today's America it is the right-wing that is radical and the left-wing that is conservative…. That is the political essence of reverse configuration.

68. George Condo. "YouTube, Nietzsche and the Vietnam War: George Condo on his biggest cultural influences." Interview. *The Art Newspaper*, May 20, 2020.
69. George Condo quoted by Simon Baker, *George Condo. Painting Reconfigured*: 227.

This is what radical conservatism aims to point out it's not just a trendy catch-phrase."[70]

Two years before the outbreak of the second Iraq war, the Enron scandal had heralded a dangerous evolution in global capitalism. The world was stunned to discover that one of the United States' largest energy companies had implemented a sophisticated system of accounting fraud and financial manipulation on an unprecedented scale. Enron's "creative accounting" practices revealed capitalism's moral drift in an age of intangible economies and financialization.

The scandal disclosed the existence of tax havens and the collusion between capitalist megacompanies and the accounting firms meant to audit them (the firm Arthur Andersen faced charges in the scandal). When the dust settled, twenty-seven thousand Enron employees had lost their jobs—and the retirement savings plans they were counting on as well.

Political satire has always made free use of obscenity and sexual debauchery. Picasso, to denounce Francoist violence, transformed "El Caudillo" into a priapic chimera in 1937. In the late 1960s, Philip Guston excoriated Nixon's politics by sexualizing the latter's nasal organ. Likewise, Condo seized upon the events of his time and overlaid them with the sexual obsession that runs through his work.

To depict the immorality and generalized transgression of the Enron scandal, Condo revisited the iconography of the final days of Sodom and Gomorrah. Under his brush, the incestuous relationships between accounting firms and the companies they audited, between industrial production and financial securitization, became the spectacle of a massive orgy. This debauchery stands as a metaphor for an age whose unbridled economic liberalism flouts all sense of ethics and responsibility. When asked what spurred him to explicitly depict sexual desire, Condo answered, "I think it is the uptight conservative climate that got me going. They are a reaction to the façade of morality that hides the fanatical undercurrent that we are faced with today."[71]

America and its values were sinking. The superheroes that had shaped the imagination of several generations of young Americans couldn't escape the general catastrophe. In one scene, a perverse Batman poses side-by-side with a Playboy Bunny. "I think the pedestals

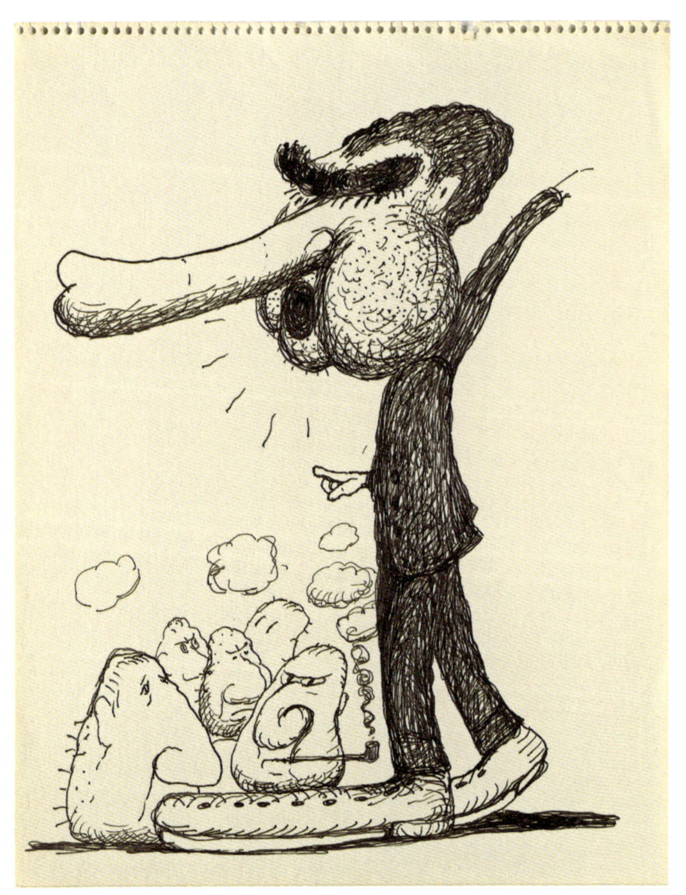

Philip Guston, *Untitled*, 1971. Ink on paper, 14 × 11 in. (35.6 × 27.9 cm)

70. George Condo quoted by Peter Fleissig in *Memories of Manet and Velázquez*: XXXII.
71. George Condo. *George Condo. Existential Portraits*. Interview by Ralph Rugoff: 10.

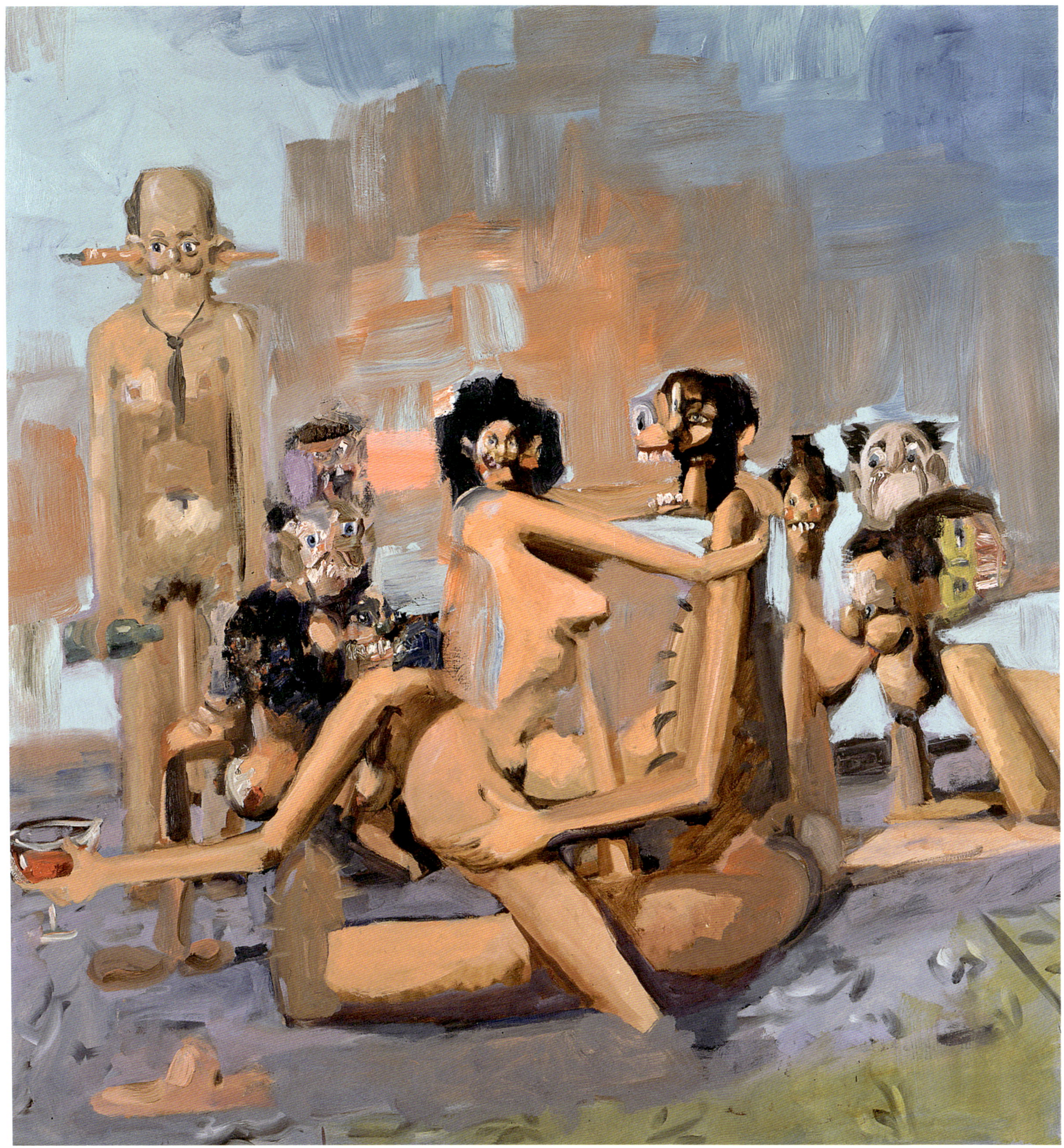

George Condo, *The Last Days of Enron*, 2004. Oil on canvas, 3 ft. 10 in. × 4 ft. (116.8 × 121.9 cm)

these heroes once occupied in the American psyche have degenerated.... They are burned-out superheroes, they're ghosts of themselves," says Condo.[72]

Institutional guarantees of social order and morality were collapsing as well. Painting a priest, Condo turns him into a lascivious creature leering at a nun. These apocalyptic paintings culminated in four works exhibited at the Luhring Augustine gallery in New York in 2008. One painting is an image of God; the other three present the figures of Christ, the good thief, and the bad thief, set against dark, Zurbarán-esque backgrounds. *Dismas* (2007), the good thief, and *Gestas* (2007), the bad thief, hang on either side of *Jesus* (2007) who partly disappears behind a burst of confetti—the sacred figure fused with *homo festivus*. Perched on a bed of clouds, God wears a priestly surplice and a Hare Krishna sling bag. His face is that of the Pods who first appeared a few years earlier—and, indeed, the values he preaches are the polar opposite of those of Wall Street, where the masters of the universe hold sway a few blocks down the road.

In 2005, Condo's little troupe of actors welcomed a new figure, Jean-Louis. His profession is mysterious even to Condo himself: "Is he a waiter, a chef, a driver? or a real person?"[73] In any case, Jean-Louis is the archetype of the simple man who casts a dismayed glance upon the turpitude of the world. He would soon be joined by Uncle Joe, "a kind of Thoreau type," as Condo puts it. "[He] is a pure existentialist: faced with despair, he decided to grab a little plot of land and live way out there beyond the reach of society."[74] But can one have faith in Uncle Joe's wisdom? The bottle clutched in his fingers and his flagrant nudity imply that his asceticism is only of a very relative kind.

In 2011, an exhibition of Condo's works at the Hayward Gallery gave the artist an occasion to pay homage to the music of his youth. In London, as Maurizio Cattelan invited him to make works for *The Wrong Gallery* installed at the Tate Modern, Condo painted a series of burlesque portraits of Queen Elizabeth II. Condo's stay in London also inspired the creation of a new character, the figure of a contemporary artist whose suits bedecked with multicolored circles evoked the most famous, and wildest, artist on the British scene: Damien Hirst.

Savage Love

In 2006, Condo painted the caveman, a Dionysian counterpart to the sophisticated figure Condo is expected to incarnate as an artist. The caveman's

72. George Condo. *George Condo. Existential Portraits*: 11.
73. George Condo, email message to author.
74. George Condo, *George Condo. Existential Portraits*: 13.

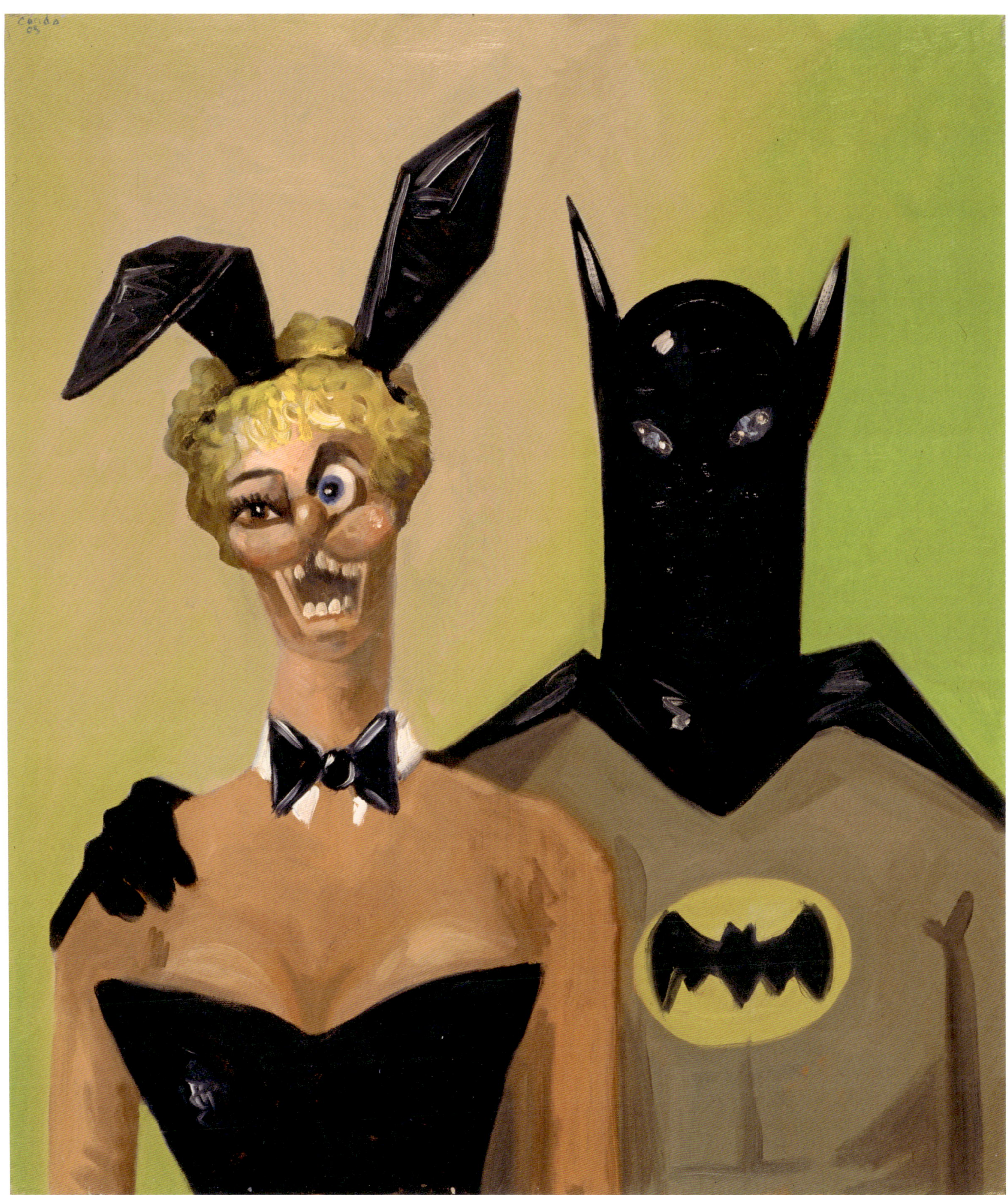

George Condo, *Batman and Bunny*, 2005. Oil on canvas, 32 × 28 in. (81.3 × 71.1 cm)

postures and gestures show him to be prey to his most basic drives, help-less to his animal instincts. His female counterpart spends most of her time throwing decidedly unpolished stones at the male half of humanity. This is savage love, of a kind first given to the American avant-garde by the car-toonist George Herriman in *Krazy Kat*, the love story between a cat and a mouse that knows no way to express her love for the feline other than to throw bricks at its head.

Comic strips once again became a main source for Condo's work in his exhi-bition *Cartoon Abstractions* at the Galerie Jérôme de Noirmont in Paris in 2010. Here, Condo borrowed characters from Tex Avery, Hanna-Barbera, and Walt Disney, using them as pretexts for visual explorations. Once again, Condo revisited the golden age of American art, the post-World War II years. Cartoon characters are the contemporaries of Jackson Pollock, Willem de Kooning, and Arshile Gorky. They are the purest emanation of the demo-cratic genius of America, the same genius later brought to light by the work of Andy Warhol.

As their shared name with Renaissance "cartoons" implies, toons belong to the graphic arts. Through them, Condo reconnected with line drawing. The paintings he exhibited in Paris inaugurated another series of "expanding canvases," an homage to the abstract expressionists.

Black and Red Compression (2011) transforms the graphic density of drip painting into an "all-over" assemblage of cartoons characters. Revisiting the now-legendary tale of American modern art, Condo tells the story of the graphic arts, from Picasso's cubism and Matisse's color fields to the works of Newman and Rothko, all "tooned" in *Downtown New York* (2012).

Bad States

Around 2015, something went haywire in Condo's pictorial mechanics. The cubism he applies to his figures malfunctioned, atomizing them and soon annihilating their coherence, disintegrating their readability. *Beginnings* (2014) unleashes a painterly lyricism that finally destroys the figure, leaving nothing but a panicked eye. The crisis unfolding in Condo's art took explicit form in a canvas that assembled four self-portraits. Condo titled the painting *Self Portraits Facing Cancer* (2015).

The illness that afflicted Condo affected the very heart of his painting. Humor temporarily vanished from his work. Black overwhelmed his palette and soon invaded his canvases. Once more, Condo turned to Goya. *Portrait*

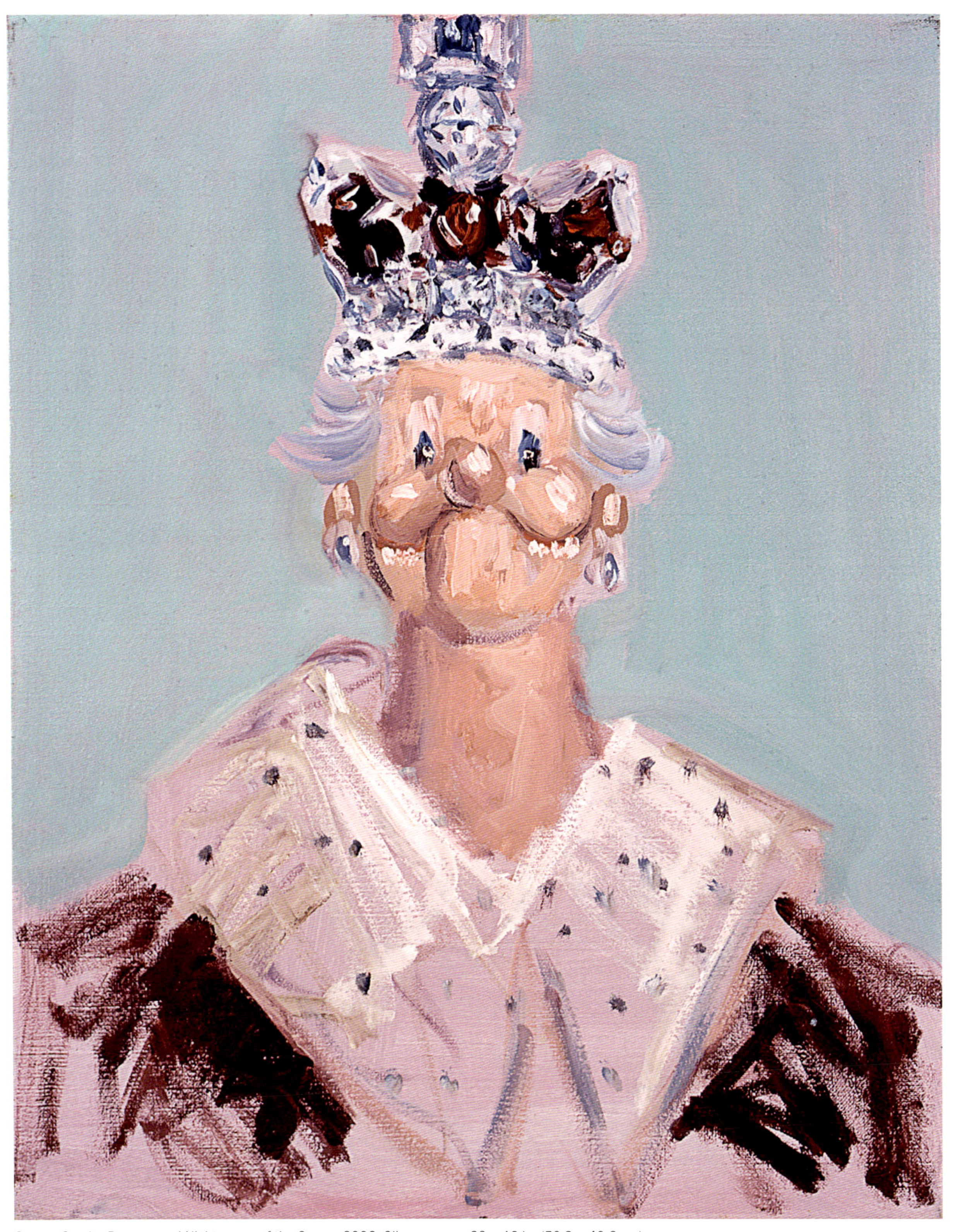

George Condo, *Dreams and Nightmares of the Queen*, 2006. Oil on canvas, 20 × 16 in. (50.8 × 40.6 cm)

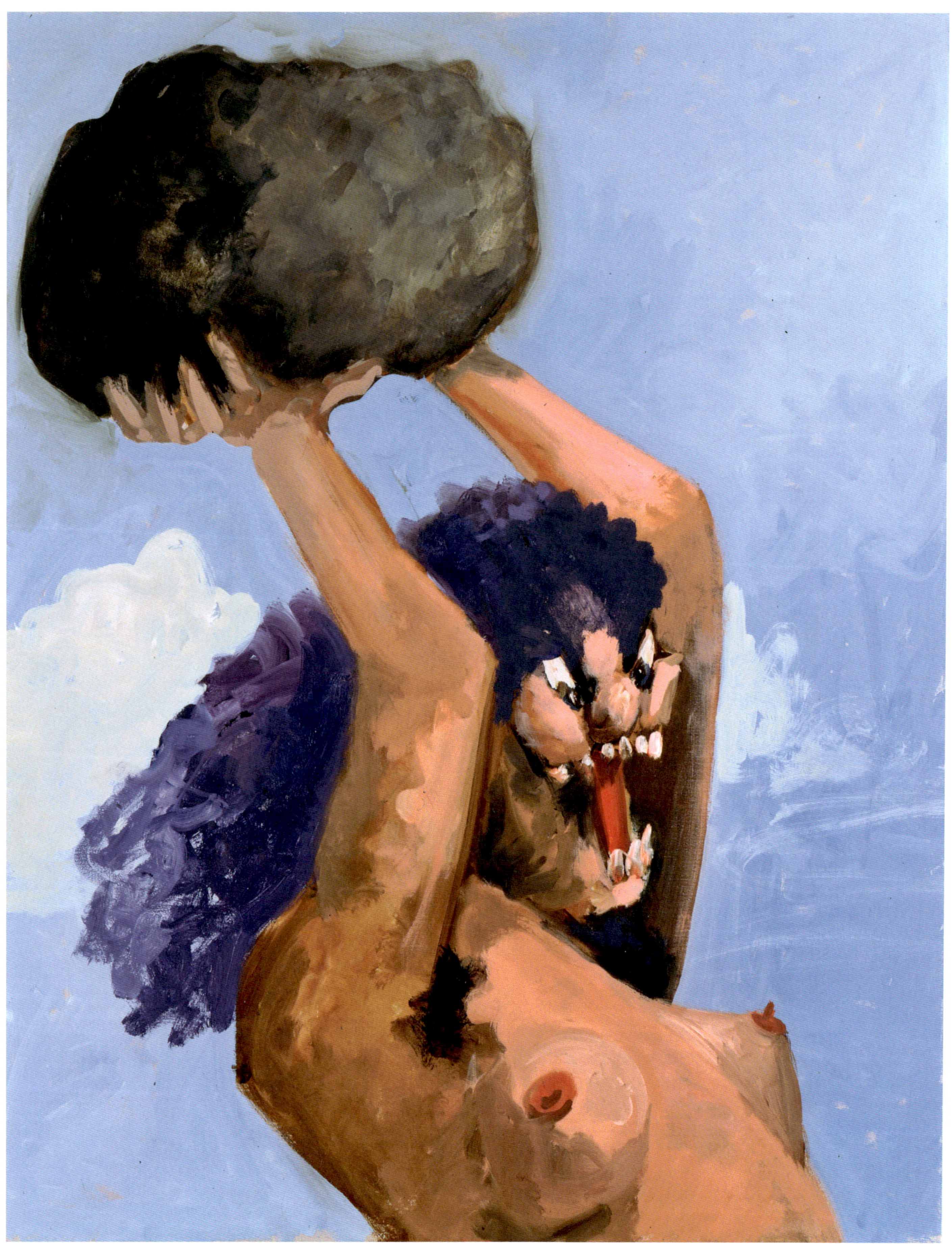

George Condo, *The Cave Woman*, 2006. Oil on canvas, 5 ft. × 4 ft. 2 in. (152.4 × 127 cm)

of the Marquise de la Solana, long contemplated in the Louvre, returned to his memory. He covered her face in black paint, a reminiscence of the series Goya painted at his home, the Quinta del Sordo.

Hugely, Trump

In 2017, Condo's "artificial realism" became reality. A character straight out his most burlesque, or nightmarish, paintings became the 45th president of the United States.

Antipodes be damned. Fox News, chronicle of the Trump presidency, began to supply America with a daily offering of grotesque creatures. Under Condo's brush, *The White House* (2017) becomes an aggregate of lewd, threatening figures, floating among a mass of feminine forms—Ingres's *The Turkish Bath* (*Le Bain turc*) seen through the lens of a porno magazine. *Infiltration*, painted the same year, is marked by the paintings of Joan Miró, whom Condo had yet to summon in his work. The painting evokes the Kafka-esque world of social media, particularly Twitter, as a carrier for the president's speech. Derived from trolls, bots, social media and what's influenced the American election, these paintings reflect a fleeting feeling, that of the rapid changes in today's political environment.

Not since Nixon had a president offered such inspiration to artists.

The controversy surrounding the Trump campaign's suspected collusion with Russia inspired Condo to make a new political painting, *The Trial* (2017). "I'd gone down [to Washington] for my drawings exhibition at the Phillips Collection," says Condo, "and I was staying at the Hay-Adams hotel. In the bar area, they had all of these caricatures of politicians all over the walls. I thought of Philip Guston's caricature of Richard Nixon. And the events in Washington with Michael Flynn happened simultane-ously.[75] So I came up with these caricature-like images of Flynn…. When something this complex is happening on a world stage and the entire coun-try's reputation is at risk—it gives you more reason to express yourself as an artist." By its title, the painting evokes Kafka, extracting itself from the Washington political-judicial context and becoming a timeless allegory of paranoia. "I thought of the Kafka book, *The Trial*, where nobody knows why [the protagonist] was arrested or who was arresting him," Condo says. "With this guy [Flynn], we don't know what he did—we can't figure out what's real and what's fake. So it's less of a caricature and more of a para-

75. In 2017, Michael Flynn was charged with making false statements to the FBI about his contacts with the Russian ambassador.

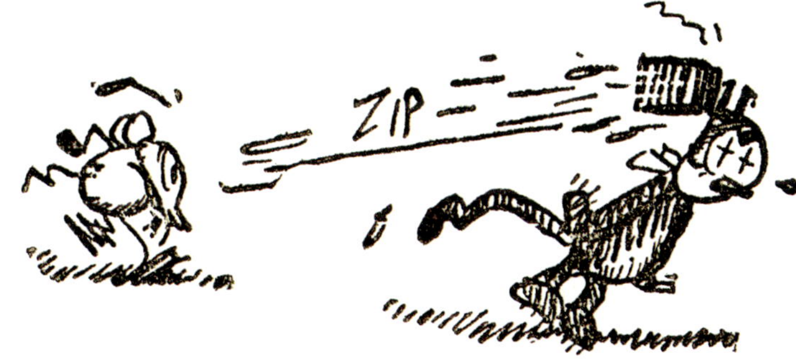

George Herriman, *Krazy Kat*, 1920

noiac painting." Condo is too well-versed in art history to fall into the trap of political militancy. He has learned the lessons of *Guernica*, analyzed how Picasso's reliance on allegory universalized a historical event. "A lot of political art—funny paintings of Clinton or Bush—looks dated," he says. "If they capture a sense of paranoia or oppression or freedom, those images become locked in our minds."[76]

After the illness that had just afflicted him, darkness now fell upon America as a whole.

The optimism that drives political struggle, and a remnant of hope for the future, inspired Condo to paint a series of portraits with lyrical undertones. *Triple Head Composition* (2017) presents merry female figures against a background of color planes taken from Mondrian. The source of Condo's painting was his daughter's participation in the Women's March on Washington in January 2017.

Double Elvis

For the 2019 Venice Biennale, Condo made a painting that reopened his dialogue with Andy Warhol. The model was Warhol's Elvis series from 1963. Condo's interpretation presents two drunkards pitifully armed with beer cans. The work's flair for farce and caricature is far from nihilistic. It is a critical mirror held up to an age of universal cynicism. Condo says that his *Double Elvis* testifies to the "loss of American values"—the values that made it possible to believe in equal opportunity and a fair chance at happiness for all. These bums, whose "reach-for-the stars" hopes have been shattered by the cruelty of current times, are Condo's riposte to the American dream. He adds that these poor derelicts embody humanity more deeply than tech-industry golden boys or Wall Street sharks ever will. It's no use to look here for the pompadours and carefree glamour of the age of rock 'n' roll that Warhol celebrated. That's over. The heroic stagecoach rides of the pioneers who tamed the West have given way to the wanderings of homeless people through city streets. Cowboy pistols have been replaced by beer cans, insidious weapons of mass self-destruction.

Condo had heard the official lies that led the way to unjust wars and terrorist crises. He had seen his country sink into the murky waters of populist politics. His painting is a reflection of the nightmare that the American dream has become. "I tend to turn everything into a battle against the world," he says.[77]

76. George Condo. "Can't Wait for Michael Flynn's Trial? Now George Condo Has Painted It in Advance." Interview by Julia Halperin, *news.artnet.com*. June 9, 2017.
77. George Condo. "George Condo by Anney Bonney."

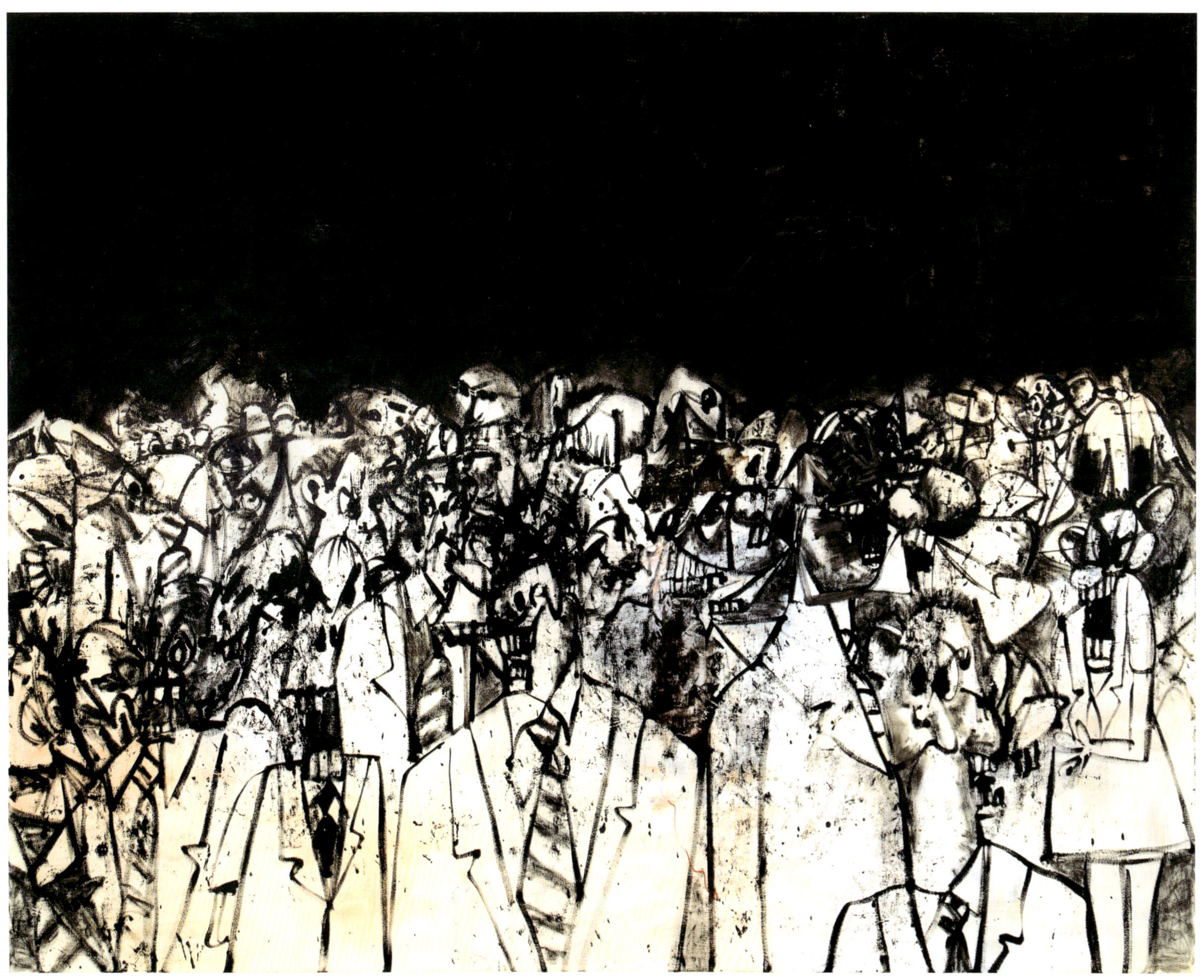

George Condo, *The Trial*, 2017. Oil and acrylic on canvas, 6 ft. 4 in. × 8 ft. (193 × 243.8 cm)

Internal Riot

The coming decades will reveal what effect the COVID-19 lockdowns had on works of the spirit. Condo's paintings will then constitute an invaluable object of study. Scholars will be able to measure there what happens when a mind in isolation is bombarded with current events. And not just any events: the spread of a killer virus that paralyzed the world and turned metropolises into ghost cities.

Condo's studio lies sheltered away, far from New York City. Hearing him describe it, one gets the impression of an afterworld, a post-apocalyptic decor: "There's a small one-car garage to paint in and a guest house that's empty. Both have been completely turned upside down and look like a tornado went through of flying papers ripped up everywhere, random tubes of new and old paint, brushes that should have been thrown out years ago … it's quite a mess. But I must say that's how I like it.… I started making the drawings when I got out here in about the second week of March, say the 14th or 15th. So these have been made while in quarantine and represent the feelings of distancing and missing human contact. They are figures who are distanced from one another or, in fact, even distanced from themselves."[78]

When the chaos of our times cannot be exorcized through public critique, it works its way into our minds. Our skulls echo with its noise and entropy. Condo calls this cacophony "internal riot." He has devoted to it a series of paintings that he exhibited in New York at his new gallery Hauser & Wirth from November 5, 2020, to January 23, 2021. All the paintings are the same format. Their titles reflect an age of fear, of paranoia: *Hysteria*, *End of Reason*, *Shades of Darkness*, *Human Rage*. Once again, the spirit of Warhol was a guiding principle, as Condo lined these paintings up along the walls like Warhol's Shadows series.

Condo's new paintings are battlegrounds. They are images of a fragmented face, of puzzle-like features whose pieces have grown hostile to each other. They take form through a clash of techniques, a maelstrom of colors. Condo calls this "the fraction aspect of today's society." These works are seismographs of a world that is falling apart. For the first time, Condo inscribed the date of completion on each canvas, offering future historians the chronicle of a lockdown, of a world reduced to the space of a skull. In a video by the painter and video artist James Kalm, we ironically glimpse an impromptu band playing "What a Wonderful World" outside the gallery in which the exhibition was held.[79]

78. George Condo. "Distanced Figures: George Condo. Quarantine painting, drawing and listening." Interview, *hauserwirth.com*. April 10, 2020.

79. James Kalm. "George Condo 'Internal Riot' at Hauser & Wirth." Vimeo, November 20, 2020, 24:32, https://vimeo.com/481893367.

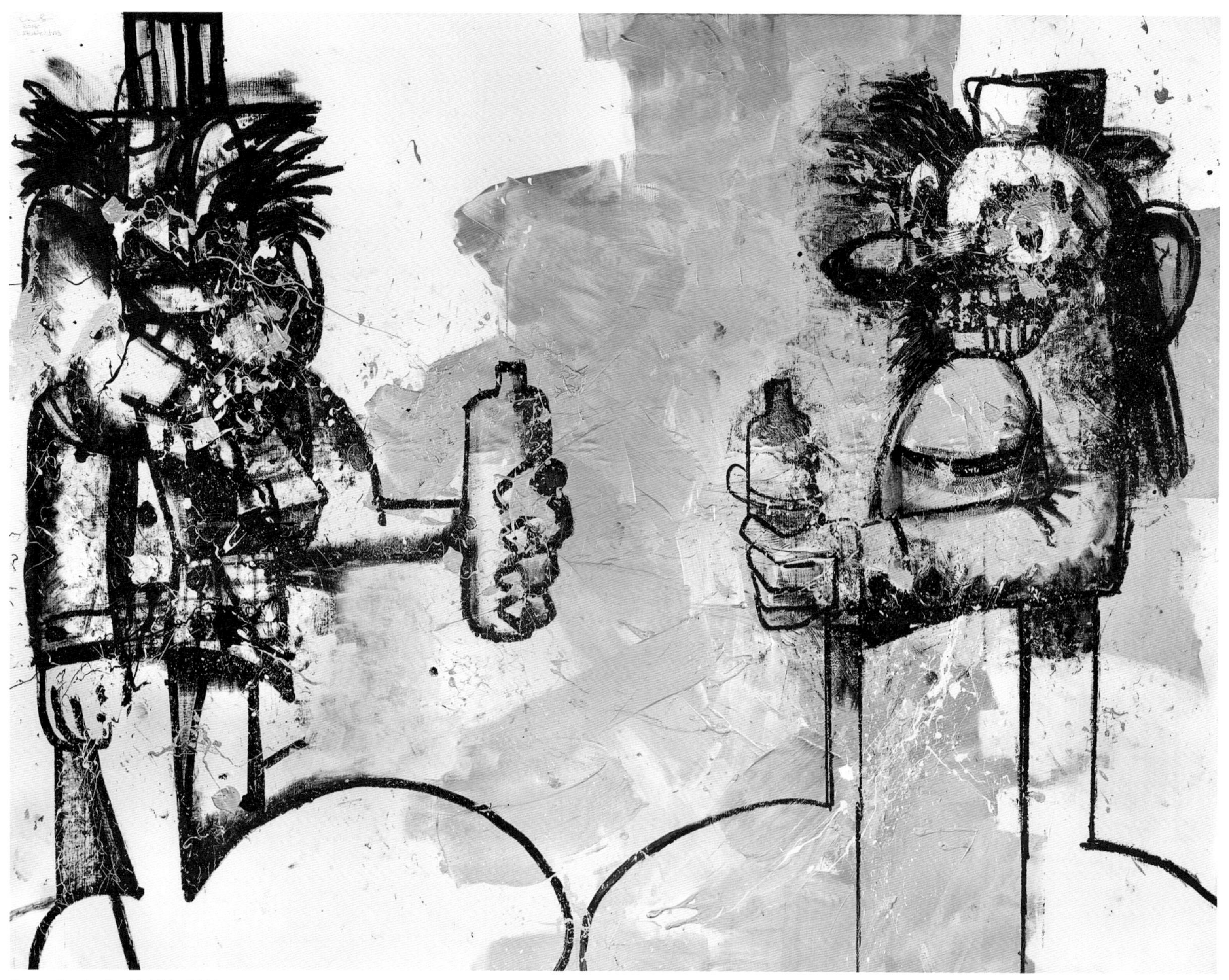

George Condo, *Double Elvis*, 2019. Acrylic, silver metallic paint, and pigment stick on linen, 12 × 16 ft. (365.8 × 487.7 cm)

After the internal riot of the lockdown canvases, the paintings presented at the exhibition *Ideals of the Unfound Truth* in fall 2021 reconnected with the fundamental principles of George Condo's art. The female form—endowed with all the beauty of the classical rules his great-great-uncle Albano once upheld—becomes the central theme of these new paintings. Female forms are everywhere, whether central to the compositions (*The Cocktail Drinker*) or implied (*The Day They All Got Out*). They save the canvases from radical abstraction, offering the curve of a breast in counterpoint to strict geometry. Ever since he read Nietzsche, Condo has known that the Apollonian order—the perfect, pure beauty evoked by these figures—cannot exist without its entropic, trivial counterpart, the Dionysian. Lascivious comic-strip gnomes therefore intermingle with Condo's ideal pinup models. From neoclassical grace to the triviality of cartoon characters, the dialectic between kitsch and high art enacts itself again. Grafting a cubist head onto an all-too perfectly beautiful body, Condo recapitulates the original drama of modern painting: the founding crisis of *Les Demoiselles d'Avignon*. At least since the days of Manet, the schizophrenia that Condo sees as the distinctive characteristic of his painting has been one of the fundamental values of art as defined by Baudelaire. Condo updates the cocktail that Baudelaire proposed back then: a shot of "the eternal and the immutable" (the invocation of classical beauty, Uncle Albano's impossible legacy) and a zest of the "modern" ("the ephemeral," "the fugitive," "the contingent": cartoons and pop-culture icons extracted from a prosaic and trivial present). After all, as Lyotard once claimed, postmodernism was perhaps simply a way of updating art's fundamental values.

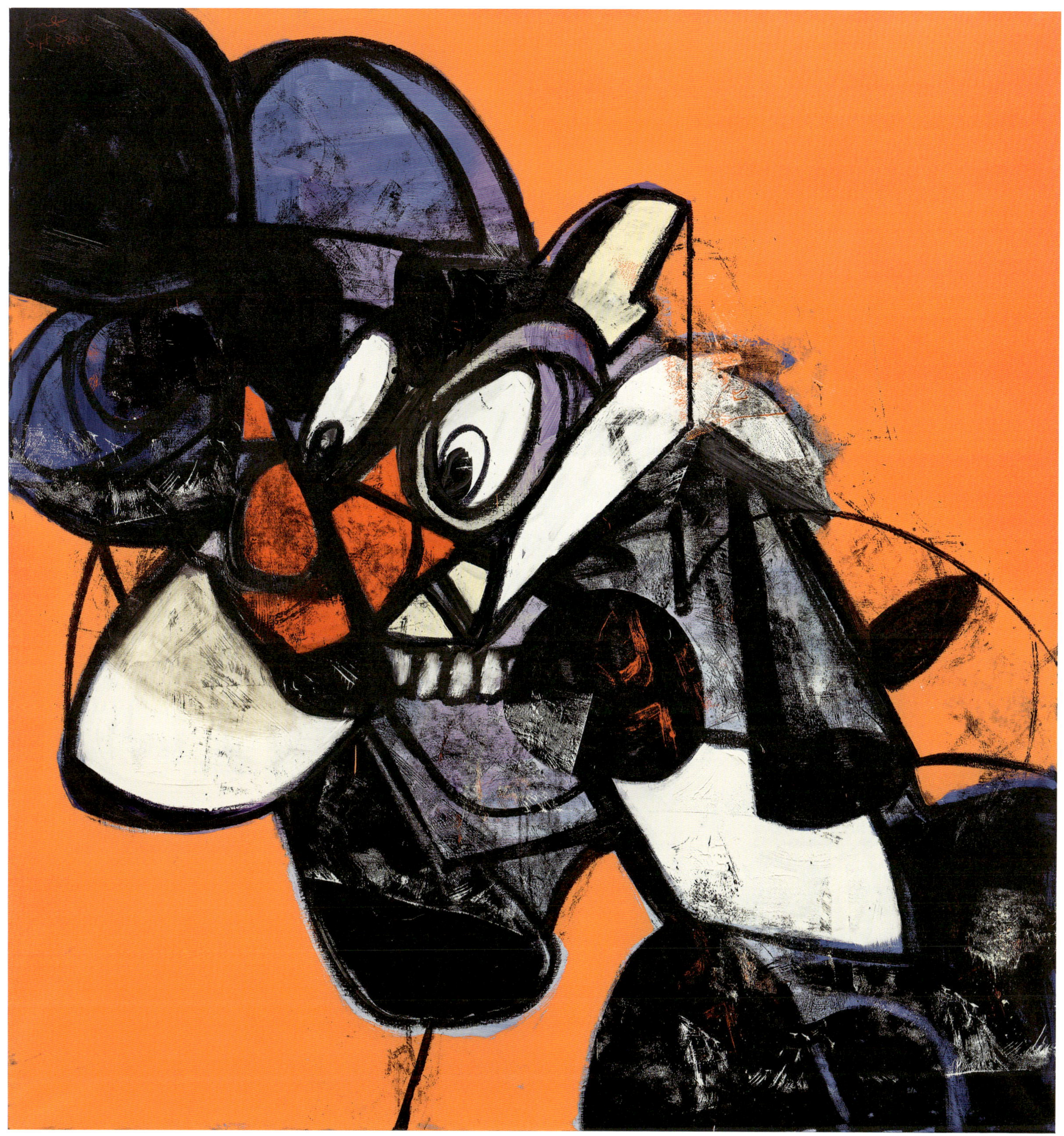

George Condo, *Human Rage*, 2020. Acrylic and pigment stick on linen, 6 ft. 10 in. × 6 ft. 8 in. (208.3 × 203.2 cm)

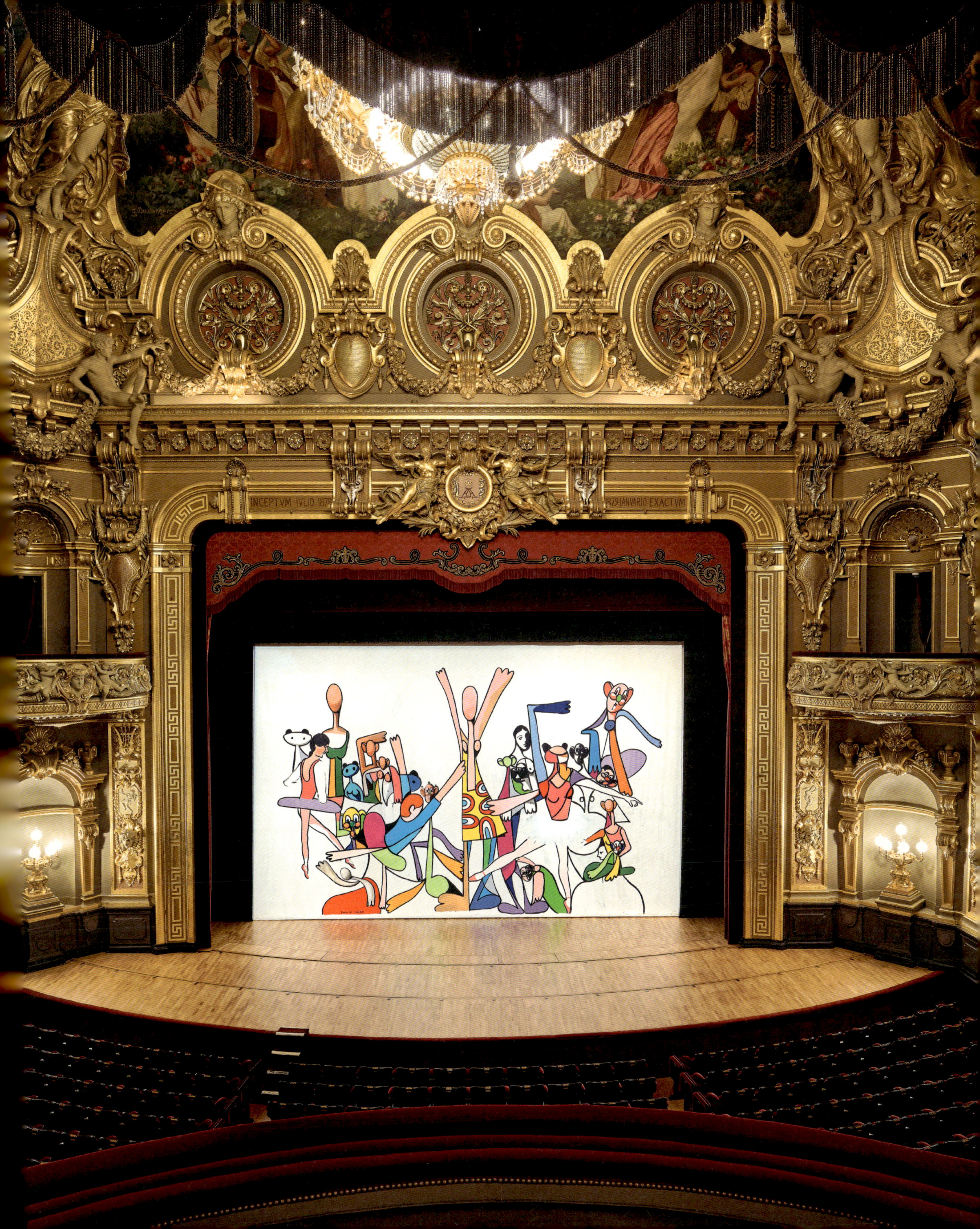

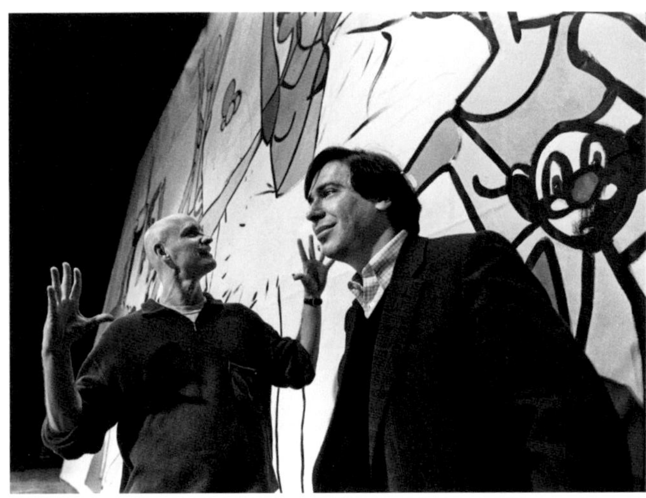

JEAN-CHRISTOPHE MAILLOT & GEORGE CONDO: BEHIND THE CURTAIN

Interview by Guillaume de Sardes

Guillaume de Sardes: You have been the director and choreographer of Les Ballets de Monte Carlo since 1993. The company is heir to the Ballets Russes, whose founder Serge Diaghilev often collaborated with avant-garde artists. He would commission sets, costumes, and stage curtains from painters like Léon Bakst, Georges Braque, Giorgio de Chirico, Sonia Delaunay, André Derain, Natalia Goncharova, Marie Laurencin, Henri Matisse, and Pablo Picasso. What made you want to maintain this tradition?

Jean-Christophe Maillot: To direct a ballet company is to continue its history. I'm not one of those people who makes a clean sweep of the past. I think it's more interesting to find a way to make the past your own: get to know it, understand it, bring it back to life in contemporary forms. For Les Ballets de Monte Carlo, that came naturally to me since I grew up around total artworks. My father was a set designer and painter, and he created hundreds of theater sets and stage curtains. His friends were actors, musicians, dancers. They all spoke about the productions they were working on.

Not long after I arrived at Les Ballets de Monte Carlo, I commissioned a first stage curtain from Ernest Pignon-Ernest, whose paintings Princess Caroline had called to my attention. At the time, I was staging *Romeo and Juliet*. Ernest had already worked on a lot of Italian themes and artists: Caravaggio, Pasolini, etc. It went so well that I repeated the experiment with Philippe Favier. I liked the idea of commissioning a stage curtain from an artist who specializes in miniatures and small-format black-and-white work.

G.S.: In 1998, you commissioned George Condo to paint a stage curtain. He was forty-one years old at the time, an American painter. What made you think of him?

J.-C.M.: There again, it was thanks to Princess Caroline. He was friends with her and Ernst August of Hanover. George Condo and I got on well immediately. Why? Maybe because we were about the same age; maybe because we've both kept a part of our childhood alive within us; maybe because we share a similar artistic situation, namely a (too) great natural aptitude. George possesses incredible technical mastery—he can do anything. It isn't easy to find your own style in those circumstances. In any case, we had a few drinks and decided to work together.

G.S.: George Condo painted this 23 × 36 ft. (7 × 11 m) stage curtain himself. How did the work go, from the first sketches to the final form?

J.-C.M.: George works by instinct, so it all went very quickly. He spent a lot of time with us, with the company. The dancers fascinated him. It only took him a few sketches to find the general composition. Once that was decided upon, the canvas was rolled out on the floor of the Diaghilev studio where we used to rehearse—a space not very well suited to dance, but which is part of so many memories—and George started painting. People don't necessarily realize what a feat it is for an easel painter to work at such large scale. To go from the initial sketch to the curtain, artists generally rely on decorators, or even mechanical processes like silkscreen printing. George did it all on his own, like Picasso for the *Parade* curtain. It only took about three weeks in all.

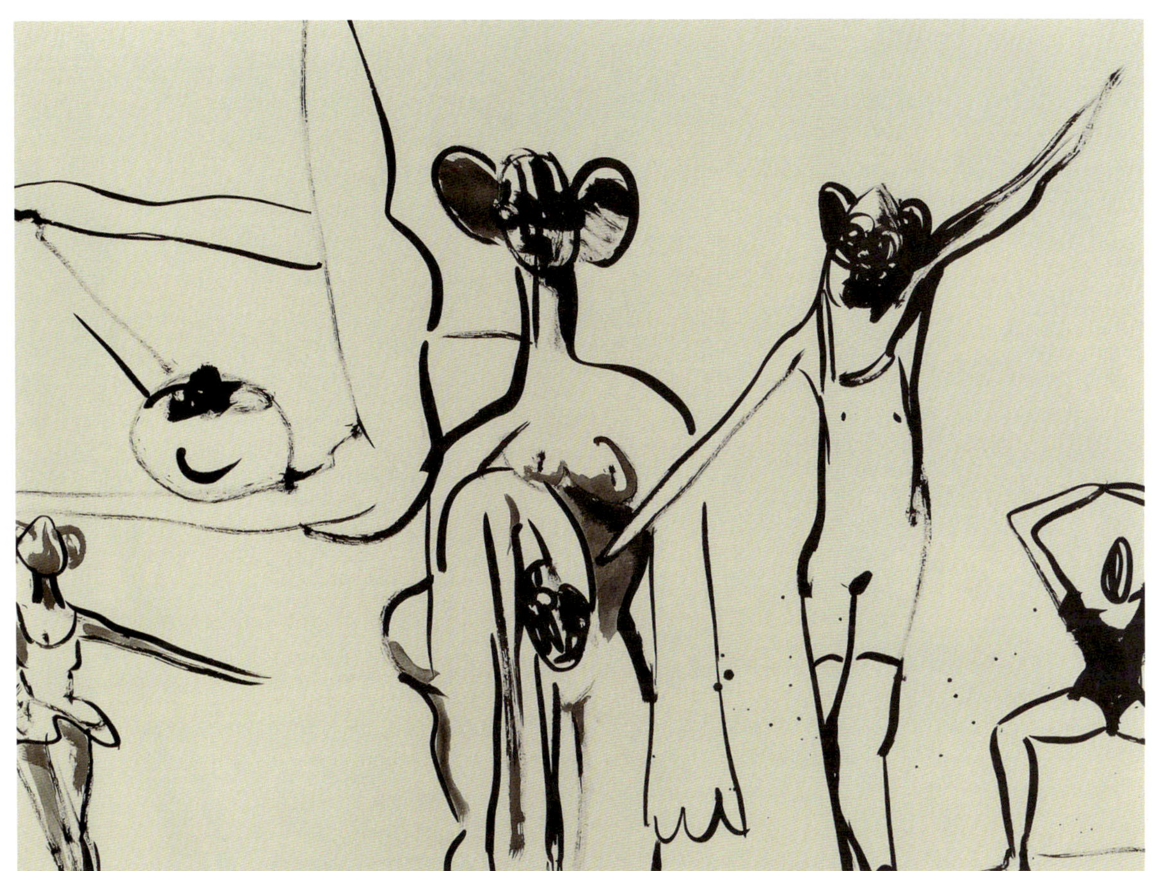

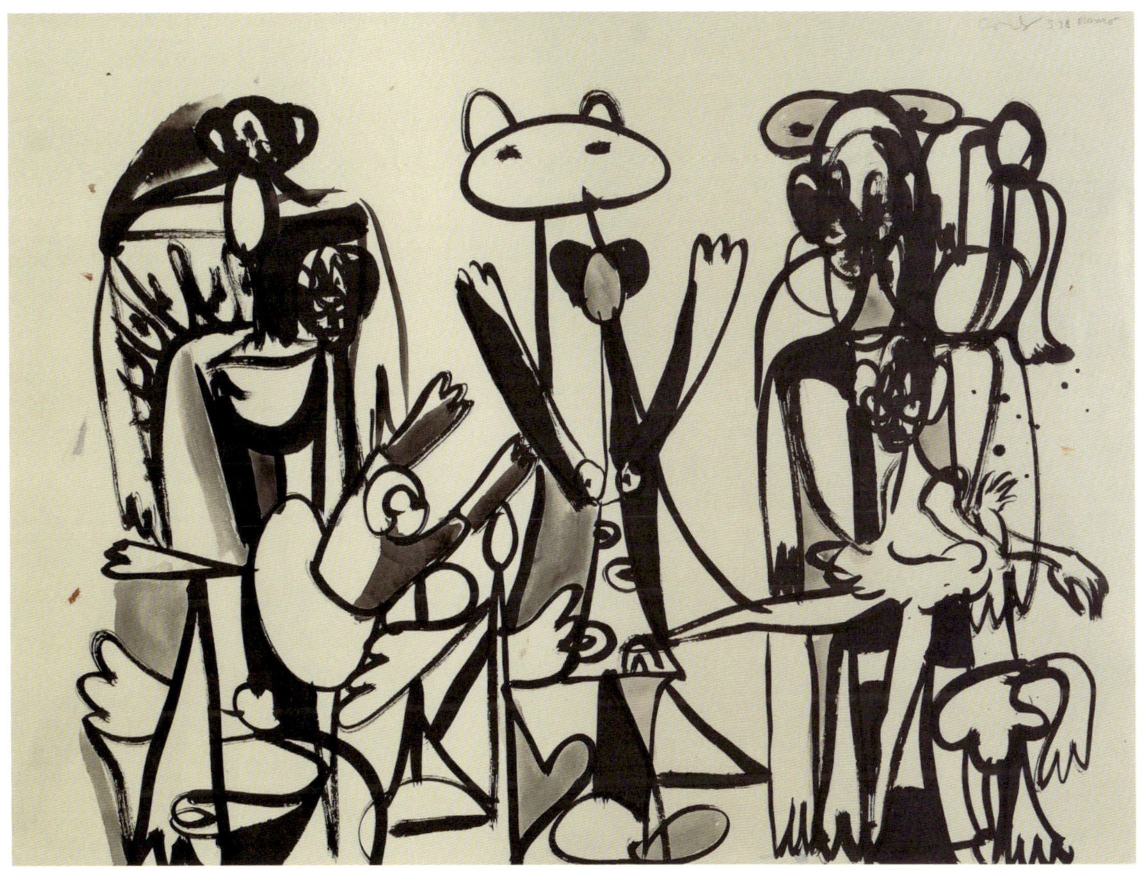

Page 181: George Condo, *Dancers in Motion*, 1998. Acrylic on fabric.
Ballet curtain displayed at the Opéra de Monte-Carlo
Above: George Condo, *Studies of Dancers at the Ballets de Monte-Carlo*,
1998. Drawings, 21¾ × 30 in. (55.5 × 76 cm) each

G.S.: You once told me that a profile portrait of you was added to the curtain at the last minute....

J.-C.M: Yes, when George had finished the stage curtain, some mutual friends came over to have a look at it. One of them jokingly said, "But you left out Maillot!" George immediately picked up a brush and, right there in front of us, added my profile in a few strokes, bottom right. It's a pretty close likeness, and I see it as a kind of dedicatory inscription.

G.S.: Two years after that first collaboration, you commissioned George to create the sets and costumes for your ballet Opus 40. *How did that new project come about? And what was the process like?*

J.-C.M: The creation of the curtain had gone so well we wanted to keep working together. You might say it served as a test. The way I am, I can only collaborate with artists if I appreciate not only their work but also their personality. *Opus 40* is an ode to childhood and our earliest emotions. There's a childlike element to George that you can see in his paintings. They have a certain energy, enthusiasm … joy, even. So I thought he'd be the right person for the project. And he was—he served the choreography very well. He didn't try to make his mark too heavily. On the contrary, his contribution was well balanced, delicate. He created a very simple set formed of two large grey walls. For the sixteen dancers, he wanted short dresses whose colors he carefully determined. We still have the prototypes of the costumes on which he placed a dab of each color he wanted.

G.S.: Opus 40*'s score was composed by Meredith Monk, a New York artist like Condo. Was that a coincidence, or was it deliberate? Did you want to place your ballet in the New York avant-garde tradition?*

J.-C.M: I pay attention to how the various elements of my ballets fit together. Everything contributes to the impression of the whole. The first time I heard Meredith Monk, I was at a big event in New York. I immediately liked the playful complexity of her music. After the performance, I went up to her and asked if she would let me use the piece for *Opus 40*. She's a choreographer herself, so I didn't expect her to say yes. But she did! When George heard the music, he immediately

understood why it was right for the ballet: several passages evoke the babbling of an infant, or a teenager's annoying laughter. Not many people know this, but George is a great music-lover, crazy about Bach. Several of his friends are composers, and he himself plays the cello and the lute beautifully. In fact, it's thanks to him that I met and worked with Danny Elfman.

G.S.: George Condo once wrote, "The Humanoids are my imaginary people, ones who can play the role of all the lovers and the mad and lonely, the hierarchy and the lowlife...." In closing, I'd like to ask you what that description calls to mind. Under that definition, do you think the Humanoid who plays all the roles might not also be a dancer?

J.-C. M: What I like about that quote is the idea of metamorphosis. It's the metamorphosis of the dancer I once was, of course, passing from one role to another. But it's also the metamorphosis of the choreographer I am now, moving from one style to another. While some of my fellow choreographers always work in the same vein, like William Forsythe or JiĐí Kylián—to the extent that you can recognize one of their pieces in a few seconds—I prefer to explore the fields of what is possible, to pass from a narrative ballet to an abstract piece, from the grammar of classical dance to a strictly modern grammar, or even to mix them together. I don't like categories, and I've always done my best not to belong to any of them, except maybe that of the "Humanoid," constantly reinventing itself.

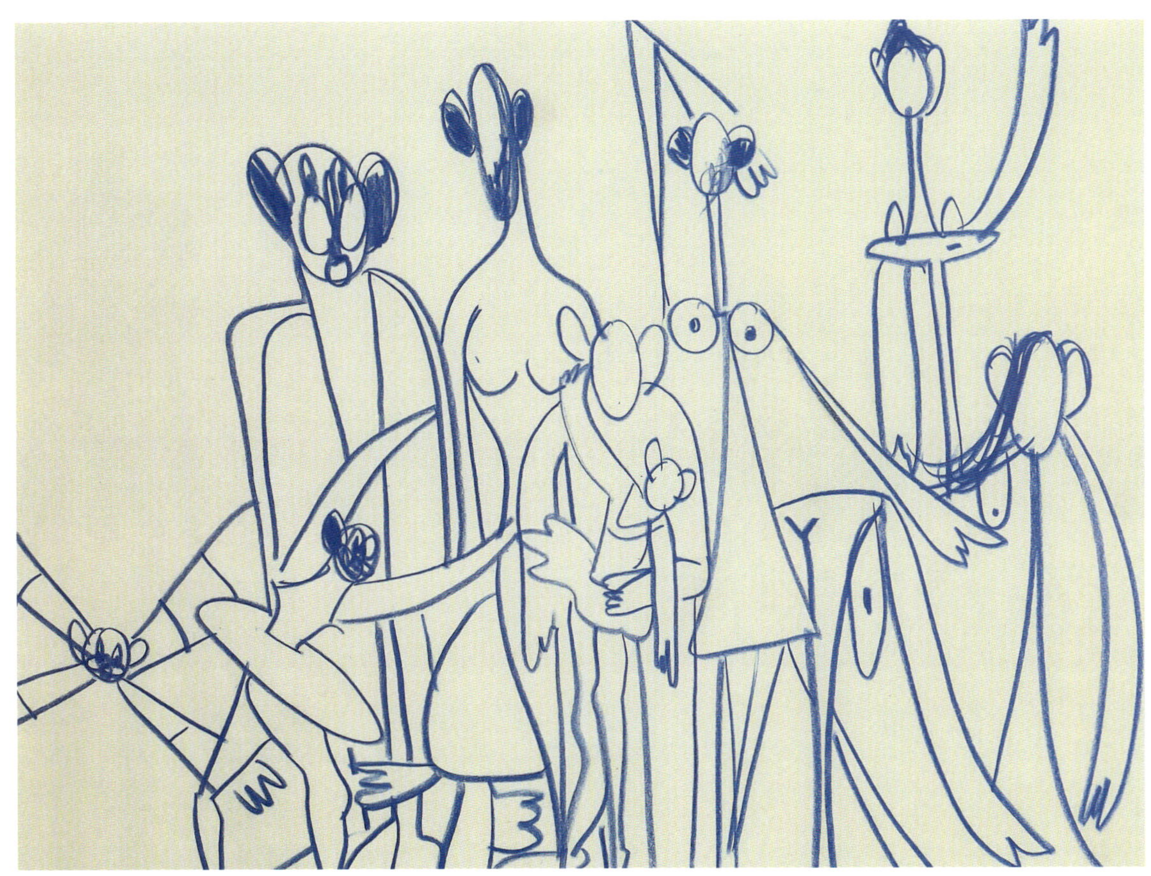

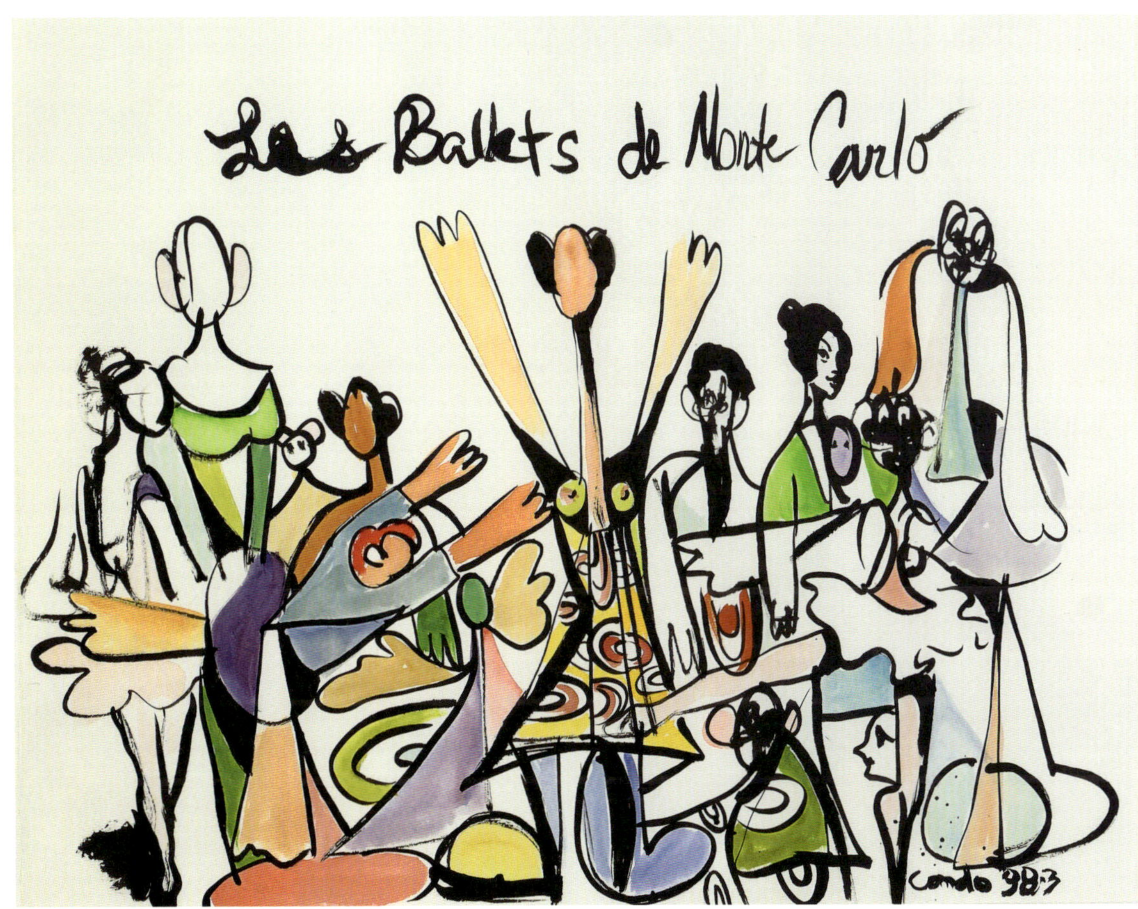

Above: George Condo, *Studies of Dancers at the Ballets de Monte-Carlo*, 1998.
Drawings of 21¾ × 30 in. (55.5 × 76 cm, top) and 19¾ × 25¾ in. (50 × 65.5 cm, bottom)
Pages 186–87: George Condo, *Dancers in Motion*, 1998. Acrylic on fabric.
Ballet curtain displayed at the Opéra de Monte-Carlo

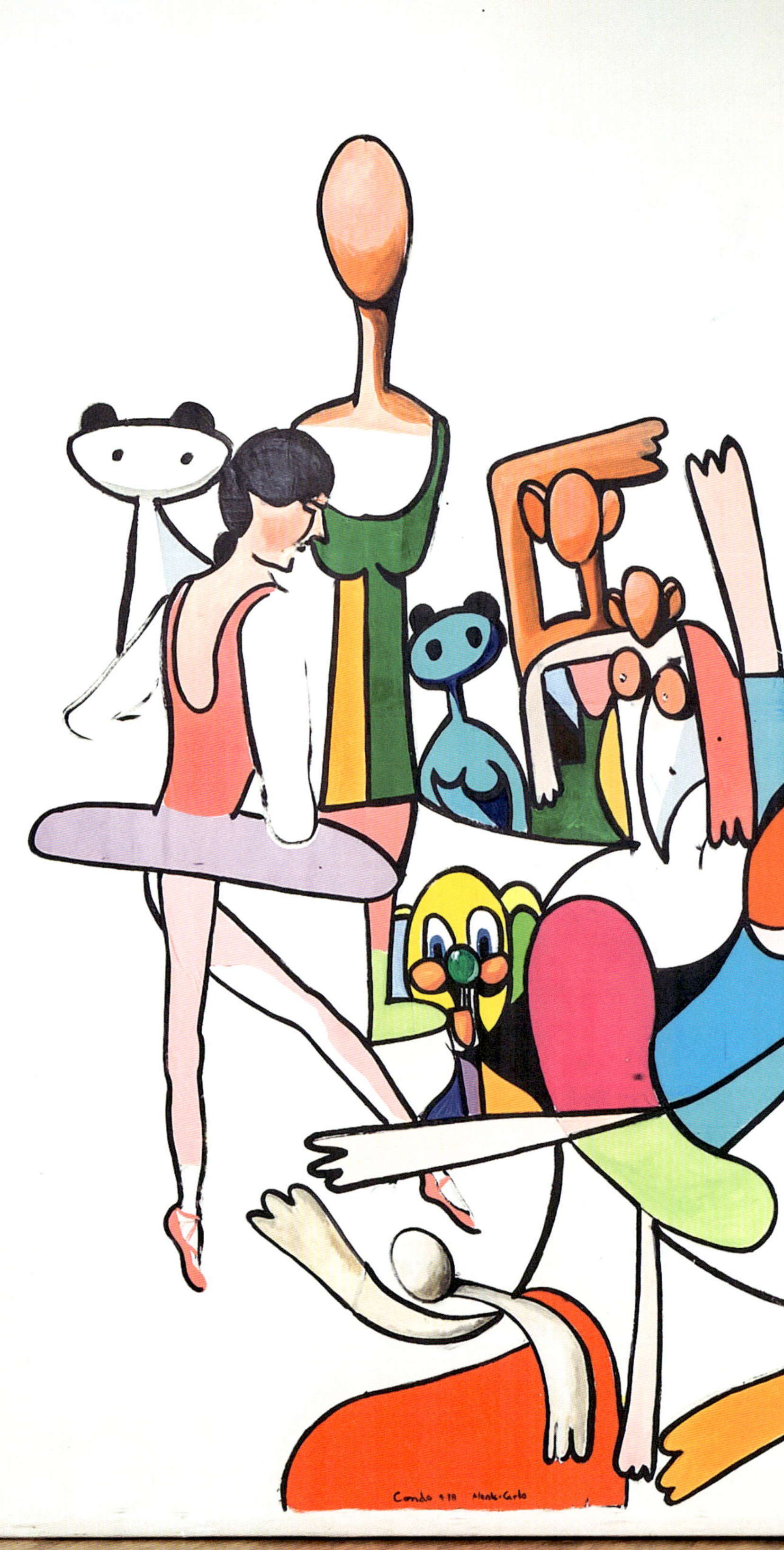
Condo 9.99   Monte-Carlo

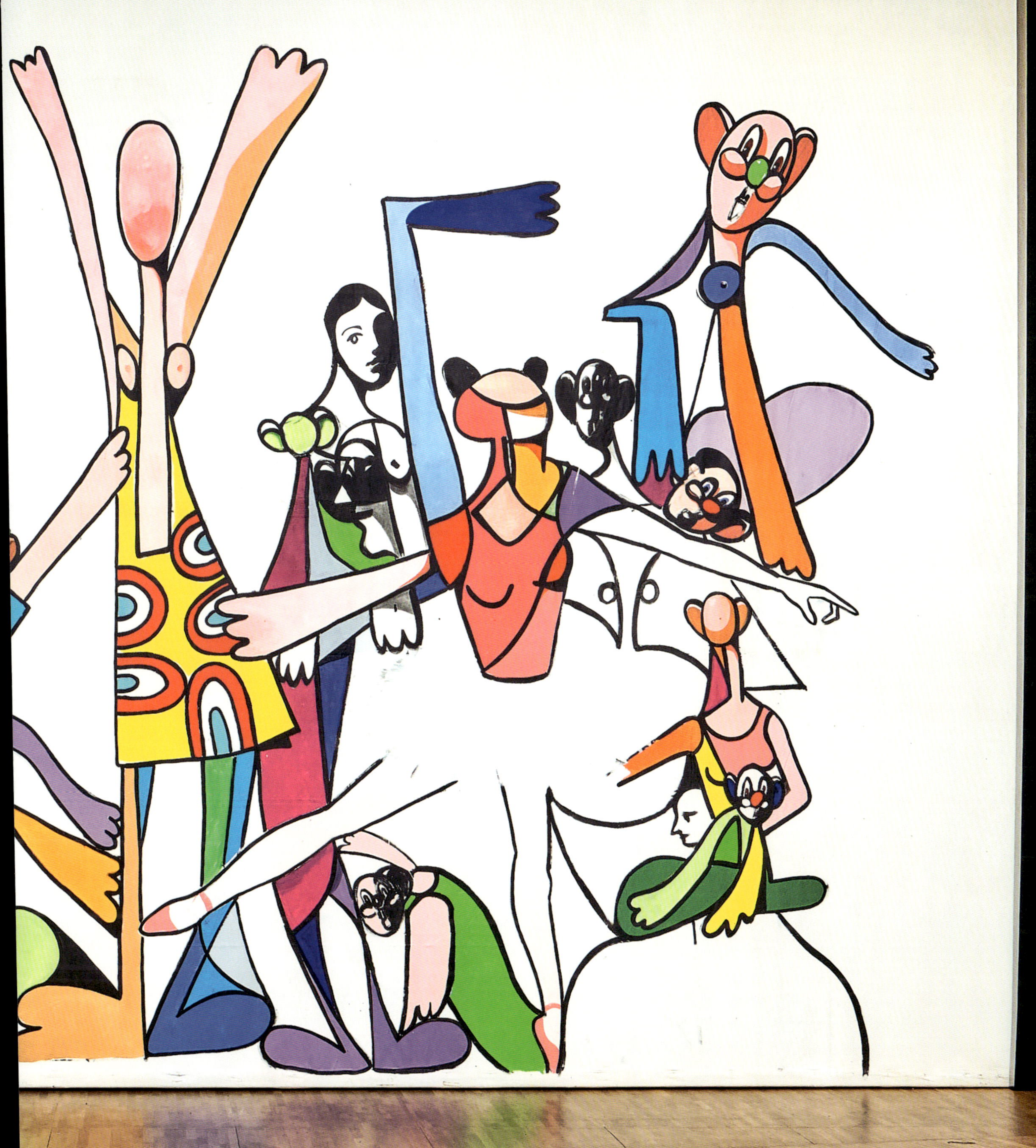

Bibliography

2022

Baker, Simon. *George Condo. Painting Reconfigured.* 2015. London: Thames & Hudson.

2019

Ruiz-Picasso, Bernard. *George Condo. Life Is Worth Living.* Paris: Almine Rech Editions. Exhibition catalog.

2018

Martinou, Atalanti, Aphrodite Gonou, and Carlos Picón. *George Condo at Cycladic.* Athens: Museum of Cycladic Art. Exhibition catalog.

2017

Condo, Eleonore. *George Condo. Recent Sculptures.* New York: Skarstedt Gallery. Exhibition catalog.

Kosinski, Dorothy. *George Condo. The Way I Think.* Washington, D.C.: The Phillips Collection; Humlebæk, Denmark: Louisiana Museum of Modern Art; Minneapolis: Shapco. Exhibition catalog.

2016

Kittelmann, Udo, Felicia Rappe and Olivier Berggruen. *Condo. Confrontation.* Berlin: Museum Berggruen; Nationalgalerie, Staatliche Museen zu Berlin. Exhibition catalog.

2015

Condo, George. *Mister Nicotine. The George Condo Purple Book.* Paris: Purple Institute.

2014

George Condo. Ink Drawings. London: Skarstedt Gallery. Exhibition catalog.

Whitfield, Sarah. *George Condo. Headspace.* London: Simon Lee Gallery. Exhibition catalog.

2013

George Condo. Paintings & Sculpture. Berlin: Sprüth Magers; Distanz Verlag. Exhibition catalog.

2011

George Condo. Drawing Paintings. New York: Skarstedt Gallery. Exhibition catalog.

Rugoff, Ralph, Laura Hoptman, David Means, and Will Self. *George Condo. Mental States.* London: Hayward Gallery. Exhibition catalog.

2010

Troncy, Éric. *George Condo. Cartoon Abstractions.* Paris: Galerie Jérôme de Noirmont. Exhibition catalog.

2009

Kellein, Thomas. *George Condo.* Brussels: Xavier Hufkens. Exhibition catalog.

Ottinger, Didier, Bertrand Lorquin, and Massimiliano Gioni. *George Condo. La Civilisation perdue/The Lost Civilization.* Paris: Gallimard; Musée Maillol. Exhibition catalog.

2008

Patsukov, Vitaly. *George Condo. Artificial Realism.* Moscow: Gary Tatintsian Gallery. Exhibition catalog.

2007

Willberg, Peter. *George Condo.* London: Simon Lee Gallery. Exhibition catalog.

2006

Rugoff, Ralph. *George Condo. Existential Portraits. Sculpture, Drawings, Paintings 2005/2006.* Berlin: Holzwarth Publications; New York: Luhring Augustine. Exhibition catalog.

2005

Husslein-Arco, Agnes, and Thomas Kellein (eds.). *George Condo. One Hundred Women.* Ostfildern, Germany: Hatje Cantz. Exhibition catalog.

2004

Fleissig, Peter. *George Condo, Memories of Manet and Velazquez.* Paris: Galerie Jérôme de Noirmont. Exhibition catalog.

2003

Kellein, Thomas, and Malcolm Green. *George Condo. Sculpture*. Zurich: Galerie Bruno Bischofberger. Exhibition catalog.

2002

Rugoff, Ralph. *The Imaginary Portraits of George Condo*. New York: powerHouse Books.

2001

Condo, George, and Bernard Marcadé. *George Condo. Physiognomical Abstraction*. Paris: Galerie Jérôme de Noirmont. Exhibition catalog.

1999

Berggruen, Olivier, and Paul Miller. *George Condo. Portraits Lost in Space*. New York: PaceWildenstein; Deitch Projects. Exhibition catalog.

1998

George Condo. Televised Silkscreens. New York: Sandra Gering Gallery. Exhibition catalog.

Fitzgerald, Michael. *George Condo. Collage Paintings*. New York: PaceWildenstein. Exhibition catalog.

1995

Kuspit, Donald. *George Condo. Paintings and Drawings*. New York: PaceWildenstein. Exhibition catalog.

Moody, Tom. *George Condo. Recent Paintings*. Houston: Contemporary Arts Museum. Exhibition catalog.

1994

Burroughs, William. *George Condo. Recent Paintings*. New York: PaceWildenstein. Exhibition catalog.

1992

George Condo. Obra 1990-1992. Madrid: Galería Soledad Lorenzo. Exhibition catalog.

Bonet, Juan Manuel. *George Condo*. Barcelona: Galería Salvador Riera. Exhibition catalog.

1991

Burroughs, William, and George Condo. *Ghost of Chance*. New York: The Library Fellows of the Whitney Museum of American Art.

Dickhoff, Wilfried. *George Condo. Recent Paintings*. New York: Pace Gallery. Exhibition catalog.

Tsuzuki, Kyoichi. *Art Random: George Condo*. Kyoto: Kyoto Shoin International.

1990

Guattari, Félix. *George Condo*. Paris: Galeric Daniel Templon. Exhibition catalog.

1989

George Condo. London: Waddington Galleries. Exhibition catalog.

1988

Geldzahler, Henry. *George Condo. Paintings and Drawings*. New York: Pace Gallery. Exhibition catalog.

1987

Dickhoff, Wilfried. *George Condo. Paintings and Drawings 1985–87*. Zurich: Galerie Bruno Bischofberger. Exhibition catalog.

Dickhoff, Wilfried (dir.), and Demosthenes Davvetas. *George Condo. Gemälde/Paintings 1984–1987*. Munich: Kunstverein München. Exhibition catalog.

1986

George Condo. Paintings. Tokyo: Akira Ikeda Gallery. Exhibition catalog.

Dickhoff, Wilfried. *George Condo*. New York: Barbara Gladstone Gallery. Exhibition catalog.

Index of George Condo's works reproduced in the catalog

Exhibited works

Complementary works

Photographic Credits

The publisher would like to thank all those who have kindly given their permission for the reproduction of material for this book. Every effort has been made to obtain permission to reproduce the images and texts in this catalogue. However, as is standard editorial policy, the publisher is at the disposal of copyright holders and undertakes to correct any omissions or errors in future editions.

Works by George Condo: © 2023 George Condo/Artists Rights Society (ARS), New York

p. 21, 27: Photo: © NMNM/François Fernandez
p. 45: © PONCET Georges
p. 128: The National Pedagogical Museum and Library of J. A. Comenius, Prague, S II 8790
p. 129: © Photo12/7e Art/Universal Pictures
p. 135: © Milan Kunc • Collection Groninger Museum: Photo © John Stoel
p. 138: © Walter Dahn/Courtesy the artist and Sprüth Magers
p. 140: © Estate of Jean-Michel Basquiat. Licensed by Artestar, New York. • © The Estate of Jean-Michel Basquiat/Adagp, Paris, 2023
p. 141 (bottom): Keith Haring Artwork © Keith Haring Foundation
p. 142: © Adagp, Paris, 2023/Wifredo Lam • © NPL - DeA Picture Library/Bridgeman Images
p. 149: Photography: Benoit Pailley, George Condo, New Museum, 2011
p. 150: © Succession Picasso 2023 • Photo © Photo Josse/Succession Picasso/DACS, London 2023/Bridgeman Images
p. 152: Photo © Fine Art Images/Bridgeman Images
p. 156: Photo © Photo Josse/Bridgeman Images
p. 157: © Adagp, Paris, 2023/Jacques Hérold • Photo © Centre Pompidou, MNAM-CCI, Dist. RMN-Grand Palais/Philippe Migeat
p. 158: © Eredi Aldo Rossi, courtesy of Fondazione Aldo Rossi • Photo © Centre Pompidou, MNAM-CCI, Dist. RMN-Grand Palais/Georges Meguerditchian
p. 166: © The Estate of Philip Guston • Courtesy Hauser & Wirth/Photo: Genevieve Hanson
p. 173: © Photo12/Alamy/Old Paper Studios
p. 181, 186–87: Photo: © NMNM/François Fernandez, courtesy of the SBM
p. 183, 185: Photo: © ML.Briane/Les Ballets de Monte-Carlo
On the front cover : *Rodrigo's Wife*, 2011. Oil on linen, 4 ft. 6⅛ in. × 4 ft. ¼ in. (137.5 × 122.6 cm). © 2023 George Condo/Artists Rights Society (ARS), New York

© Éditions Flammarion, Paris, 2023
ISBN: 978-2-08-041968-2
© Nouveau Musée National de Monaco, 2023
ISBN: 978-2-492121-12-8
L.01EBTN001028
No. 560544
Legal Deposit: 03/2023
Printed in Italy by Musumeci
in February 2023